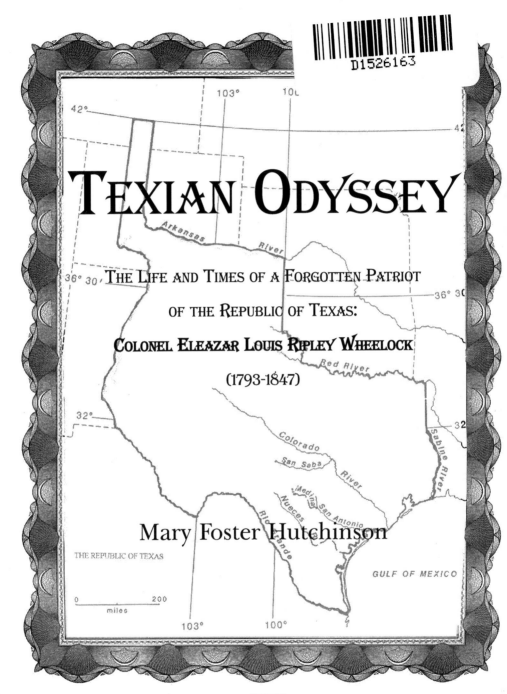

TEXIAN ODYSSEY

THE LIFE AND TIMES OF A FORGOTTEN PATRIOT

OF THE REPUBLIC OF TEXAS:

COLONEL ELEAZAR LOUIS RIPLEY WHEELOCK

(1793-1847)

Mary Foster Hutchinson

THE REPUBLIC OF TEXAS

0   200
miles

GULF OF MEXICO

SUNBELT EAKIN   Austin,

Library of Congress Cataloging-in-Publication Data
Hutchinson, Mary Foster, 1924–
    Texian Odyssey : the life and times of a forgotten patriot of the
Republic of Texas, Colonel Eleazar Louis Ripley Wheelock (1793-1847) /
Mary Foster Hutchinson.– 1st ed.
        p.   cm.
    Includes bibliographical references and index.
    ISBN 1-57168-686-X
    1. Wheelock, Eleazar Louis Ripley, 1793-1847. 2. Pioneers—Texas—
Biography. 3. Texas—History—To 1846. I. Title
F389.W58 H88   2002
976.4'503'092–dc21   200215231

IN MEMORY OF

GEORGE RIPLEY WHEELOCK
1819-1888

BUENA WHEELOCK BERRY
1868-1899

CARRIE ANNETTE BERRY FOSTER
1892-1977

History is not what happens.
History is what gets written down.
—M.F.H.

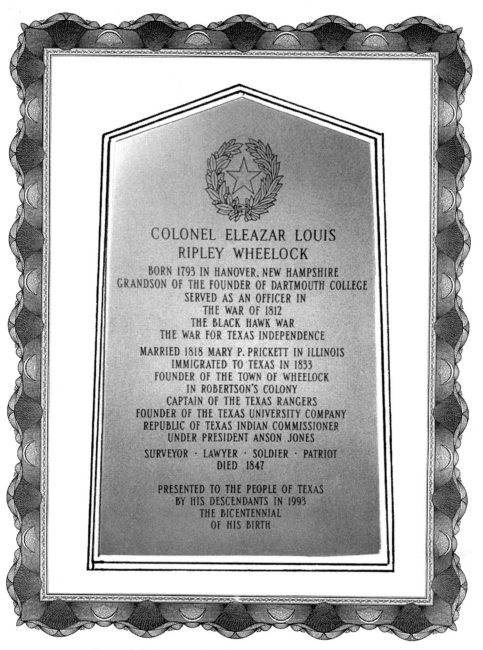

Cenotaph for E.L.R. Wheelock at Texas State Cemetery, Austin.

CONTENTS

ACKNOWLEDGMENTS

Many people and institutions have contributed to these pages over two decades of research. I confess that I cannot remember them all, but they were all appreciated, and I thank them all. I am especially indebted to the following:

My children, who have shared their professional expertise and patiently suffered throughout;

My sister, Phoebe Foster Hughes, for help and companionship during many hours in dusty courthouses and libraries;

My brother, William H. Foster Jr., *sine qua non;*

Seymour E. Wheelock, M.D., Denver, Colorado, an encourager without peer;

Carter Wheelock;

The late Ray Cameron Cox;

The late Joyce Shaw and family;

The Reverend Emmett M. Waits;

Dr. Edwin C. Bearss, Washington, D.C.;

T. R. Fehrenbach, San Antonio, Texas, whose *Lone Star* taught me that history can make sense in human terms;

Dr. Malcolm McLean of Georgetown, Texas, without whose monumental nineteen-volume work no student of Robertson's Colony could possibly function;

Adams County (Illinois) Historical Society;
Arkansas State Archives, Little Rock;
Cincinnati Historical Society;
Courthouses of Adams and Madison Counties, Illinois, and
   Franklin and Fayette Counties, Texas;
Dartmouth College;
Edwardsville (Illinois) Public Library;
Greenville (Bond County, Illinois) Public Library;
Historical Society of Quincy and Adams County, Illinois;
Illinois State Historical Library (Springfield);
Kentucky State Archives;
Libraries of the University of Texas at Arlington;
Libraries of the University of Texas at Austin;
Louisiana State Archives and Museum, New Orleans;
Mason County Museum, Maysville, Kentucky;
Ohio Historical Society, Columbus;
Ripley (Ohio) Heritage;
Southern Methodist University Libraries;
Tennessee State Archives, Nashville;
Texas/Dallas History and Archives Division, Dallas Public
   Library;
Texas General Land Office;
Texas Rangers Library, Waco;
Texas State Archives;
Texas State Historical Association.

INTRODUCTION

Plenty of things have happened in Texas that the records say nothing about.

—J. Frank Dobie

In the beginning, every Texan had his odyssey. It started in Tennessee or Virginia, in Scotland or Germany, in Alabama or New York. It ended in a broad, largely uninhabited wilderness. Each brought himself, for good or ill. Together, they made a nation.

Each has his tale to tell. This is the story of a New Hampshire boy and his journey from the Dartmouth College campus where he was born to the town of Wheelock in Robertson's Colony, state of Coahuila and Texas. This is also a serious history of Texas, but not the usual history about movers and shakers or generals and presidents. Generals and presidents will appear, but as minor characters. This is a book about one of the ordinary settlers who came to Texas by the hundreds and then the thousands and made Texas out of nothing but courage and sweat.

Eleazar Louis Ripley Wheelock's life line was to lead him from fortunate beginnings as the grandson of the founder of Dartmouth College through poverty in pioneer Ohio, the clash of famous battles during the War of 1812, law studies in Kentucky, love and marriage in Illinois, peril on the Arkansas frontier, and finally, in 1824, an exploratory journey across Texas which transformed his life.

Captain of the Texas Rangers, silver miner, founder of a fort and town on the Old San Antonio Road, foe and friend of the Red Man, would-be establisher of Texas's first university, surveyor, rancher, land agent, lawyer, failed politician, and partisan of General Houston; few men have enjoyed and endured such an adventurous life. He brought his Yankee integrity into the rough and careless world of the southern squatter and speculator, who over and over rejected him and his ideas. But by golly he gave them a run for their money.

Wheelock's papers have lain moldering in attics and libraries for more than one hundred and fifty years. I tell his story not because I am anyone in particular, let alone a professional historian, but because no one else has told it. It deserves to be told. It is the story of the settlers in Robertson's Colony, who came early to Texas to make a new life, only to be engulfed by revolution and betrayal.

In agreement with Andrew Forest Muir, who edited the work of the unknown Ohioan I have called the Anonymous Buckeye, "in order to distract as little as possible, I have silently expanded initials, modernized spelling, redivided paragraphs, rectified grammatical errors . . . and cleaned up untidy punctuation."

Unattributed primary material throughout the book is from the E.L.R. Wheelock Papers, Center for American History, the University of Texas at Austin.

Mary Foster Hutchinson
Dallas, Texas, 2002

Book One

Getting There

. . . the fateful repositioning of the physiological IBM card that is called inheritance.

—Seymour E. Wheelock, M.D.

Wheelock Mansion, 1776.
—Courtesy Dartmouth College Library
with permission of artist, Donald Johnson

CHAPTER 1

BOYHOOD:
1793-1812

Hanover

A fourteen-year-old boy stood on the banks of the swollen, pewter-colored Connecticut River as it roiled past his home on the Dartmouth College campus in Hanover, New Hampshire. The year was 1807. He was saying good-bye. They—his father, his mother, his little sister, his four little brothers, and himself— were leaving to settle in the new state of Ohio. His Uncle John was sending them away, or so it seemed to Ripley.

He could not help feeling outcast. It was a feeling he would never truly shake the whole of his life. He knew he should try to pretend that the migration was a fine upward move for his parents, one they had chosen and desired, but Hanover was home and the seat of his heart. Besides, it was a great thing to be a Wheelock at Dartmouth College. That was why he had such a long name, Eleazar Louis Ripley Wheelock. Eleazar after his father, his grandfather, and his great-great-grandfather. (Uncle John had told him that the name meant "God will hear me" in Hebrew, but Ripley was not sure about this.) Ripley after his Uncle Sylvanus Ripley, Aunt Abigail's husband. And Louis after

3

an old friend of his father's.[1] But three Christian names were too much for a boy, so he was simply called Ripley.

His grandfather, the Rev. Dr. Eleazar Wheelock, had been a great and famous man and a celebrated preacher and missionary to the Indians and had founded the college, and voices were special when he was spoken of. His father was Col. Eleazar Wheelock Jr. Voices were special when the family spoke about his father, too, but in a different way.

Although raised in the Puritan tradition which believed in the breaking of childish wills, Ripley's father had proved recalcitrant. Nevertheless he became the founder's favorite and went on to graduate from Dartmouth College and later to receive his master's degree. But conformity eluded him; he developed into the black sheep in a large and conventional family. Perhaps he preferred the fishing in Mink Brook or the wild game on Moose Mountain to theology.

Children sense these things. For a long time Ripley had known that there was something wrong with his father. Uncle John, the second president of Dartmouth College, was very distinguished and wore the great jewel about his neck at commencement. Uncle James owned a merry tavern in the village of Hanover where he, Ripley, was not supposed to go, but the tavern did not seem to keep people from liking Uncle James. Even ailing Uncle Ralph, holder of a bachelor of arts and a master of arts degree from Yale, had the respect of the community. No one showed this same respect for Ripley's father. Still, to be a Wheelock, even the least one, was somehow a distinction.

His mother's people, the Pennocks, were less distinguished. Loyal to the Church of England, they had settled in Strafford, Vermont, with a group of co-religionists who hoped to exist modestly apart from the encircling Puritans. War shattered their dreams. Ripley's maternal grandfather had been killed at the Battle of Saratoga fighting for King George. Confiscation by the victorious Yankees had left the family poor.

Ripley's father had fought for the rebels. Of Eleazar Jr.'s soldiering, beyond his service as a lieutenant in the York Light Infantry under his brother, John, nothing is certainly known. Military records of the time are incomplete and to the confusion of historians several of his distant cousins, also called Eleazar Wheelock, joined the rebel cause.

In 1787 he is referred to in the Hanover Town Records as Col. Eleazar Wheelock.[2] Like that of his son, the colonelcy may have been a militia title.

His father's death left him well off, but he did not remain so. Financial failure was not considered an admirable trait in Calvinist society. Of the Wheelock heirs, John alone had the acumen to build on his inheritance and by shrewd management and a discreet marriage to acquire a large fortune. Having most of his father's talents, except his greatness of mind, John took up the reins of college government and the remainder of his odd life is well documented.

Eleazar Jr.'s path, on the other hand, led downhill.

One year, 1784, proved memorable. President John sent his two younger brothers to the Old World to fetch home some college supplies, a telescope, and other scientific instruments. This, their first visit to Europe and their first long sea voyage, must have been both a daunting and an enlightening experience, decanting them into the Europe of Mozart and Beethoven, Goya and David, Schiller and Kant, Blake and Fanny Burney. Britain was busy taking over India while Russia annexed the Crimea. Samuel Johnson had just died. Frederick the Great ruled Prussia, and the French Revolution was only five years in the future.

After such a smorgasbord of a continent, New Hampshire must have looked like plain fare indeed. But there is no indication that any of the Wheelocks regretted their ancestor's immigration 147 years earlier or wished to reverse the process, just as no record comes down to us that they missed the aesthetic feast being placed so triumphantly on European tables. Art had little place in the Puritan psyche.

On his return from Europe, Eleazar Jr. hastily married Tryphena Young, the daughter of John Young of Hanover, a widower. Two months later, a daughter, Abigail, was born to the pair. Perhaps the long sea voyage had prevented a more timely marriage. In March of 1786 Eleazar Jr. was chosen town constable and a second daughter, Mary (known as Polly), was born to the couple. In 1787 four shillings were voted to Col.

Eleazar Wheelock for services and Elizabeth (Betsy) joined the family.

In 1790 Tryphena died in childbirth, taking a fourth daughter with her. Eleazar Jr. now found himself as a Hanover town surveyor, the father of three motherless children, and a man with a bleak financial future. In 1792 he solved his domestic problem by marrying a twenty-one-year-old woman named Thankful Pennock.

Thankful gave Eleazar Jr. his first son, Eleazar Louis Ripley, on March 31, 1793. Twenty-nine days before, on March 2, a child named Sam had been born to Samuel and Elizabeth Houston in Rockbridge County, Virginia.

Nancy Marie, the Wheelocks' only daughter, was born in 1796, followed by John in 1802, George in 1804, Thomas in 1805, and William in 1806.

As they reached the appropriate age, Ripley and his brothers attended school with their Wheelock cousins, first at the Wheelock mansion to learn reading and writing from the Bible and plain figuring from the house accounts, and later with other students—some Indian, some white—being prepared for entrance to the family college. Almost certainly the Wheelock children expected to receive the same education their father enjoyed.

The college was the nexus of family life. Ripley could tell that founding a college brought great respect. Some day, he dreamed, he too would found a college and become a famous man like his grandfather. But did he ask himself, when he left for Ohio, where his own college education would come from?

The bustle when the whole Wheelock family came together in its fine mansion for the three great annual holidays— Election, Commencement, and Thanksgiving—with aunts and uncles to fuss and turn stern eyes and the jibes of critical cousins to bear, these gatherings would not be missed perhaps. But the warmth of the great family cocoon enveloped them all in a sense of place and belonging which was deep and satisfying. All this Ripley was to lose.

Amongst a natural preoccupation with their own infant republic, did he hear New Hampshire men discuss events in Hispanic America, where Ripley's still unimaginable future lay?

At the time of Ripley's birth, New Spain contained seven million people, about twice as many as the young U.S.A. Mexico City alone was a city of 150,000. Spain held title to all lands west of the Mississippi plus most of the Gulf Coast. Did anyone in Hanover speculate that all of this immensity north of the Rio Bravo would one day be part of their own nation, and that young Ripley would be a cog in the machinery which made it so?

Ohio

Even before Ripley was born, events were taking place which would pluck him from the safety of New Hampshire. Once forbidden country under the British, Ohio and the rest of the Northwest Territory were now open for settlement.

Land was the medium of this migration, its goal, and its glory. It was ringed in dollar signs. "Speculation in land was (and is) a widespread business activity that, as a form of capital investment, runs like a thread through the history of the United States."[3]

In 1787 a man named John Cleaves Symmes applied for a million acres between the twin Miami Rivers (the word means "mother" in the Ottawa language) in repayment for a debt owed him by the U.S. government. He received 311,682 acres, including the area where Ripley and his family were to live.

Clermont, the eighth county created in the Northwest Territory, was formed December 9, 1800, by proclamation of Territorial Governor Arthur St. Clair and at the instigation of William Lytle, a speculator following in the footsteps of Symmes. Lytle was one of the greatest of land speculators, and in many cases his activities were—from the point of view of the settlers— highly suspect. He owned a clouded title to one of the finest sections of Clermont County, which he sold off at an enormous profit. Early buyers often ended up with invalid titles and some had to pay twice for their holdings or lose them altogether. It was from this man that young Ripley got his early lessons in land speculation. When he finally arrived in Texas, he would know to be wary.

By 1805 someone else was living in Eleazar Jr.'s rambling

house on Dartmouth Hill. Whether through misfortune, mismanagement, or other woes, he had come to the end of his financial rope. He himself said, in a letter written from Milford, Ohio, to Lytle in 1810, that "a failure in a large commercial London connection is the cause of my being here." After his death, his brother John wrote that unsteadiness and irregularity had reduced his property. Tradition labels Eleazar Wheelock Jr. an alcoholic. For whatever reason, family money was found to finance his emigration.

At first the Wheelocks settled in Milford, near Cincinnati, and it was from Cincinnati on February 8, 1808, that Eleazar Jr. wrote to President Thomas Jefferson asking for a grant of land based on his Revolutionary War service.[4] No such grant was issued, and in 1810 the father of the family approached Colonel Lytle. On August 24 the Wheelocks contracted with Lytle to pay $800 for 200 acres, which they reached by traveling upstream and debarking at a tiny landing called Boat Run on the vast banks of the Ohio. This majestic stream is a third of a mile wide at Boat Run, and the Kentucky shore looks far away, like a foreign country. It must have acted like a magnet to frontier children, drawn to view with wide eyes a stately procession of adventurers gliding inexorably at three miles an hour toward fabulous New Orleans.

Although, as a Puritan, he had been raised to manual labor as a natural corollary of study, pioneer life must have been hard for Eleazar Jr., already over fifty years old, in a land where most men wore out at thirty, and probably in poor physical condition.

On Thankful fell the whole burden of raising six children, clothing a family of eight in linen and linsey-woolsey, gardening, cooking, keeping the house, doctoring (tansy for worms, lard for the itch), instructing the young ones, and helping with the animals. It must have been a great solace to her when one of her grown stepdaughters came out from Hanover to help.

Of course, all but babes in arms worked. As Ripley grew, more and more of the hardest labor fell on him. Ohio was his dress rehearsal for Texas.

Fortunately, Ripley's father was able to draw a second string to his financial bow. Among the first teachers in Clermont County is listed "a New Englander named Whelock."[5] As the holder of bachelor's and master's degrees from Dartmouth, he must have offered a tutelage superior to most, and the community must have counted itself lucky to have him. Hard as life was, ambitious settlers were filled with dismay at the idea of their children growing up unlettered. When they could, the fathers chipped in to support a subscription school.

The struggle to establish the Wheelock family in Boat Run turned out to be short. Only sixteen months after writing his hopeful letter to Lytle, Col. Eleazar Wheelock Jr., B.A., M.A., son of the founder of Dartmouth College, Revolutionary War veteran, died of a stroke in Clermont County, Ohio, just three weeks before the turning of the new year of 1812.

A Dartmouth College alumni note describing the event reads, "Sixteen miles above Cincinnati was Boat Run where Eleazar Wheelock Jr. died on December 7, 1811, at the age of 55. Merchant in Hanover, but becoming embarrassed in business emigrated to Ohio about 1805. While in the act of felling a tree, he was seized with a third shock of apoplexy, and in a few moments expired in the arms of his wife, who saw his fall and flew to his assistance."[6]

Ripley, at eighteen, was left in charge of his mother, his fifteen-year-old sister Nancy, and his small brothers John, nine, George, seven, Thomas, six, and William, five years old. Their situation was desperate.

In early January 1812, with Colonel Wheelock scarcely cold in his grave, a representative of land speculator Lytle wrote to President John Wheelock in Hanover demanding payment for 200 acres of land in Ohio purchased by his dead brother. No mention was made of a clouded title.

Thankful Pennock Wheelock seems only to have been sustained by her husband's needs. She shortly followed him in death, probably in late 1812 or early 1813, and with her went seven-year-old Thomas, perhaps succumbing to the annual swamp-fed typhoid epidemic. All three may have been buried in the Clermont County cemetery, but no markers have ever been found. No doubt the orphans lacked money for such a luxury.

Of the children left stranded in Ohio, Ripley was the only one full grown and the only one to remember clearly the comfort and security of Hanover and the Wheelock mansion.

Conscious of his father's failures, his memories must have been tormented ones. Still, an appeal to Uncle John had to be made, and it was not made in vain. Younger brothers John, George, and William were suffered to return to New Hampshire with their older half-sister. There the two younger boys were adopted into the family of cousin William Woodward, son of the founder's daughter Mary and Prof. Bezeleel Woodward. John was sent to live, unhappily, with the Rev. William Allen, another cousin, in Pittsfield, Massachusetts. Nancy already had her eye on the man who would be her husband and was reluctant to leave Ohio, so arrangements were made for her to remain temporarily with a neighbor's friendly clan.

Ripley had turned his soul away from his native clime. He never entered the state of New Hampshire again. Free now of family obligations and anxious no doubt for a fresh start in life, Ripley went to war.

CHAPTER 2

SOLDIERING ON OUT WEST: 1813-1820

Mr. Madison's War

President James Madison declared war on Great Britain on June 18, 1812, inspired by political motives and greed for Canadian and Amerind-held western lands, both motives carefully sheltered behind a screen of moral indignation at imagined and real grievances against the mother country.

Some of his cohorts, suspecting that Canadian ambition might bite into American territories, hoped to establish a buffer Indian state in the area between Canada and the United States. This idea aroused nothing but fear in the minds of the United States frontiersmen, who saw a huge, united Indian nation blocking their way west. This fear was the torch which lit Wheelock's first war.

E.L.R. Wheelock was sworn in as a private of the Second Regiment, Ohio Militia, on September 4, 1813, in Clermont County, Ohio. A pension application filed by his widow years later states that he was twenty years old, a prosperous farmer, six feet tall, with grey eyes, fair complexion, and dark hair. Prosperous must have been an exaggeration, as E.L.R.'s only known

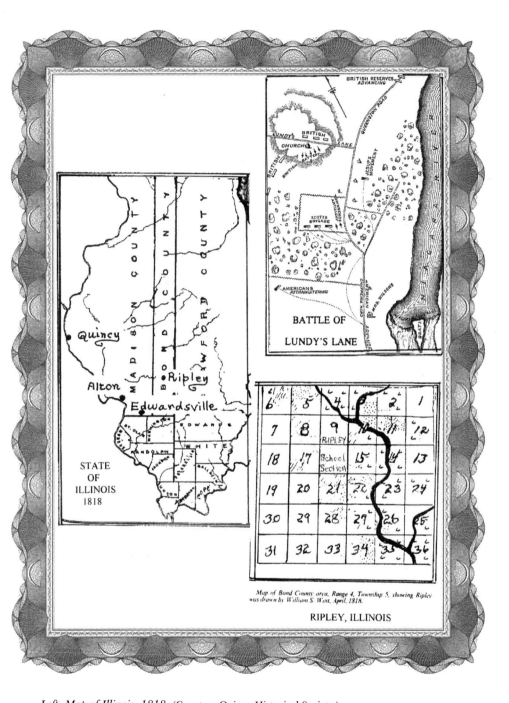

Left: Map of Illinois, 1818. (Courtesy Quincy Historical Society.)
    Upper right: Battle of Lundy's Lane, sketch by Benson Lossing in Pictorial Field Book of the War of 1812.
    Lower right: Map of Bond County, 1818, with sketch of Ripley. (Sketch by William S. Wait, courtesy Bond County (Il.) Public Library.)

assets were youth, strength, and freedom from family obligations. It must have been with a sense of release and adventure
that he set out to free the Northwest Territories from British and
Indian domination.

Wheelock marched with his regiment across Ohio and
southern Michigan and survived the cold, the semi-starvation,
the rotten equipment, the boredom, and the constant threat of
disease typical of this campaign. The hardships of his youth
had made him tough, and he was young; he was soon chosen
to be a noncommissioned officer. Perhaps he enjoyed the challenge of command, which came to him naturally, but he knew it
wasn't war.

As one of 1,300 Ohio militiamen under Gen. Lewis Cass, he
was left to garrison Detroit after its recapture. Here he met even
worse conditions: a disgusting amalgam of confusion, disarray,
frontier drunkenness, petty crime, and poverty. By November
28 over a thousand troops in occupied Detroit were ill with fever
and many of the healthy guilty of "much slovenly conduct, selling of clothing, assault of civilians, distilling grain, etc." [1] For
most Ohioans, the war was over. They just wanted to go home.
The army agreed.

On March 4, 1814, E.L.R. Wheelock was discharged from
the Ohio Militia in Detroit with the rank of sergeant major and
issued a sum of money for his three-hundred-mile journey back
to Clermont County, Ohio. But Clermont County no longer
held any attractions for him. In New York he had a first cousin
who was a general and might be persuaded to befriend his
mother's brother's child. Wheelock took his money and followed
the war to New York.

The Niagara Campaign

Third Lieutenant E.L.R. Wheelock, age twenty-one years,
the junior officer's uniform still stiff around his legs and shoulders, was commissioned into the Twenty-first Infantry Regiment
of the U.S. Army in June 1814, in upstate New York only a few
weeks before the beginning of Napoleon's exile on the island of
Elba. His odd rank was one sometimes given to a young officer

awaiting a vacancy in the roster of ensigns, normally the lowest commissioned rank in the army. The Twenty-first Infantry Regiment was assigned to one of the hottest battle zones of the two-year-old United States–British war. His regiment was commanded by his first cousin, Brig. Gen. Eleazar Wheelock Ripley.

The Battle of Chippewa

As part of Gen. Jacob Brown's Army of the Niagara, Lieutenant Wheelock did not have long to wait for action. On July 3, 1814, his army crossed the Niagara River into Canada and recaptured Fort Erie, obtaining a toe-hold on foreign soil. On the night of July 4, Gen. Phineas Riall's British army arrived, camping a mile and a half from the United States Army near the Chippewa River, about a mile above the great Niagara Falls.

At this point in history, infantry organization was founded on the need to form a line, control it in battle, renew it when it collapsed, and maneuver it so as to place the enemy at a disadvantage. Battle formations were thus lines of men two ranks deep with the soldiers virtually elbow to elbow, as is seen today during close-order drill.

What followed the next day was a classic eighteenth-century battle, with drummer boys crisply sending out orders through the coded music of their drums. General Winfield Scott, backed up by General Brown, personally led the Eleventh Infantry on a bayonet charge, pushing enemy units backwards over the Chippewa Bridge. The Battle of Chippewa was "a stunning victory" for the United States.[2]

The Battle of Lundy's Lane
(Also known as the Battle of Niagara)

Eager to follow up his advantage, General Brown now advanced deeper into Canada, but was soon forced back southward to the Chippewa River. On the night of July 24, the Army of Niagara, 2,600 strong, camped on the Chippewa battlefield. Early the next morning the British sent a column of 950 men to take a defensive position north along a road called Lundy's Lane.

At 5:00 P.M. on a sultry, hot July 25, General Scott was ordered by General Brown to advance along the road that connected the American position to that of the British. Scott launched his attack about 6:00 P.M. and by 8:00 P.M. had only 600 effectives remaining. The United States sent for reinforcements. Both Americans and British had cannons on a single hill, and the confusion was so great that the noise of exploding powder almost drowned out the roar of nearby Niagara Falls. In more than one case the cannoneers "limbered up and brought off an enemy piece, mistaking it for their own."[3]

General William Drummond arrived with reinforcements for the British, while General Ripley arrived with United States reinforcements. At about 10:00 P.M. Brown ordered Ripley to silence the enemy cannons. General Ripley personally took the Twenty-third Infantry to strike the British left, and gave to Col. James Miller and 300 men from the Twenty-first Infantry Regiment the honor of attacking the battery proper.

All his life Lieutenant Wheelock was to remember with pride his participation in this battle. "The two columns advanced in bright moonlight that was streaked with the comet-like tails of the British Congreve rockets."[4] "Miller worked his men up through brush to a rail fence, fifteen yards from the hostile cannon. He ordered them to rest their guns on the fence, take careful aim, fire once, and rush the battery. They were inside the British position before the defenders knew they were threatened."[5] Lieutenant Wheelock emerged unscathed.

"Meanwhile General Ripley, with equally brilliant action, had broken the British left."[6] Repeatedly, the British tried to take back their cannons, in vain, until both Generals Brown and Scott were gravely wounded. General Brown then ordered General Ripley to withdraw, and as he did so the captured British cannons were left behind, forgotten, to be recovered by the British intact.

The next morning, stung perhaps by the loss of the cannons, General Ripley marched his exhausted troops out again towards the British lines, but finding them much reinforced and himself outnumbered two to one, he returned to his base. In spite of his brilliant charge, which gave General Ripley the so-briquet "The Hero of Lundy's Lane," honors went to the British. "Lundy's Lane—the sharpest fight of the war in the Canadian border—was a tactical standoff, but strategically a victory for Drummond."[7]

Still, it was the stuff of which old soldiers' tales are made. Years later in Texas, G. H. Love remembered that he "often heard him (E.L.R. Wheelock) speak of the battery he was in and of Lundy Lane."[8]

The United States Army under General Ripley, including his young cousin, now retreated to Canada's Fort Erie which had been captured by the United States on July 3. Here he put his men to work to improve the fortifications of batteries, trenches, blockhouses, and earth works. The force had twenty-seven heavy guns and 3,000 men in place, while the nearby British were severely weakened by an epidemic of typhoid fever. When General Ripley retired, Lieutenant Wheelock remained with the veterans defending Fort Erie.

On August 13 Lieutenant Wheelock again came under fire. The British and Canadians under General Drummond attacked Fort Erie and maintained a bloody siege until September 21. General Ripley, called up at the last moment, was severely wounded in the neck, a trauma from which he never fully recovered. Young Wheelock's regiment, the Twenty-first Infantry, was active throughout, and on September 17, 1814, he was rewarded by a promotion to the rank of ensign.

When Drummond finally retired, his army and Brown's were "mere skeletons of the confident regiments of early July."[9] On November 5 the dispirited Americans blew up Fort Erie and retreated to United States soil, ending the invasion of Canada with "both a bang and a whimper."[10] The Canadians regained their fort by default. Neither side had gained an inch of ground.

On November 14, 1814, Wheelock was appointed regimental quartermaster, a post he filled until June 1815, the date of his honorable discharge from the army. He was now responsible for burying the dead and providing food, shelter, and clothing for the Twenty-first Infantry Regiment. It was a skill he would take with him to Texas along with the glory of having

participated in the perilous Niagara Campaign. But as far as
military action was concerned, Wheelock's first war was over.

By June 1815 he found himself once again mustered out of
the military. Free to make of life what he could devise, he chose
not to return to New Hampshire or Ohio, both places of unhappy memories for him. The frontier was expanding and reasonably safe, offering the only real opportunity to the impecu-
nious and the dispossessed. His skills were farming and fighting,
both in high demand in the borderlands. His cousin and erstwhile commanding officer, E. W. Ripley (having quarreled with
Jacob Brown and the state of New York), was planning to move
his family south. E.L.R. Wheelock decided to go west. Neither
could have guessed that the former would serve briefly as
shadow president of a shadow land called Texas, though he
would never live there, while the other would make Texas his
home.

Kentucky

October 13, 1815, found Wheelock witnessing a sale of
Negroes and land in Mason County, Kentucky, just across the
river from his old home in Boat Run, Ohio. Here he paused to
see to the welfare of his sister and no doubt to assure himself
that ownership of his father's 200 acres had reverted to General
Lytle, as he must have surmised.

He had left Boat Run a boy. He was now a man and a war
veteran, reassured by experience that he could measure up to
life. Others saw this quality in him. In Washington, Kentucky, he
was befriended by attorney James Campbell, who, recognizing
something of promise in the young ex-officer, took him in to
study law and reflect on his future. The Kentucky legal documents which Wheelock carefully copied by hand during this period were to form the basis of his law practice in the Republic of
Texas.

During 1816 he journeyed to Philadelphia, perhaps on his
master's business, perhaps simply to satisfy the curiosity of a
country boy about a famous city. On October 2 of that year his
only sister's future was secured as Nancy Marie Wheelock was

joined in marriage in Mason County, Kentucky, to James
Hillman, with E.L.R. Wheelock as bondsman. Hillman, like his
new brother-in-law, was a veteran of the War of 1812, where he
served in Rayen's Regiment of the Ohio Militia as a sergeant's
mate. The two men became lifelong friends, and Wheelock was
to show his regard for Hillman by naming a son in his honor.

Ripley Wheelock, in whom family feeling ran strong, had
never intended to relinquish his young brothers permanently.
Now that he was in a position to care for them, the time had
clearly come to reestablish communications with New England.
No doubt he wrote to Hanover to announce the wedding of his
sister and give his own address. First cousin William H.
Woodward, an attorney who had succeeded his father as treasurer of Dartmouth College, had adopted George and William
and given them the Woodward name. It was he who answered
the letter from Kentucky. About his own charges, his news was
good. George and William were growing up peacefully in the
Woodward household in Hanover. John, now thirteen, was a
different story. Miserable in New England, he had run away the
previous spring. Nothing had been heard of him since.

Woodward tried to give E.L.R. what encouragement he
could. John was described as robust and healthy, equal to protecting himself even among strangers. The family had specu-
lated that he might have gone to sea. Woodward, however,
feared that "John's mind was unstable and his passions without
restraint."[11] Yet he hoped that John, being so young, would yet
settle down and follow the good example of his family.
Altogether, it was a very Puritan letter. It must have worried the
recipient a good deal.

Nevertheless, with the newlyweds off to homestead in Pike
County, Indiana, E.L.R.'s attention turned to even newer country, and for the time-honored reason. He had met a girl who
lived in Illinois.

The Prairie State

In 1808 one of the many settlers arriving in infant Illinois
from Kentucky was English-born George Prickett, accompanied

by his wife, Sarah, and their nine children. The Pricketts settled in what is now St. Clair County, in the midst of the fertile American bottom. There they finally found haven after a rambling journey which had carried them from Maryland through North Carolina and Georgia (where daughter Mary was born), to Kentucky, and finally to Illinois.

By 1813 Abraham Prickett, their eldest child, had set up a store in Edwardsville (now part of the St. Louis Metropolitan District, then a brisk town of 1,000 inhabitants), been elected justice of the peace, and become a founder of the First Presbyterian Church. He seemed destined to stand tall in this Illinois community for the rest of his life. Yet it was he who would die along the Red River and E.L.R. Wheelock, the Texan, who was destined to die in Edwardsville.

Sometime in 1816 or 1817, Abraham Prickett and Wheelock must have met in Kentucky where the Pricketts still had relatives. As their friendship ripened and came to include Abraham's sister Mary, the smitten Wheelock began to realize that the practice of law could move too slowly. Through Abraham he heard that fortunes were being made—and made in a hurry—in Illinois land deals. He was very much in love. This attachment was classic, a life-long devotion which the years seemed only to strengthen. Twenty-nine years later he would declare to Mary Pope Prickett Wheelock in a letter written in Philadelphia, "The ladies are gay, sprightly, and intelligent, but I have seen none . . . I would exchange my Mary for."

In late 1816 or early 1817, he was reunited with his runaway brother John in Kentucky and took the boy under his wing as a junior partner in a scheme to invest in land in southern Illinois. This must have been a heady moment, remembering as he had to do their parents' difficulties in Boat Run.

It was in Bond County, Illinois, that Ripley decided to plant his life, and from 1817 he was listed as a voter in that place. Sometime in the same year, amid the oaks and hickories, dogwoods and redbuds, he and John established a new town on Shoal Creek named in honor of their cousin and co-investor, General Ripley, who had already been distinguished in the same way by the town of Ripley, Ohio.

In Hanover, Uncle John had died, and the family was losing control of Dartmouth College. Circumstances were opening the door for E.L.R. to reclaim his two younger brothers.

The town of Ripley, Illinois, became an important trading post where people from within a radius of fifty miles came to do business. When neighbor Samuel Lee erected the first water mill in the county on Shoal Creek, Wheelock and a partner quickly erected their own water mills on the east side of Shoal Creek to meet the needs of surrounding farmers.

Wheelock understood how to diversify, but his main business was to buy and sell land, sometimes investing his own funds and sometimes those of General Ripley, Abraham Prickett, and others. Much lay in fecund Madison County.

But Bond County remained the focus of his new life. It was in this town of Ripley, now filling up with North and South Carolinians, that Wheelock saw his future unfolding, and to this village of his own making he brought his bride. It was to be their home forever.

Manifest Destiny, although it had not yet received its name, was America's rising doctrine. It was "the natural outgrowth of the Puritan belief that they were God's chosen people"[12] "The Puritan's code of behavior was highly effective in developing a doctrine of success."[13] Those with grim determination, optimism, strength, and diligence succeeded on the frontier and succeeded in reestablishing the standards of civilization they had left behind in the east. Those who were indolent and weak lapsed into barbarism easily enough. So spoke New Hampshire.

When the Rev. William Kinney rode out to George and Sarah Prickett's farm in St. Clair County on March 22, 1818, to join together Mary Pope Prickett and Eleazar Louis Ripley Wheelock, Illinois had just achieved statehood and was full of piss and vinegar. The bride's brother, Abraham Prickett, a member of the First Constitutional Convention of Illinois, had had the honor of making the speech which proposed statehood for Illinois.

The Wheelocks settled into the Village of Ripley with a household consisting of E.L.R., his wife, and his three brothers John, George, and William. To augment income from the mill on Shoal Creek, the head of the family established a distillery and ran a small store. In the same year he had the town of Ripley formally platted so that lots could be made ready for sale.

Furnishings for the honeymoon house arrived by river. In 1818 almost everything not made at home came up the Mississippi from New Orleans in keel boats hauled by ropes or down the Ohio from Pittsburgh. Ripley's homesteading experience in Ohio and the help of neighbors erected their modest log house. Roads were scarce and primitive. On April 6, 1818, Wheelock appeared before the circuit court to urge the building of a road between Ripley and Alton, a major port on the Mississippi. If approved, the road would be built by the settlers themselves as a service to their community.

The society of Ripley was a Ulster-Scot southern society, not a Puritan one, and must have seemed as strange to Wheelock as it was comfortable for his wife.

Illinois frontiersmen, like any others, took pride in being their own men. They obeyed no laws save those of community opinion enforced by lynch law. They had no enemies save Indians and nature. As in the Rev. Dr. Wheelock's day, "The wilderness to the American pioneer was no mother but a terrible foe."[14] Its hero was Andrew Jackson.

Jackson had won the heart of the west when he wiped out the Creek Army in Alabama at Horseshoe Bend during the War of 1812. He was the embodiment of T. R. Fehrenbach's stricture that only the Scotch Irish, of all settlers, were mean enough and tough enough to defeat the Amerinds. All his life he was their adversary, and the settlers knew it. This fact formed the base of much of their affection for him.

On February 1, 1819, Ripley and Mary welcomed their first child. Deciding to drop the awkward Eleazar, the couple named their son George after Mary's father, giving him E.L.R.'s third Christian name, Ripley, as a middle name. Like his father, he was known in the family as Ripley.[15]

On the frontier, newspapers arrived as early as churches and mills and even babies. E.L.R. Wheelock Esq. was listed as the agent in Bond County for the *Edwardsville Spectator* as soon as it began publication. Pioneer newspapers printed not the activities of the frontier (with which everyone was already familiar) but national and international affairs. Editors in isolated spots copied the articles of those in busy seaports like New Orleans, which got international news more quickly. By this route E.L.R.

Wheelock received his first news of Texas, which even then had become a focus of national attention.

The Adams-Onis Treaty, "one of the most important agreements that the U.S. has ever made," [16] defined the United States' western borders and contained America's express renunciation of all lands west of that border. In it Spain ceded Florida to the United States. This treaty was to cause much controversy among Anglos wishing to expand into Texas, of whom there was already a large number. How, they argued, could one renounce what one had never had? And if one had had it, could not one take it back? And perhaps after all Texas had been part of the Louisiana Purchase? On August 17, 1819, the *Clarion and State Gazette* of Nashville, Tennessee, declared that the treaty "gave away a valuable district which we ought to have, and which we can get, if ever an appeal to arms is made, and that consequently it will publish occasional articles until the public attention is drawn to that delightful country enslaved by miserable wretches." [17]

The delightful country was, of course, Texas, and the miserable wretches were those traditional enemies the Spanish.

The Adams-Onis Treaty was not ratified until 1821. In that year the *Arkansas Gazette* reprinted an article which had been published in the *Louisiana Advertiser* on the previous January 3.

The Florida Treaty

We have understood from a source entitled to confidence that this treaty has been ratified by the Cortez of Spain, and received by our government at Washington. The influence of the Executive will no doubt get this treaty through the Senate of the United States.

But when the House of Representatives come to approve $5 million to pay for the sand banks of Florida—we should be glad to know whether they are prepared to tax the people even for the interest, especially after surrendering Texas, worth about Five Floridas, even if Florida were worth, $5 million.

So were all restless men within the reach of these newspapers encouraged to dream of Texas as an El Dorado—far away, hazy, almost but not quite unobtainable.

The year 1820 was not a good one for Wheelock. Seeking to explore the boundaries of his self-made world, he ran for the state legislature. On August 7 the largely southern Bond County electorate defeated the Yankee, whom they respected but viewed as an alien. The defeated candidate thought he detected fraud and contested the election. His challenge was dismissed. He was deeply chagrined by this rejection, which violated both his amour-propre and his sense of justice. It was many years before he ran for public office again.

There are only two safe ways to meet injustice: with anger or with indifference. Wheelock chose a third, dangerous way. He burned up inside. Life henceforth was never quite as promising, never quite as friendly.

To add injury to insult, the land boom prophesied for Illinois, which was to make him rich, did not materialize.

> 1820—*Arkansas Gazette* for Nov. 18,, p. 3, Edwardsville, Illinois, Oct. 17. The public sale of lands in this town closed on Saturday last. Of the 38 townships which were offered, only 15 half-quarter sections were sold, and none above the minimum price of $1.23 per acre.

This disaster was a reaction to the Financial Panic of 1819, now being fully felt in the West. By 1820 almost everyone was in debt. Banks in Ohio and Kentucky failed. Banks in Illinois ceased business. The great tides of immigration into the Prairie State which everyone had counted on after the War of 1812 never rose. Illinois was hurt by its ambiguous stand on slavery and saw itself bypassed by southerners on their way to Missouri, which welcomed slave-holders.

Like the rest of the country, E.L.R. was all but wiped out by the Panic of 1819. Family responsibilities put any dim dreams of Texas, which may have been awakening in his mind, on hold. Something had to be done at once to recoup the young family's fortunes. He was obliged to sell his distillery and his water mill. The buyer was Dr. John Todd of Edwardsville, formerly of Lexington, Kentucky, uncle of future first lady Mary Todd Lincoln.

Wheelock's second child and only daughter was born on
April 8, 1821, and named Annette Woodward Wheelock after
her father's cousin back in New Hampshire, Annette Woodward
Searle. It was another mouth to feed.

His military skills were the only thing the young husband
and father could now put to work to bring in steady money. He
knew that his wife and children would be safe under the care of
the large Prickett clan. We next hear of him and his brother John
in Arkansas and in uniform.

CHAPTER 3

OVER THE EDGE: 1821-1832

Little Gibraltar on the Arkansas

In 1817 Maj. Stephen H. Long, a Dartmouth graduate, and Maj. William Bradford, an old war chum of Wheelock's, had sailed down the wide Mississippi from Saint Louis to Arkansas Post and up the Arkansas River to select a site for a new fort. They chose Belle Point, a bluff overlooking the rocky and heavily wooded junction of the Poteau and Arkansas Rivers.

Fort Smith stood sentinel between the westward retreat of the Amerinds from their Atlantic homes and the inexorable westward expansion of the Europeans. Military groups such as E.L.R. Wheelock and his brother John now joined were used to control Indians and to restrain illegal settlement on the ragged edges of United States territory.

Wheelock's friend Major Bradford was Fort Smith's first commandant. He and Wheelock must have been close, because thirty years later, when Mary Wheelock filled in her application for a widow's pension, his was the only name she could remember from among her husband's many army associates.

Her husband's sojourn in Arkansas was the couple's first

25

Quincy, Illinois, showing Prickett's Addition and Wheelock's Addition.
—Courtesy Adams County Historical Society

separation for any substantial length of time. It boggles the mind to think of the stoicism required of the wives of these peripatetic pioneer husbands, who cheerfully bade their wives good-bye for jaunts which lasted many months and then expected to return home to find the children all in order, the wife healthy, the farmwork accomplished, the taxes paid, and a good meal on the table. Amazingly, pioneer women produced all these things.

Although the Texas card was yet to be played, it hovered just out of sight to the south. Bradford allowed Thomas Nuttal, a visiting British naturalist, to accompany him on one of his routine patrols down to the Red River. At the mouth of the Kiamichi they came upon a group of squatters. Nuttal described them as "of worst moral character imaginable, being many of them renegades from justice, and such as have forfeited the esteem of civilized society. When further flight from justice became necessary, they passed over into the Spanish territory." [1] In modern terms, they went to Texas.

Another of Major Bradford's duties was to provide proper licenses and papers regulating trade and travel in Indian country, which became legal after 1819. When the Adams-Onis Treaty was ratified in 1821, Bradford acquired the additional duty of policing the newly established Spanish-United States border, now defined as the Red River and the 100th meridian. Texas was just over the river.

When in 1821 Florida became part of the United States, military tensions lessened in the southeast. The Seventh Infantry was withdrawn from its civilized post in Georgia for service on the western frontier. Half went to Fort Seldon in Louisiana to confront the Spanish if necessary, and half to Fort Smith. Many officers, knowing from the reliable army grapevine what life was like in Arkansas, resigned their commissions rather than undergo the hardships of life in the Ozarks. Others died of dysentery on the journey. The regiment departed New Orleans on the steamer *Tennessee* on November 6, 1821, arriving at Fort Smith the following February with a new commander, Col. Mathew Arbuckle. Lt. John Wheelock put on the tar bucket hat and white pompom of the Seventh Infantry as one of its replacement officers.

E.L.R. Wheelock's military status is harder to pinpoint. Although he was a patient in the spring of 1822 at the Fort Smith infirmary, his name does not appear on any official United States Army lists from this era. He may have been an officer of some militia group for which the records are long lost.

First Mexican Probes

Through the 100-degree heat of this same sultry spring, a group of men assembled in Nashville, Tennessee, to found a society to promote Texas settlement which would permanently change Wheelock's life. Closer to his temporary home in Arkansas Territory, a portentous father and son, Moses and Stephen Austin, had surfaced three years before to recruit Texas emigrants, and were still much talked of. There is no evidence that Wheelock ever met Moses Austin, but he might easily have heard and read of his Arkansas sales talks. As a contemporary source declared, "The Spanish country is all the rage in the southern end of the (Arkansas) territory."[2]

E.L.R. Wheelock's recovery from the seasonal fevers, which plagued all frontiersmen and killed many more soldiers than the Indians ever did, is evidence of his tough constitution. Not everyone was so blessed. There were usually several funerals each week at the fort during the sickly season. When an officer died, a procession marched to the cemetery to the sound of muffled drums and the mournful tones of "Roslin Castle" played on the pipes. His fellow officers wore a badge of mourning for thirty days as tribute, sent a message of condolence to his family, and drank toasts to his memory. This was the rite celebrated at Fort Smith for Lt. John Wheelock, age twenty-one, on February 21, 1823. It was E.L.R.'s first serious loss since the death of his parents and small brother Thomas in Ohio. He felt it keenly.

Soon afterwards he returned to Bond County, carrying with him the necessary documents for a trip into the alien land south of the Red River, now the property of the two-year-old Republic of Mexico. Later in 1823 he left his affairs for the second time in the capable hands of his wife Mary and headed south. Illinois had proved disappointing and Texas was beckoning, but with Yankee shrewdness he wished to see Texas for himself before buying. Fort Smith was the closest major fort to the Texas road, and it is probable that E.L.R. was familiar with at least its beginnings. He traveled through Arkansas, across the Red River, alone and on horseback, trading along the way with Amerinds and settlers alike. Unfortunately, no account of this epic journey has survived. Did he hire himself out to some military group or visit Stephen F. Austin's Anglos in south Texas, waiting and hoping for legal title to land promised them by his father? Did he visit San Antonio or Nacogdoches? Was he aware of the determined group of Anglo empresarios (Leftwich, Austin, and about a dozen others) waiting in Saltillo for permission to populate Texas with their own kind? Perhaps.

Overreaching the extent of modern Texas, he ended up in 1824 in Tampico, on the Gulf coast of Mexico. Heretofore Wheelock's travels had taken place within the Anglo nexus. Now for the first time he found himself in a foreign land and experienced a culture which contrasted sharply with that of New Hampshire. The language, the religion, the clothing, the manners, the climate were all new to him. Even the trees were foreign. It is indicative of some deep and unexpected response from the disinherited Puritan boy within the man that he lingered there.

During his stay in Tampico, the city paid Wheelock a city lot (25 by 50 varas in size, or about 725 by 1,650 feet) for his services as a surveyor. Perhaps he learned a little Spanish, even ventured within the cool cavern of the Roman church. Perhaps this long visit to Tampico awakened the first faint vibrations of sympathy for a still-alien religion, which he would one day embrace. Nothing is known of his trek back to Illinois, only that during this prodigious journey a deep affection was born in him for an empire not his own.

By the spring of 1825 Wheelock was back in Ripley, Illinois, to take up his neglected business affairs. The village of Ripley, like the country as a whole, still sagged under the effects of financial panic. Soon after the birth of his second son, William

Hillman, on February 1, 1826, Wheelock began to think again about heading south.

It would be hard to praise Mary Prickett Wheelock too much for her endurance during her restless husband's wanderings. When he left her in Ripley in 1821-22 to mend their fortunes in the militia, and when he went to survey Tampico in 1823-24, she had two small children. Now, on his second trip to Mexico in 1826, she had three—George Ripley, Annette, and William.

Perhaps Wheelock returned from Tampico in 1825 ready to immigrate. Austin's Colony was finally legal and open, and he may have visited there. By then San Felipe, its capital, already consisted of a couple of dozen cabins strung out along the Brazos River, housing perhaps 200 people. Indeed the community must not have seemed to differ greatly from Ripley, Illinois.

During his second trip to Texas in 1826, however, Wheelock met a future empresario in San Felipe whom he found more appealing than Austin. He was Maj. Sterling Clack Robertson of Nashville, Tennessee. From this time Wheelock's Texas hopes were centered on a colony once known as Leftwich's Grant, then the Tennessee Colony, and finally Robertson's Colony.

Robertson's family had been prominent among those citizens of Nashville who sought to establish a colony of Anglos in Texas. On January 21, 1826, Dr. Felix Robertson, in Texas inspecting their grant, had written home: "The Brazos lands are as rich as any land in the world. I measured a piece of cotton ground this morning twelve yards wide and sixty five long, off which the owner said he picked 900 lbs of cotton. Better farming land I am certain is not to be found on the globe."[3]

Among the leagues surveyed by Dr. Robertson's party were those earmarked for himself, Sterling Robertson, and twenty others, presumably some of the young Tennesseans who came with them to Texas. By April 1826 the doctor, considering his duty done, had returned to Nashville, but among those staying behind was Sterling Robertson, who in the same month carried a letter to S. F. Austin in San Felipe. It was probably at this time that Sterling Robertson met E.L.R. Wheelock and interested him in becoming a settler in the Tennessee Colony.

Quincy

But no matter how alluringly Texas may have beckoned, when Wheelock returned to Illinois, he found his wife determined to give Illinois a second chance. Her brother Abraham Prickett had sold out his interest in his Edwardsville store to brother Isaac and gone to seek his fortune in the new town of Quincy, north of Alton on the Mississippi River. He wanted his brother-in-law as his partner, and no doubt Mary preferred to stay in Illinois, close to her family. Perhaps a little wifely persuasion was applied. At any rate, the Wheelocks moved to Quincy and E.L.R. tried his hand for the second time at the development of a new town. He planned to do much the same thing he attempted in Ripley, but without a financial panic to negate all his hard work.

Again Wheelock augmented his income from real estate by rejoining the militia. On July 24, 1827, in Adams County, he was appointed paymaster of the Third Division with the rank of major by Brig. Gen. Nicolas Hankin (or Hawkins). Militiamen were needed because there was new Indian trouble on the frontier, the so-called Winnebago War.

It was during his stay in Quincy that Wheelock received the military title by which he was known for the rest of his life. A visiting Englishman, G. W. Featherstonhaugh, had written of Virginia that "almost every person of the better class is at least a colonel."[4] This rule also held in Illinois and other frontier places. Wheelock, evidently considered a person of the better class, was from this time on Colonel Wheelock by courtesy of some long forgotten militia election.

In 1830 the Wheelocks added a third son to the family, David Prickett Wheelock, named in honor of Mary's lawyer brother, now clerk of the House of the General Assembly of Illinois. On September 15, 1832, Wheelock was sworn in as justice of the peace for Adams County, and in the same year he became paymaster for the Second Regiment.

Unfortunately, at about this time he and Abraham Prickett began to find their partnership burdensome. The exact nature of the problems between them, which must have been very

painful to Mary, are not known, but they were serious enough
to cast shadows which reached out long after both men were
dead.

In April 1832 the colonel was enrolled in his second war.

The Black Hawk War

In the words of John Carrol, "A democracy is only a mob.
If we tolerate ours, it is because every year we can push our innovators out west."[5] By 1832 the "innovators" had been pushed
at least as far west as Illinois. The Black Hawk War was the usual
uneven struggle of settlers versus nomads. Conflict began on a
minor note when on April 4 Gen. Henry Atkinson (known to the
Indians as White Beaver) was ordered to chastise the Sauk and
Fox Indians and make peace between them and the Sioux, with
whom they had a boundary dispute.

The Sauk and Fox were originally from Canada and were
related to the Algonquin. Pushed west, they exchanged land for
treaties as they went. The Indians had little concept of the private ownership of land and were easy to hoodwink.

The Sauk and Fox became divided into the Peace Party and
the British Band. Keokuk (the name means "he who has been
everywhere"), his blue eyes proclaiming his French blood, led
the Peace Party. Black Hawk, who wore his King George III
medallion proudly all his life, continued to lead the British
Band.

The first shot of the brief Black Hawk War was fired on
April 11 by settlers shooting at turkeys. This gunfire so alarmed
the edgy countryside that women and children took refuge at
the local fort. Black Hawk seized the opportunity to cross the
river into Illinois, and General Atkinson asked Governor
Reynolds for militia with which to push him back into his allotted territory. The odds were far from equal. Black Hawk had 500
braves. Illinois had a pool of 157,000 male citizens eligible for
military service.

Militia camp was undisciplined. There were no roll calls, no
drills, and no order, although there seem to have been plenty of
mud, liquor, and rattlesnakes. E.L.R. Wheelock served with this

ragtag from April 23 until May 28, 1832, as paymaster under Col. Jacob Fry, Second Regiment, Whitesides' Brigade of Mounted Volunteers. His appointment came directly from Governor Reynolds and he had to ride 250 miles to the muster point, Rushville, where he took over his duties on April 30.

After much maneuvering, Black Hawk tried to surrender, but met accidentally with a certain Major Stillman who had not heard about any surrender and thought he was being attacked. Black Hawk decided on a suicide charge. Terrified, the drunken, muddy Americans ran for their lives, leaving eleven dead. The amazed and victorious Black Hawk returned to Iowa.

After this setback for the state of Illinois, many of the volunteers had had enough and many deserted. Disgusted with the militia, General Atkinson moved his army of regulars across the Rock River where Black Hawk went on the attack once more. The countryside was in a panic, and Chicago was filled with refugees.

When their thirty days enlistment was up, the majority of the volunteers went home, including Wheelock, who was mustered out on May 30 at the Fox River. Perhaps the Wheelock family tradition of sympathy for the Indians in concert with what he had seen inhibited him from re-enlisting. The Rev. Sam Kirkland, famous missionary to the Indians in Illinois (whose son John served as president of Harvard College from 1810 to 1826), was married to a distant cousin, Sarah Wheelock, and from them Wheelock may have developed some empathy for the Sauk and Fox.

A purely military decision was now to provide the worst distress of the war, so far as the Americans were concerned. At the same time it would produce the immediate reason for the Wheelocks' long contemplated immigration to Texas.

President Jackson replaced General Atkinson with Gen. Winfield Scott, the Virginia gentleman familiar to Wheelock during the War of 1812 who once dismissed an aide de camp for not recognizing a quotation from Dryden. Scott's men brought with them from the east coast a cholera epidemic, which lasted three years and killed far more Illinoisans than the war. The Indians looked on and thanked their gods for divine intervention.

On July 28 the Illinoisans, with greatly superior numbers, won the Battle of Bad Axe and the Black Hawk War was essentially over. A brutal slaughter of Indians by the United States followed. Of the 1,000 Sauk who had crossed the Mississippi in April, 40 remained as prisoners, mostly women and children, and less than 100 escaped across the river.

Wheelock must have been glad to put this disgraceful affair behind him and arrive home to Quincy in time for the birth on November 9, 1832, of Thomas Ford Wheelock, named for a future governor of Illinois who was a close friend of the family. During the same period, a decision was made by the Wheelocks to leave Illinois for Texas and make their third try for a permanent home.

As with their efforts in the town of Ripley, affairs in Quincy had not developed according to plan. Wheelock and Abraham Prickett had fallen out, and their real estate partnership lay in ruins. Memories of hardship during the recent Winter of the Deep Snow were fresh and distressing. The cholera epidemic had killed thirty-three of their Quincy neighbors within five days. It was the last straw.

Besides, after a hiatus, Texas was open to Anglo settlement again.

BOOK TWO

MEXICAN TEXAS

We have been trying to find out what really happened in Texas in that vague and mysterious period before the Texas Revolution.

—Malcolm McLean

CHAPTER 4

TEXAS ON THE HORIZON: 1493-1821

Explorers

By the time the Wheelock family finally decided to emigrate, the substructure of Texas history had already been laid. In 1493, only one year after Columbus touched ground in the New World, Pope Alexander VI published the papal bull *Inter cetera divina* dividing it between the two Iberian nations, Spain and Portugal. In 1494 at the Treaty of Tordesillas these favored kingdoms worked out details. Territory which would some day be known as Texas was the spoil of Spain, at that time the most powerful nation in Europe.

Spain espoused two interests in its new domain, religious conversion and revenue, not necessarily in that order. Texas, which contained neither significant gold nor significant numbers of souls to be saved, largely escaped her attention. By 1741 a portion of her area was incorporated into the Mexican Province of Coahuila; the desolate remainder was known as the New Philippines. Spain's desultory efforts to establish itself in Texas did not thrive. Alone of several Spanish settlements, San

Antonio de Valero (if not exactly flourishing) had survived. Yet Spain clung to its empty province.

Others coveted Spain's enormous overseas empire. In 1763 her political strangle-hold on the Gulf of Mexico was eased as the Treaty of Paris ceded parts of Florida to the English; the Spanish were now increasingly annoyed by reports of English ships in its Gulf waters and Englishmen on land in its Gulf territories, along the Trinity River and in Louisiana. In 1775 a party of Englishmen squatted near the Neches River long enough to grow crops before disappearing, and in 1777 what was apparently another serious effort at Anglo colonization was aborted in the same area. The Spanish became aware of an Anglo menace.

The Cortes also had reason to be nervous about encroachments into Texas from the United States. Sinister Americans such as Gen. James Wilkinson were casting rapacious eyes west of the Brazos River. In 1791 this double agent (USA/Spain) sent a clerk named Philip Nolan into Texas, ostensibly as a peddler; his real mission was to obtain military information. Nolan was one of the first Texas explorers, the "bold, restless men, impelled by the fascination of wild adventure" to make "their way into new regions, reckless of danger and hardships." Spain notwithstanding, Texas could not remain "a closed garden of Hesperides to such spirits."[1]

Nolan was a filibusterer. The term means freebooter, an adventurer who invades a foreign land for personal gain but with semi-official authority. He met the customary end of such, killed by Spanish troops on March 21, 1801. The convoluted General Wilkinson saw that Nolan's maps and reports reached the right hands in Washington City.

Wilkinson's interest in Texas was not dampened by Nolan's death. In 1806 Wilkinson teamed up secretly with Aaron Burr to stage an invasion of Mexico. The next year, evidently losing confidence in this scheme, he denounced Burr as a traitor. Acquitted at his trial, Burr confessed to a friend later in life that "I did hope to establish an empire in Mexico and become its emperor."[2] No wonder the Spanish were alarmed.

Not a bit discouraged, later in 1806 Wilkinson dispatched Zebulon Pike to explore the headwaters of the Arkansas and Red

Rivers and if possible take a look at Spanish settlements in New Mexico. After being captured and released by the Spanish, Pike returned home along the future Robertson Colony's Old San Antonio Road (El Camino Real) in 1807. His favorable account tallies well with that of David Ingram, first English explorer of Texas, written two hundred years before. "Herds of mustangs, good land, ponds and small dry creek beds, prairie and woods."[3] No doubt Wilkinson was gratified.

Accounts of all these adventures were published throughout the United States (nowhere more than in the state of Tennessee) and followed with avid interest by prospective settlers. In 1812 would-be Texans were inspired by the writings in Tennessee newspapers of James Patteson, who had been incarcerated by the Spanish in 1809 while seeking a trade route to Santa Fe. The Spanish thought that his mercantile party was a nest of Napoleonic spies. While in Mexico Patteson witnessed the execution and decapitation of Fr. Miguel Hidalgo, the great revolutionary. When he returned to Nashville after three miserable years in a Mexican jail, Patteson testified that such barbarians as the Spanish did not deserve to rule in the Americas.

The desire to free Texas from Spain was becoming a disease. In the same year (1812), while the United States focused on war with Britain, the Gutierrez-Magee Expedition assembled at Natchitoches, Louisiana. It invaded Spanish territory and proclaimed Texas independent, but was soundly defeated by Spanish troops at the Battle of Medina River. Jose de Toledo (one of the conspirators who stayed home) subsequently took his tale to Nashville. Tennessee was again well supplied with first-hand information about Texas.

The involvement of the Wheelock family in the fate of Texas began in Louisiana. Along the United States side of the Sabine River, Cajuns had begun to worry about their foreign neighbors. Would the Spanish provoke Indian raids into their settlements in reprisal for the American forays into Texas? As early as 1816 Louisiana Gov. W.C.C. Claiborne had "urged the establishment of a post on the Sabine but was told that the hoped-for gain would not justify provoking the Spanish."[4] Gen. E. W. Ripley, now commander of the Eighth Military Department of New Orleans, agreed that the post on the Sabine was needed. The nearest United States stronghold, Fort Claiborne, was a two-day march east. But in 1806 a neutral ground between Spain and the United States prohibited military presence along the river. This was the year during which General Ripley was engaged in investment ventures in Illinois in partnership with his cousin E.L.R. Wheelock, and no doubt the latter heard all about General Ripley's plans for a Sabine fort.

In 1818 nervous Spanish troops moved east. General Ripley countered by stationing the First Infantry Regiment on the American side of the Sabine at newly christened Camp Ripley, which was maintained on neutral ground well into 1821. In 1822, after the international boundary was officially established and the neutral ground agreement abolished, Camp Ripley was replaced by Fort Jesup. But General Ripley's Texas career was not over. He was soon to occupy a bizarre and unique position in her history.

In 1819 the indefatigable General Wilkinson's nephew-in-law, Dr. James Long, resolved to free Texas from Spain. He established a fort at the beautiful Falls of the Brazos, destined to be briefly the capital of Robertson's Colony, later destroyed by a change in the river's course. There he proclaimed Texas free and independent. On June 23, 1820, Long wrote to his long-time friend, General Ripley:

Headquarters
Republic of Texas

To Major General E. W. Ripley
New Orleans, Louisiana USA
Sir:
I do myself the honor to announce to you that (I) having resigned that office, you have been duly elected President of the Republic by the Supreme Council thereof, convened conformable to the constitution, and as generalissimo of the armies and navy thereof. . .

A salary of $25,000 per annum out of the Treasury of the Republic and "twenty miles of land" were attached to this offer of employment.[5] Where they were to come from, no one knew.

General Ripley replied, "I have received with lively sensibility your communication . . . I have reviewed the present state of the colony (Texas) . . . paralyzed by the despotic and intolerant colonial system of Spain. . . And I have come to the determination to accept the appointment which the people of Texas have conferred upon me."

President-elect Ripley must have known all about Dr. Long's invasion and may have helped to finance it. The detailed plans he envisioned for Texas survive. But before any of these could be carried out, or indeed before he set foot on Texas soil, Long's dream of empire collapsed. He failed to secure the hoped-for military help of buccaneer Jean LaFitte, and his entire party was defeated and captured by Spanish troops. Long escaped and later joined a man named Ben Milam and one John Austin in attempting to aid Mexican rebels, only to be betrayed, imprisoned, and executed by the Spanish. E.L.R. Wheelock must have heard this tale of his cousin's ephemeral glory with intense interest.

These abortive Anglo efforts to free Mexico from Spain and open Texas to English-speaking settlers were well known in Mexico as well as in the United States, and formed the foundation upon which E.L.R. Wheelock and others like him built their dreams.

The Would-Be Empresario

Over a hundred years after the first futile English efforts to colonize Texas from Europe, an Englishman was born in Connecticut whose attempt almost succeeded. Moses Austin, after managing a family store in Philadelphia, married and moved to Virginia, where the curiously modern sounding boom-and-bust pattern of his ambitious life began. For a while, the young couple had the grandest house in Richmond; then money troubles forced Moses to leave his stately house and seek another source of income.

In 1792 Moses persuaded the Commonwealth of Virginia to lease and later sell a group of moribund lead mines to him and his partners. The Austins were soon prosperous again, selling shot, bar lead, and sheet lead from their factory outlet in Richmond.

This boom was followed by another bust, and Moses Austin decided to try his luck in the lead mines of Missouri, then a section of the Spanish territory of Louisiana. Here he again achieved great prosperity.

When Missouri became part of the United States through the Louisiana Purchase, Austin's wealth declined. Maimed by the financial Panic of 1819, the bank he had founded closed and his other problems proliferated. Ruined, he was imprisoned as a debtor. Although soon released, Moses Austin found himself a social pariah. Disgraced but never discouraged, he decided to begin again in another Spanish territory. As Colonel Morgan, the first American empresario, had been to Spanish Louisiana, so he would be to Spanish Texas. His knowledge of the Spanish empresario system used in Louisiana would give him a third chance for glory.

This system, later to be adopted by Mexico, allowed individuals to contract to settle stated numbers of colonists in stated territory within a stated period of time. In return, the empresario received substantial rewards. At this time Texas was part of the Eastern Interior Provinces of New Spain, under the civil and military jurisdiction of Gen. Joaquin de Arredondo. The governor of Texas serving under him was Antonio Martinez, and it was to him that Moses Austin applied to become a Texas empresario. Martinez's duty, however, was to evict Moses from Texas, which excluded all foreigners.

Moses Austin was ready to abandon his hopes and depart, when the intervention of an old friend saved him. A native of Dutch Guiana, Philip Hendrik Nering Bogel was fleeing embezzlement charges in the Netherlands when he arrived in Texas in 1805. Self-denominated from that year as the Baron de Bastrop, and obviously a man of great personal charm, he was already the recipient of Spanish permission to establish a colony between San Antonio and the Trinity River in the Province of Texas and stood high in the esteem of Governor Martinez.

Within three days Martinez had yielded to the Baron's persuasion and sent Moses' application for a colonization permit (in which he lied about his age and religion) on to General de Arredondo, with a strong positive recommendation. General de Arredondo approved this application for the settlement of 300

Anglo families in Texas and on December 29 the successful applicant left for home. Less than three months after his return to Missouri, however, Moses Austin died.

His elder son, Stephen, who was studying law in New Orleans, may have hoped to step smoothly into his father's shoes, but history intervened. In September 1821 Mexico declared its independence from Spain. The colonization permit issued by the Spaniards to Moses Austin became null and void.

CHAPTER 5

LEFTWICH'S GRANT: 1821-1825

The New Republic

Moses Austin was not the only man to lose his shirt in the Panic of 1819 and seek redress in Texas. Before 1821, according to popular wisdom, "Spain would not even let a bird cross the Sabine."[1] A Virginian named Robert Leftwich was to clear the air for many such birds, and E.L.R. Wheelock would be one of the flock.

Robert Leftwich was born about 1777 in Virginia and prospered as a Kentuckian until in 1819, like just about everyone else in America, he was caught up in economic catastrophe. Wiped out by this cataclysm, Leftwich looked around for new opportunities. On February 25, 1822, he became the legal representative of fifteen citizens of Russellville, Kentucky, who signed their names to "an article of association or agreement forming a Company to be composed of fifty persons or more for the purpose of obtaining a grant of land from the new Mexican government."[2] Texas, they felt, was a land of opportunity whose time had come.

Area in which Leftwich was granted permission to introduce families, April 15, 1825.
—Reproduced with permission from
McLean, *Papers Concerning
Robertson's Colony,* II, 301.

Other investors in the Texas scheme were needed. On
March 2 (prophetic date) Leftwich carried his agreement to
Nashville, Tennessee, where it was melded into a memorial by a
group of seventy prominent citizens. Nashville was a happy
choice. The city had followed the development of Anglo involvement in Texas with keen interest and was the home of James
Patteson, who had been a prisoner of the Spanish for three years
and whose account of the decapitation of Fr. Hidalgo had turned
so many American stomachs. His father, Nelson Patteson, became the moving spirit behind Nashville's Texas venture.

Among these signatories, in addition to the Pattesons, were
representatives of some of the most prominent families in
Tennessee. The Hardings ran horse-proud Bellemeade Plantation. The Robertsons were co-founders of Nashville. The
Childresses occupied one of its most elegant mansions. Soon-to-
be U.S. Congressman Sam Houston signed this document, perhaps the first to connect him with his land of destiny.

Leftwich and a Tennessean named Andrew Erwin were selected to represent the group in Mexico and soon set out by river
boat for New Orleans to obtain their colonization grant. Amos
Edwards, a signatory of the Tennessee Association, advanced
$6,500 for expenses.

The Tennessee Association must have realized that their
group was not the only one going hat-in-hand to Mexico for permission to settle Texas, but this did not worry them. Surely,
Texas was large enough for all. Later they were to discover that
not everyone agreed.

Arriving in New Orleans, Leftwich and Erwin called on
Attorney Andrew Duncan, a long-time friend and financial sup-
porter of the Mexican revolutionary movement, and signed him
up as a member of their association. For further financial support, they approached Joseph H. Hawkins, an attorney and former United States congressman, who had in the past financed
the Moses Austin family and owned a half interest in any Texas
lands the Austins might acquire there in the future.

Leftwich and Erwin, two innocents abroad, now began an
adventure which was to last three years and end in Leftwich's
mysterious death. On their journey from New Orleans to Mexico
the two ran into a sea captain, Thomas Reilly, to whom they had

a letter of introduction. This encounter was the preamble to a long history of false promises of help and insincere assurances of good will which would dog their footsteps in Mexico. Reilly spoke to them fairly, but unbeknownst to them was a lobbyist for the Austin interests, which were secretly hostile to competition and hoped to become the sole purveyors of Texas lands to American settlers. After meeting the representatives from Nashville, Reilly reported prophetically back to S. F. Austin through Hawkins in New Orleans that "there is every probability that Mr. Robert Leftwich will receive a Grant of Land—I cannot refrain from expressing my opinion of the whole Transaction that it is a Most singular and extraordinary One. In my Opinion the Austin Grant will have as much to fear from the encroachment of new grantees as from any other cause."[3]

S. F. Austin had, of course, no legal standing in Texas at this time—his father's grant from Spain having been voided by the Mexican Revolution—and was obliged to stand in line in Mexico City to ask for empresario status just like everyone else.

The inexperienced Tennesseans now faced a labyrinth of polite misdirection, accidental and deliberate misunderstandings, devious political maneuverings, and repeated frustration. Like most Anglos, they had little knowledge of the Latin psyche and cultural differences which controlled the environment into which they had ventured. Naively, they expected to travel to Mexico City, present their petition, gain approval, and return to Nashville in a few weeks. Austin had the advantage over them through his greater understanding of the Mexican mental climate. Leftwich was to struggle in this alien weather for over three years, and only his tough perseverance saved Nashville's grant in Texas.

Before any foreigner could obtain an empresario contract, however, two things had to happen. First, the new nation of Mexico had to hammer out a colonization law. This was difficult because many Mexicans quite rightly feared that Anglo colonization would lead to United States takeover. After that, each application had to be individually approved. Used to Yankee briskness, the Tennesseans needed some time to adjust to the leisurely pace of Latino business.

On April 29 Leftwich and Erwin got a roommate. It was
S. F. Austin, newly arrived to press his father's claim with the infant Mexican government. The three became part of a small but
potent American colony in Mexico City which developed under
the eye of Joel Roberts Poinsett, the American minister. A net-
work of Americans and Mexicans with American bias seemed to
support the future Anglo empresarios in their applications, as
did former Americans such as Col. Benjamin Rush Milam, who
was second in command to Gen. Jose Trespalacios, governor of
the province of Texas. Milam would later become a hero of the
Texas Revolution.

On April 30 Leftwich and Erwin had a private talk with S. F.
Austin, who promised to give them "all the aid in his power." He
assured them that it would be good for his colony to have other
American grants in Texas. They also received promises of support from William Taylor, United States diplomat in Mexico
City, Juan Davis Bradburn, a top government official, Gen.
James Wilkinson, and Anastacio Bustamante, captain general of
the Interior Provinces, which included Texas. Nothing could
have been more encouraging.

The gentlemanly Leftwich's diary and letters show that he
bowed gracefully to the Austin family's priority in the Texas land
grant race. Was there not plenty for all? Outwardly, the wily
Austin promised to help his compatriots in their suits, treat-
ing them with great cordiality. Behind the scenes he did all he
could to frustrate their hopes. Later Austin was to deny that he
had American friends in Mexico City during this period.
Andreas Reichstein excused him by writing, "If Austin did
not describe all this [his sharing quarters with Leftwich and
Erwin and promising them help], then it was because the others
were not primarily friends but competitors whom he accompanied everywhere . . . but he did not help them as promised."[4]
At the time, the unsuspicious Leftwich took Austin's word at
face value.

The Tennesseans and the Austin interests were not, of
course, the only petitioners. Milam (an old Texas hand), the so-
called Baron de Bastrop, General Wilkinson, and several others
including at least two Europeans were also applying for colonization grants. One of the latter was British General Arthur

Goodall Wavell. In July 1822 Austin made a contract with General Wavell, promising to divide between them any lands either might be granted. Wavell trusted Austin (whose manner must have been ingratiating when he wished) and returned home to England. Austin was later awarded ample grants, but Wavell was never to receive an acre in Texas from Austin, in spite of repeated pleas and later demands that their contract be honored.

The Mexican Empire

On May 13, 1822, the Tennessee Association and S. F. Austin both presented memorials to the Republic of Mexico Congress. But again revolution intervened. On May 18, 1822, Agustin de Iturbe was proclaimed Emperor Agustin I and all previous legislation was rescinded. Applications for colonial grants now had to be resubmitted to the government of the Mexican Empire.

In July Andrew Erwin was forced to leave for home to fulfill his obligations as a member of the Tennessee legislature, leaving his power of attorney from the association with General Wilkinson. This did not suit Leftwich, who wrote home, "Your acquaintance with the character of the General (which I do not admire) precludes the necessity of my saying any thing to you on that subject . . . He is very popular here and I have never seen a Spaniard that could exhibit more deception in common place salutations . . . he deals in flattery . . . nor does he refuse to receive the coin he passes."[5]

Left behind to carry on as best he could, Leftwich found Mexico in a holiday mood. As a guest of the United States minister, he occupied a diplomatic seat of honor in the cathedral at the coronation of the new emperor and empress. His account of this event is vastly entertaining, and shows a proper attention to what everyone wore. "The Empress was first conducted and seated on her throne attended by two gentlemen dress'd in full uniform and five maids of honor bearing the train of her dress (which was white trimmed with gold) accompanied by the Emperor's sister and her three small daughters dress'd in white and a crimson silk velvet robe trimmed with gold lace."[6]

Leftwich wrote to Hawkins in New Orleans, "We are yet between hope and despair relative to our memorial which is before the Mexican Congress for lands in Texas."[7]

After this ceremonial interlude, the imperial government finally took up routine business. On January 4, 1823, a new general colonization law was signed by the emperor, a law written "entirely according to Austin's conception and wishes,"[8] and again Leftwich applied on behalf of the Nashville group, proposing to site 600 families between the Brazos and the Navasota Rivers. He called on his big guns for support with the administration, but was disappointed (although not surprised) to find that General Wilkinson, although he had been willing enough to accept membership in the Nashville Company in exchange for his services, now found that he owed allegiance elsewhere.

On February 18 S. F. Austin's grant was singled out from the pile of waiting applications and signed. No others were approved, although many had been received before or at the same time that Austin's was presented. There were several reasons for his favored status. His father having received a grant from a previous government was no doubt considered, and the fact that some settlers were actually in place on his prospective land, albeit illegally, may have weighed in as an advantage. Reichstein theorizes that Austin's membership in the Masonic Order (favored by many Mexicans of republican persuasion) was another. Austin's skillful political maneuvering with influential Mexicans behind the scenes and his bluffing of rivals were certainly factors.

But in February Leftwich, not a bit disconcerted by Austin's success, wrote guilelessly to John Erwin in Nashville, "There are a number of applicants for lands from the United States which I fear has excited alarm, as the Govt. at this time are frightened of their own shadow."[9] Leftwich still had not identified Austin as an adversary.

In the meantime, the emperor's rule was not going smoothly. A certain Gen. Antonio Lopez de Santa Anna had taken arms on behalf of republican rebels and captured the city of Vera Cruz. On March 19, 1823, the emperor abdicated under pressure, voiding the S. F. Austin empresario contract, and leaving all applicants to reapply to a third set of officials.

The Second Republic

Leftwich had had no idea of the difficulties and time frame he would face in Mexico, and was now running short of money. But he was not discouraged. Nor was Austin. Without waiting for the passage of a revised colonization act by the new Congress, Austin resubmitted his request for a grant on April 5, and on April 14 it was again signed. Leftwich wrote, "It may not be amiss here to remark that Austin's application was considered by the Mexican Govt. on a very different footing from the other applicants, having a grant from the former Govt. and a large number of already settled and open farms on said grant. This alone was the cause of his succeeding at that period."[10] But there was probably more to it. Austin knew how to handle the Mexicans. He had the advantage of early exposure to Spanish manners in Missouri and had been advised by his father. In 1835 he was to write to his sister:

> They are a strange people, and must be studied to be managed. They have high ideas of National dignity should it be openly attacked, but will sacrifice national dignity, and national interest too, if it can be done in a still way, or so as to not arrest public attention. . . . God punishes the exposure more than the crime is their motto. This maxim influences their morals and their politics. I learned it when I was there in 1822 and I now believe that if I had not always kept it in view and known the power which appearances have on them, even when they know they are deceived, I should never have succeeded . . ."[11]

The successful Austin now sought to deflect the Nashville Company's plans by attempting to persuade Leftwich disingenuously that Texas had no future. Leftwich, who had no doubts about Texas, offered to buy Austin out. This offer was of course refused. Later on, Austin tried the same ploy on Wavell with the same result. That dog was not hunting.

Austin's next maneuver was to propose that Leftwich buy a

league of land from him at six and a half cents per acre and travel with him to Texas. He even caused a passport to be issued in both their names. On their arrival in Texas, Austin prophesied, Leftwich could again apply for land. Leftwich had the good sense to refuse.

Accordingly, on April 18 Austin traveled alone to Texas to bring the news to his colonists that they were now on legal ground, although it would not be until August of 1824, fifteen months later, the year of E.L.R. Wheelock's first Texas journey, that the Old Three Hundred received legal titles.

Leftwich remained in Mexico City and wrote a new memorial.

Austin continued to be worried about the Tennessee Association and its probability of success. On April 23 he wrote to Leftwich enclosing a letter of introduction to a certain Don Juan Arizpe, a man supposed to have influence with the government, proposing that the Tennessee Association grease his palm in return for help with its application. A sum of five or six doubloons was mentioned. But bribes did not work any more than words.

On May 16, 1824, Texas and Coahuila were combined into one state, with its capital in Saltillo, and the states of the Second Mexican Republic were given power to create and administer their own colonization law. Shortly thereafter, Leftwich moved his campaign to Saltillo. Undefeated when many would have given up long since, abandoned financially by the Tennessee Association, now operating on a personal loan from Haden Edwards, he made his last application for a colonization grant in his own name.

On October 20, 1824, Leftwich presented his petition to settle 800 Catholic families in Texas on eight million acres to the Provincial Congress.

Two months later, S. F. Austin wrote a remarkable letter to Gaspar Flores, alcalde of San Antonio de Bexar, proposing that all of Texas be portioned out to two individuals, himself and Erasmus Seguin, to the exclusion of all other empresarios.

When the Baron de Bastrop, Leftwich, and others seeking empresario grants received a copy of Austin's letter to Flores, they were thunderstruck. Here indeed was betrayal, hard proof that Austin was trying to shut out all competition for Texas in favor of himself and his associates.

Robert Leftwich's purgatory finally came to an end as on March 24, 1825, the State Colonization Law of Coahuila and Texas was passed, and on April 15 his grant made official along with those of Americans Green DeWitt, Haden Edwards, and Frost Thorn. Leftwich's ordeal was over, nine applications and three years after his departure from Nashville.

His grant included land "beginning on the western bank of the Navasota Creek, at the point where it is crossed by the upper road leading from Bexar to Nacogdoches, thence with the said road westwardly to the summit of the heights which divide the waters of the Brazos and the Colorado. Thence from the said heights to the road leading from Nacogdoches to the Comanche Indian nation, thence east with the said road to the aforesaid Navasota Creek, and thence with said creek downward to the place of beginning." [12]

On this land, E.L.R. Wheelock would found his last town.

CHAPTER 6

ADVENTURES AND MISADVENTURES: 1826-1834

Colonel Foster's Tenure:
The Texas Association's Colony

Illinois resident E.L.R. Wheelock must have known a great deal about developments in Texas between 1826 and 1833. He was aware of his cousin General Ripley's fleeting term as president of the Republic of Texas in 1820, a non-event which would nevertheless have heightened the family's already keen interest in the fate of this far-off province. He read the St. Louis and Quincy newspapers with zealous attention, at times punctuated with dismay and at other times with hope. No doubt letters were exchanged from time to time with General Ripley, now a confirmed Texas watcher.

Texas's tale as seen from the point of view of eventual settlers in Robertson's Colony was convoluted and baffling. The government of the Republic of Mexico disputed among themselves as to whether Anglos ought to be in Texas at all. Immigration rules were altered. Already established colonies were determined to maintain their pre-eminence by hook or by crook, even at the expense of other grants.

On the home front, by 1826 the board of directors of the Texas Association needed a new agent. Robert Leftwich, their original representative, had mysteriously disappeared, his fate still unknown today.[1] Dr. Felix Robertson, who replaced him informally, had inspected and surveyed a portion of the Texas grant, made his report to the association, and returned to the practice of medicine in Nashville.

To succeed Dr. Robertson, the board turned again to a prominent Nashville family, choosing Col. Benjamin Franklin Foster, the son of Robert Coleman Foster, a former state senator. Early in November 1826, armed with letters of introduction to S. F. Austin, Foster and eleven other men embarked from Nashville with high hopes of making their colony a reality. They ran into an insurrection.

On November 22, while Foster and friends were still on the river, forty Americans attacked and subdued Nacogdoches, under the instigation of Empresario Haden Edwards in reprisal for what he judged to be the Mexican government's unjust cancellation of his contract. On December 12 Benjamin Edwards, the brother of Haden, proclaimed the Fredonia Republic and proceeded to sign a treaty with the Indians giving Fredonia the north half of Texas and the Indians the south half.

The Fredonians were sure that all Anglo settlers in Texas and many United States citizens would rally to their cause, but the time to liberate Texas had not yet come. Although American public opinion supported Fredonia, no United States troops arrived from Louisiana. Other Anglos already in Texas, under the influence of S. F. Austin (whose grant had not been annulled), supported the Mexican government. The Indians soon abandoned the sinking Fredonia ship and on January 31, 1827, the citizens of Fredonia fled to Louisiana before a conglomerate force of Mexican soldiers and Austin Colony settlers, supported by Nashville's Colonel Foster.

By his adherence to the Mexican cause against the Fredonians, Foster earned the Mexicans' respect, but not an appointment as the new empresario of Leftwich's Grant. Obliged to return to Nashville empty handed, he resigned.

Hosea League's Tenure:
The Nashville Colony

The Association hastened to frame a long memoir to the government of the State of Coahuila and Texas laying out its history and asking that Leftwich's Grant be declared null and void and transferred to the association. As its fourth leader it mistakenly chose an old Texas hand named Hosea H. League.

League was probably selected because he had just come from Texas, where he had been a kind of sub-agent for Austin, who now consented to assist in getting Nashville's contract reaffirmed. The petition included a request for an essential extension of time. In due course Leftwich's Grant legally passed to the Nashville Colony as requested. The name Nashville Colony was accidental (a mislabeling by Austin) but served well enough. League was named empresario. All the above provisions had Austin's support. Curiously, the time extension, without which League would be hard pressed to fulfill his contract as empresario, was denied.

At this juncture, League, instead of returning to Tennessee to recruit settlers for the Nashville Colony, settled in San Felipe, the capital of Austin's Colony, and began the practice of law.

Simultaneously, a catastrophe occurred back home in Nashville. Nelson Patteson, moving spirit of the Texas Association, was unmasked as an embezzler and forger and committed suicide. Serious immigrants lost faith in the Texas Association. On June 1, 1828, Amos Edwards, an original signer, took a grant in Galveston County, which was Austin country. William H. Wharton wrote League on September 12, 1828, that the Texas fever had died in Tennessee.

It was a great pity. The Nashville Colony grant was known to the Indians as *Teha Lanna*, the Land of Beauty. A party of soldiers passing through described it as a region where "the bottoms on the streams were rich and beautiful—the water pure and transparent, and the uplands of the best quality. The prairies were covered with flowers at nearly every season of the year."[2]

The only person who seemed to retain confidence in the Nashville Colony was Sterling Robertson, who had hoped as early as the fall of 1827 to take twenty to thirty families to Texas. Fate and Robertson's hot head intervened.

Robertson, "a man of commanding appearance, tall and thin, cultured, refined, honorable in all his dealings, and highly esteemed as a citizen and official,"[3] was earning his living by running a brick yard in Nashville with leased slave labor. On December 3, 1829, he was convicted of feloniously slaying another man with a knife in a dispute over a slave. Robertson did not deny the fact. He was sentenced to be branded in the inside of the left hand with the letter *M*, serve nine months in prison, and pay all costs of his trial. Robertson appealed to the Tennessee Supreme Court.

In the meantime, on April 6, 1830, the Mexican House of Deputies, again fearful of Anglo domination, passed a new law decreeing that empresario contracts which had not been completed were canceled. Because in a technical sense none of his own contracts had been completed, Austin was alarmed but able to use his influence to get the law changed to exempt his colony.

In February, out on bail and quite ignorant of what was going on in Mexico, Robertson set about actively recruiting for the Nashville Colony. One of his settlers, Noah Smithwick, remembered the eloquent speech Robertson gave to prospective clients, "the glowing terms in which he descanted on the advantages to be gained by emigration . . . Of the hardships and privations, . . . he was discretely silent."[4]

Robertson was legally able to promise these prospective settlers 177 acres of farm land, 4,428 acres of ranch land, tax exemption for six years, and imports free of duty for personal use. He offered a shining prospect. On April 5, 1830, the *Nashville Republican* published a warning that Tennesseans who disregarded this opportunity to come to Texas would "throw a pearl away richer than all their tribe."[5] The Tennesseans did not know how well that pearl was now guarded.

On April 24, 1830, the Principal Commandant of Coahuila and Texas, Colonel Antonio Elosna, was ordered to build a fort on the Upper Brazos to close the border at the Old San Antonio Road to further Anglo settlers (except those bound for Austin's Colony).

Colonel Francisco Ruiz, later to own land near E.L.R.

Wheelock's plantation in Robertson's Colony and to become a signer of the Texas Declaration of Independence, was chosen to build the fort.

General Manuel de Mier y Teran, the commandant general of the Eastern Interior States, who wished to see Texas cleansed of Yankees, had the responsibility for siting the fort. He ordered Ruiz to choose a situation halfway between Nacogdoches and San Antonio on the southern boundary of the Nashville Grant. In a letter to Lucas Alaman, Minister of Internal and Foreign Relations, Mier y Teran described his vision of a new capital here for the State of Texas, settled by Mexicans and honored by the name Tenoxtitlan (the place of the prickly pear), which was the original Aztec name of Mexico City.

Still innocent of any knowledge of these new developments, on June 4 Robertson wrote to Empresario League that he and his new partner Alexander Thomson would bring about 150 families to Texas that fall, easily fulfilling his quota by its deadline, April 15, 1831, ten months hence.

Ignorant of Tenoxtitlan and all its implications, Robertson and a company of ten mounted men passed through Little Rock on September 4 and headed for San Felipe. He found League effectively out of action. The do-nothing empresario had witnessed a murder and been arrested as an accessory. In the absence of a jail, he and the accused had been chained up on September 2 to the wall of an empty log cabin. Guilty until proven innocent under the Mexican law, he would hang for weeks awaiting a judge's arrival. When Robertson reached the official empresario of the Nashville Colony on October 10, he found a ruined man, sick, impoverished, and bereft of friends. Even his wife had deserted him. League was only too glad to turn over his power of attorney to Robertson.

Austin's Audacious Attempt: The Upper Colony

On October 25 Sterling Clack Robertson presented himself and six friends in a friendly way to Colonel Ruiz at Tenoxtitlan, where the Tennessean was apprised of the new law prohibiting Anglo immigration except to Austin's and DeWitt's Colonies.

Three days later Alexander Thomson and fifty immigrants, the vanguard of the Tennessee migration, arrived in Nacogdoches. Repulsed by authorities there, they found an alternate route and by November 12 were reunited with Major Robertson.

Thunderstruck by news of the devastating Decree of April 6, 1830, Robertson pleaded with Ruiz, who supported the immigrants' position and wrote wryly to Austin (who obviously had the ear of the state government), "What this country needs is honest, hardworking people, even if they come from Hell itself."[6]

Back in San Felipe, Major Robertson begged Austin, just elected sole Texas delegate to the State Congress, to intercede for him and his people in Saltillo. Austin promised to solicit an extension of time for them, and "on his word of honor to secure the appointment of a commissioner for the Nashville Colony to put the families belonging to same in legal possession of their lands."[7] Robertson was now to learn what Austin's word of honor was worth.

Once in Saltillo, Austin saw that his chance had finally come to seize the former Leftwich Grant. Using a power of attorney purporting to come from his secretary, Samuel May Williams, he petitioned the Saltillo government to declare the Nashville grant void and transfer it to himself and Williams, a man of questionable reputation who had entered Texas traveling with a female companion as Mr. and Mrs. E. Eckleston. Mrs. Eckleston was later repudiated, and her husband reverted to the name of Williams, supposedly in order to marry again. Austin represented to the Mexican officials in Saltillo (where there was no one to contradict him) that the Tennesseans had never sent any settlers or made any attempt to colonize. The officials believed him and granted his request.

Before he left Saltillo, Austin made deals with a group of influential Mexicans for large grants in his new colony, from now on to be known as the Upper Colony. Sixteen individuals, mostly speculators, received over a million acres in the so-called Upper Colony from Austin. This transaction was Texas's largest land speculation to date and Austin's neat theft its largest swindle.

Knowing nothing of what had happened in Saltillo and trusting Austin's word, Robertson now made arrangements for the safety and comfort of his colonists during the winter and started home for his appearance in the Court of Appeals. January 1831 found him in Louisiana recruiting settlers for the Nashville Colony.

Back in Tennessee Robertson's appeal on his manslaughter conviction was denied. The date at which he was to begin his sentence was, however, postponed until January 16, 1832. Realizing that time was running out for the Nashville Grant, Robertson sold some of his own land to raise money and boarded the Steamboat *Criterion* at Nashville on March 29, paying passage for himself and eleven colonists. One of these was future Chief Justice of Robertson County Francis Slaughter.

About the same time, Alexander Thomson shepherded in a new group of Nashville settlers by way of New Orleans, landing at Harrisburg, Texas, on April 2, 1831. The Nashville contract was to expire in thirteen days, but the Tennesseans were still confident that they could get their one hundred families on site in time.

Arriving in Texas in May, Robertson learned that Austin was back from Saltillo and hastened to discover the result of his pleadings on behalf of the Nashville Company. Although Austin was to conceal his personal involvement for several months, he must have told Robertson at this time that the Nashville grant had been canceled.

Sterling Robertson's reaction was to fight back as hard as was legally possible. He at once hired a lawyer with his own money to present the Nashville Colony's case in Saltillo. His choice was a splendid one. Thomas Jefferson Chambers was a brilliant, Virginia-born twenty-nine-year-old who had been admitted to the bars of both Kentucky and Alabama and was fluent in Spanish.

Austin did not admit his judicial theft of the Nashville Colony until fall, when General Mier y Teran gave him permission to settle Robertson's colonists in his grant and claim the land premium for himself.

As soon as his attorney had prepared all the paper work, Robertson presented his petition for redress to Francis White, alcalde of San Felipe, as required by Mexican law. It was approved on December 6, 1831, but mysteriously suspended for eleven months, until December 6, 1832. By then, of course, the time limit imposed on the Nashville Colony for the settling of 100 families would have expired.

For the moment, Robertson had other obligations back in Tennessee. On April 6, 1832, having been pardoned by the governor from the sentence of branding (which the Tennessee Legislature was even then outlawing), he served his jail sentence, being discharged on September 1. His family stuck by him, and the Texas Association, of which his nephew-in-law was now president, seemed willing to lay all the colonization burden on Sterling. Perhaps they thought he needed a new start in life in a new country. If so, he was in many ways the epitome of the Texas immigrant of story and song, a renegade in search of a new home, except that he did not pin GTT (Gone To Texas) on his door or leave secretly. To his credit, he never sought to evade Tennessee law, and honorably fulfilled the sentence imposed by its courts. Back in Texas, he was now to show his mettle as a fighter and a stayer.

While Robertson was paying his debt to society, additional tremors were shaking Texas. The town of San Felipe had unwisely called a convention (forbidden in Mexican law) to present demands for reform. To them the demands seemed eminently reasonable: their own schools, self-government, a separate state under Mexican rule, and the repeal of the Law of April 6 curtailing Anglo immigration.

The ins and outs of Mexican politics were opaque to most settlers, who were dismayed when they saw new presidents assuming office in Mexico City without the benefit of an election. General Santa Anna had become a major actor in an intricate power play going on in the capital, and it was difficult to tell who was in charge. Mier y Teran had committed suicide and his dream city Tenoxtitlan had been abandoned. Mexico City seemed to smolder near anarchy.

Robertson was now ready to present his case in Saltillo, but fearing interference from Austin supporters, he decided to take his papers directly to the state capital rather than go through local channels as required. Perhaps he was unaware that Mexicans did not take kindly to bureaucratic shortcuts.

By this time Austin and Williams had located millions of acres of speculative grants in the Nashville Colony; the litigation which would eventually be necessary to straighten out these illicit titles and reinstate true settlers would delay the settlement of Central Texas for forty years.

On February 7, 1833, Robertson and his party arrived in Saltillo, but soon afterwards the state capital moved to Monclova, Governor Veramendi's home town, and Robertson went with it. In the same month Robertson presented his documents to the governor. The congress adjourned in April without having acted on Robertson's plea, perhaps offended by his attempt to by-pass official channels.

That same month the town of San Felipe called another meeting, fired Austin as its presiding officer, and elected William Wharton to replace him. The town drew up a proposed constitution for a separate state of Texas within the Republic of Mexico and directed it on April 22 to Gomez Farias, its acting president. Austin, who must have known how subversive it would look to the Mexicans, was persuaded to carry this incendiary document to Mexico City.

In June Robertson was back in San Felipe buying supplies, and in November he again presented his plea to the ayuntamiento of San Felipe, this time going through the proper channels.

In December 1833 Robertson posted a declaration of war against what he judged the perfidy of S. F. Austin:

TO THE PUBLIC

All you who came to Texas with the intention of settling in the Nashville or upper colony are invited to come forward, make your selections, settle, claim and assert your rights, and help defend it against the General plunderers. . . Will you lie and let them keep their skinning knife employed while you see them fleece without mercy and see they have no bounds to their avarice? Rise like men and come before the world and claim your own. You have nothing to fear but two men of which nothing but a god could make anything of but traitors and swindlers. . .

Sterling C. Robertson[8]

He was also quoted as saying that he could not depend on local support in San Felipe because "the risk of exposing the conduct of their patron Saint Stephen and his trumpeter Sam was too certain."[9]

At this time Robertson had 350 settlers (including E.L.R. Wheelock) ready to move to his colony in Texas.

In Mexico City, S. F. Austin's usual powers of persuasion failed him. He presented the proposed state constitution of Texas to Acting President Valentin Gomez Farias, who was all smiles and verbal support. So was General Santa Anna, his *grise eminence*. Austin then rashly quarreled with Gomez Farias and wrote an uncharacteristically angry and high-handed letter critical of the president. The letter was intercepted, and in January 1834 Austin was arrested in Saltillo, returned to Mexico City, and cast into the Prison of the Inquisition, where he would remain for eighteen months.

On February 5, 1834, Major Robertson once again presented his compelling suit to the ayuntamiento of San Felipe, by whose hand it was soon approved and sent through channels to Monclova for further action by the Congress.

By this time, Austin probably realized that his greed for land had gotten him into trouble. He had written to Williams the previous year, "Keep clear of speculations for the future. They are a curse to any country and will be a very sore curse to me individually. I believe they will ruin me if they have not already done it. Cursed be the hour that I ever thought of applying for the Upper Colony."[10]

Sam Williams took advantage of Austin's absence to begin his own campaign to keep the so-called Upper Colony. This time fate was on Robertson's side. Williams's agent was waylaid by Indians on his journey to Monclova, and subsequently died of his wounds. Williams's next choice for advocate was former Mexican official Juan Antonio Padilla, who unknown to Williams had lost his civil rights after having served a term in jail in Nacogdoches in 1832.

Robertson wrote a very long and detailed petition, dated April 2, 1834, addressed to the Congress of Coahuila and Texas. He also sent a shorter document to Governor Veramendi. The most powerful man on the committee which would judge this case was Agustin Viesca, who enjoyed the soubriquet of the Grand Sultan. On April 23, 1834, a first reading was given to the bill, which granted Robertson four more years in which to fulfill his immigration contract, the title and office of empresario, and the same plot of land which Leftwich had originally received in 1824. On April 26 the petition was approved and sent to the governor. On April 29 the governor signed Robertson's petition.

In its final form the declaration of the governor contained these provisions:

1. Austin and Williams's contract, insofar as it concerned the Nashville Colony, was declared null and void.
2. Families who had applied before the original deadline were to be reinstated.
3. The limits of Robertson's Colony were to be the same as the limits of the Nashville Colony.
4. Any settlers introduced by Austin and Williams in the meantime were to have their grants respected, but could not be counted for bonus land by either empresario.

That same day Padillo finally got his citizenship back. His first step was to have the elated Robertson arrested and thrown in jail for slander on a complaint by Samuel May Williams. But Robertson, undaunted, wrote to the governor on May 4 citing the unsavory reputation of Williams and was quickly released.

Finally, on May 22, 1834, the official decree was handed down canceling the Austin and Williams grant to the *soi disant* Upper Colony and restoring the colony to Robertson as empresario.

From now on, it would be proper to refer to Robertson's Colony.

CHAPTER 7

ROBERTSON'S COLONY: 1833-1835

Pilgrimage

E.L.R. Wheelock had been advised to bring proof of good character with him to Texas. In 1833 he began to collect testimonial letters:

United States of America, State of Illinois
The People of the State of Illinois, To all to whom these presents shall come or may concern, Greeting.
Know Ye That the bearer E.L.R. Wheelock Esquire, a respectable, peaceable, and worthy citizen of the State, whose signature appears upon the margin, being about to emigrate to one of the States of Mexico, our Sister Republic, for the purpose of pursuing commerce, agriculture or such other employment which may be lawful:
Now Therefore, I John Reynolds, Governor and Commander in Chief of the State of Illinois aforesaid, do for the purpose of making known to the authorities of our sister Republic of Mexico, and for the further purpose of preventing inconvenience, delay, or hindrance in the pursuit of all lawful business of our worthy,

Map of Robertson's Colony, 1834-35.
—Reproduced with permission from
McLean, *Papers Concerning
Robertson's Colony,* II, 301.

good, and peaceable citizen E.L.R. Wheelock, do under the effect
of the Treaty of Amity and Commerce which so happily exists between the two countries, by these presents grant to our worthy citizen E.L.R. Wheelock Esquire, his family and domestics, a free
passport or letter of safe conduct to any of the Mexican States,
recommending him to their special protection as a American citizen,
In testimony whereof, I, John Reynolds, Governor as aforesaid,
have hereto set my hand and caused the seal of the said State of
Illinois to be hereunto affixed.
Done at Vandalia, this 16th day of November, Anno Domini
1833.

> Signed: John Reynolds, Governor
> A. P. Field, Secretary of State

The young Wheelocks had been told that the family was
pondering a move to Texas. The children were enchanted at the
idea. Annette, along with William and David (maybe George
Ripley was too old for such shenanigans):

> rigged up a little wagon with their playthings, a camping outfit
> consisting of such things as they could get together, she being
> eleven years old at the time and her brothers younger, and
> hitched up the goats to the wagon and started for Texas. They
> had a little trouble at first getting the goats going and pulling
> around the yard, when all of a sudden they bumped into a bee
> gum, the bees started stinging them, and the goats tore up the
> wagon and scattered everything all over the place.[1]

Before leaving for Texas, E.L.R. visited his sister in Indiana
to share his plans and hopes for the future. All his life he maintained a tender concern for her as well as for his brothers, to
whom he had tried to be a substitute father. John was dead.
William was settled in Alton, Illinois, where he would die in
1850, a bachelor with a fat estate. Now E.L.R. and George were
heading for Mexico. Nancy Wheelock Hillman felt the separation by nationality very keenly.
The Wheelocks' trek from Illinois to Texas lasted for several
weeks. They traveled overland with their worldly goods in

wagons, the Colonel and the other males in the party on horseback, and Mary Wheelock with her younger children conveyed
in a carriage pulled by two fine mares. On a narrow road in
Arkansas they met a man with a wagon load of bear hides.
Colonel Wheelock went ahead to ask him to pull aside so that his
mares would not be frightened by the fetid stench of bear, but
the surly driver refused. An offer of a small amount of money
was equally futile. Finally, the Wheelocks were obliged to edge
forward towards the load of rancid skins, and as they had feared,
the two fine mares would have nothing of it. They bolted, turning the carriage over, and pinning its occupants inside. Annette
remembered crawling out the back window of that carriage and
waiting by the road while her father felled a tree and made a
new tongue for the carriage. "From there on to Texas the carriage was pulled by a yoke of oxen."[2]

As they crossed over into Texas in January 1834, Col.
Wheelock was forty-one years old, his wife thirty-seven, George
Ripley almost fifteen, Annette twelve, William six, David four,
and Thomas Ford one and a half. Mary's brother Jacob Prickett
accompanied them. The colonel's brother George Wheelock was
to follow them to Texas with his family.

A Grand and Liberal Settlement

Colonel Wheelock now settled his family into temporary
quarters and set out to consider what opportunities might lie
open to him. Not surprisingly, he traveled first to San Felipe,
which he knew from previous visits. Austin was still in prison in
Mexico City, and Samuel May Williams was running Austin's
colony. Wheelock decided to approach Green DeWitt, holder of
an adjoining grant, to whom he had a letter of introduction
from an old friend, H. G. Miller. It reads as follows:

Col. DeWitt
My Dear Sir:
I take the liberty of commending to your friendship Col.
Wheelock, a friend of mine, formerly of the U. S. Army, appris-
ing you that in him you will meet one to whom any honorable

society will always owe much. But his independence unfits him for the latitude of these parts. He comes with a view to making a grand and liberal settlement in Texas. This scheme will please you both as a lover of the welfare of our country and with reference to your own Colony's interest and safety, more especially. In him I recommend to you one to whom you may fully confide with pleasure and delight.

Respectfully,
H. G. Miller

What did Miller mean by "the latitude of these parts"? Was Wheelock unable to fall in line behind S. F. Austin's deputy? What was Wheelock's "grand and liberal settlement"? There is no doubt that he had ambitious plans for himself, a vision which reached beyond the ordinary. Evidently, Miller thought these aims coincided with DeWitt's, since he would receive Wheelock with "pleasure and delight."

But it seems that Wheelock's visit with Colonel DeWitt did not please him any more than Austin's Colony had, and "on the last days of June or the first day of July 1834" Colonel Wheelock accompanied Maj. Sterling C. Robertson, Land Commissioner William Steele, and a few others into Robertson's Colony "seeking a home for my family."[3] Wheelock explored the land drained by Cedar, Copperas, and Tiger Creeks, and sited his league along the Old San Antonio Road.

Wheelock's grant was surveyed by J. B. Chance, the survey reading as follows:

> Beginning on the San Antonio Road on the east side of the Brazos River, at a stake on the north side of said road, Thence southwest following the meanders of said road, and formed a corner on a stake. Thence northwest to corner of another stake. Thence northeast crossing Copperas Creek, the southwest arm of Cedar Creek, and formed a corner on a quince tree on the southwest bank of said Cedar Creek, to the point of beginning.
>
> Villa de Viesca, January 19, 1835. Signed by Guillermo H. Steel, Land Commissioner. Assisting witnesses: Manuel Valdes Flores and M. Cummins.

His league and labor cost him $30, which went to Empresario Robertson. Next to the Colonel's parcel was the smaller strip allotted to his son, George Ripley Wheelock, as a single man, and, two strips over, a similar labor assigned to his brother-in-law, Jacob Prickett.

Accounts agree that the region occupied by Wheelock's head right, from henceforth to be known as Wheelock Prairie, was choice. It offered "rolling prairie, well-wooded and well-drained," with surface water twenty to fifty feet below ground and an annual rainfall of thirty-five inches. Shade trees such as oaks, pecans, walnuts, hickory elm, cedar willow, and cottonwood flourished. Pines for building soared above like the masts of sailing ships. In-season grapes, plums, persimmons, and blackberries ached for picking. In the spring dogwood, red bud, trumpet vine, bluebonnets (called buffalo clover by the settlers), Indian paintbrush, sunflowers, daisies, and verbena gladdened the eye. Two substantial creeks, as clear as the day, ran through the grant.

Wheelock Prairie is still a prime deer hunting enclave today. In the 1830s it must have seemed that the ark had just landed. Antelope, bison, bears, wolves, mountain lions, deer, javelina, wild horses and cattle, wild turkey, birds of many feathers, all fell to the gun almost at will.

While the Wheelocks were cutting the first pines for their log rolling near spring-fed Cedar Creek, Major Robertson was building a capital for his colony. He chose (like the Tawakoni Indians before him) the Falls of the Brazos, near present-day Marlin, a romantic and scenic setting with plentiful springs. He named his capital Sarahville de Viesca, after his mother and the Mexican politician, the Grand Sultan, who had helped him win his grant. But its official name was Villa de Viesca.

For the fourth time Wheelock stripped his muscular, six-foot frame to don working clothes and built a log cabin, principally with his own hands and those of his family. There was a central room, a loft for the children, and a shed room, which was used as a kitchen. It was much like the log cabin the colonel had prepared for his bride in Bond County, Illinois, sixteen years before, the one his father built in Ohio in 1810, and indeed the one his great-great-grandfather had built in Mendon, Connecticut, in the early seventeenth century.

Again the menfolk cleared and planted virgin fields. According to William Bollaert, "these new lands of Texas merely required scraping and a crop of corn or cotton comes up the first year."[4] The women of the family again got out their vegetable seeds and by the second season proudly served their family watermelon, muskmelon, pumpkin, peas, and corn.

Politically, the crop was not so wholesome. No one was prepared for the magnitude of Indian conflict in Robertson's Colony because its worst aspects arose only after the arrival of the settlers. Robertson's grant covered prime hunting ground claimed by tribes fiercer and wilder than any they had encountered back home in Illinois and Tennessee. It was soon necessary to make the Wheelock dwelling into a fortress. Wheelock's block house was needed for protection from marauding plains Indians for almost ten years. Known as Fort Wheelock, it was bordered by tall, spiked cedar logs with gun holes in the walls. The heavy foundation logs sat in a ditch. Another parallel ditch and cedar barricade was set up outside and the intervening space filled with dirt. Heavy logs were laid across the top and covered with more soil. Later a ten-foot stockade enclosed about three acres around this fortification.

On November 9, 1834, the first mention of the community of Wheelock which has come down to us occurs in a letter to Sterling Robertson from Joseph Chance. This long letter, headed Wheelock, November 9th, 1834, is a plea from Chance to Robertson to find a way to reconcile boundary disputes among the settlers and prospective settlers and to fight slanders by the Austin contingent. It reads:

> Unless you do resort to some means to gain friends and to put a stop to the calumny which has spread itself abroad against you, you will not get anything like a liberal proportion of the wealthy Emigration the ensuing winter and spring.[5]

Wheelock became involved in some of these boundary disputes. In November 1834 a survey was begun for an eleven league grant Robertson had given Jose Antonio Nixon in return for favors bestowed in Monclova. This parcel was run around the improvements, dwellings, and enclosures of Dread Dawson, Mrs.

Hudson, J. McGrew, and others—contrary to their express wishes and without their consent. Wheelock was troubled to discover that the survey had been almost completed before these people found out why it was being made.

Uneasily, Wheelock began to suspect that behind Major Robertson's back and perhaps without his knowledge the distribution of land in the colony was not always fairly managed. But he was a stranger and a newcomer. For the time being he held his tongue.

Robertson's Colony was now prospering. On November 14, 1834, Jeremiah Tinnin, one of the empresario's sub-agents, reported, "I am filling up my Colony very fast. The Parker tribe is removing back pretty fast. Also I understand that there is several more families of the Irish coming in. I think a few more settlers and I will be obliged to have my colony enlarged." "Benjamin Cochrum and family have arrived; also four other families at Wheelock's."[6]

The Irish coming in were Ulster Scot Presbyterians who in 1833 had established an unauthorized community called Staggers Point (probably stakers' point) on the O.S.R. near present day Benchly. After Tenoxtitlan, their settlement was the oldest in Robertson's Colony. Many Staggers Point residents were to move on to Wheelock Prairie.

On November 29, 1934, Major Robertson printed the following notice:

THIS splendid country, known by the name of the Nashville Colony, which has so long been the object of a legal contest, has at length been restored to its rightful owner, and although this interesting section of Texas has for a long time been kept a wilderness by fraud and chicanery, justice has at last gained a triumph over perfidy, and it is now open for settlement according to the terms of the contract that the Nashville Company and the law of colonization of the 24th March, 1825.[7]

Indeed, between October 1834 and March 1835, 145 grants were issued in Robertson's Colony to 132 individuals, most having their families with them. These were real settlers. During the time that Austin and Williams held this land as the Upper

Colony, their grants were mostly to "non-resident Mexican politicians, represented by non-resident American speculators who were being charged $2,000 for the privilege of locating eleven-league grants in the area. On the other hand, the typical Robertson colonist was actually in the area with his family ready to build homes, cultivate the soil, raise livestock, fight the Indians, lay out roads, and do all the things necessary to make the heart of Texas productive."[8] The distinction was an important one.

Lord of All You Survey

Austin's interference and other legal difficulties had tangled land titles in Robertson's Colony past toleration. The most pressing need of new colonists, after they chose their sites, was a reliable land survey. On September 17, 1834, Commissioner Steele appointed John G. W. Pierson as principal surveyor, and later that month he swore in E.L.R. Wheelock and several others as deputy surveyors.

"They were to scientifically survey the vacant lands in the colony agreeable to the Mexican National Colonization Law of August 18, 1824, and the State Colonization Law of Coahuila and Texas of March 24, 1825. Each surveyor was to provide himself with a good compass and metallic chain ten varas long."[9] The surveyors were to connect their surveys so that no vacant land existed between, to make a note of how much timber was included, and to state the quality of the land. Wheelock, who had learned surveying in the army and practiced it in Tampico, was recommended for the post by Commissioner Steele. His particular assignment was to survey for all persons requiring land east of the Brazos River, at or near the O.S.R., within Robertson's Colony. If the applicant had a family, Wheelock was either to survey twenty-five labors (one league) for him in a single survey, or twenty-four labors in one survey and one labor in another place. Single men were to receive one-fourth league. Each settler paid $30 to $48 (depending on difficulty) for his survey, of which $10 went to Pierson and the remainder to the man who ran the survey, and thus Wheelock was provided with a sorely needed cash income.

The mental picture evoked by this wilderness surveying is striking. Earlier in the year a surveyor in the colony had issued his crew with horses, rifles, beef, medical supplies, blankets, butcher knives, calico, caps, coats, deer skins, handkerchiefs, leggings, needles, and other articles of clothing.[10] Presumably, Wheelock had to provide all these items for himself and his crew. The surveyor scouted the frontier before the frontiersmen, and his task was often dangerous. The Amerinds were well aware that surveying parties drew settlers in behind them; the slaughter of surveyors was common. The Comanche called a compass "the thing that steals the land."[11]

The frontier surveyor needed to have a sufficient knowledge of science and law: how to compute magnetic variations, how to measure in Spanish, and how to file correctly-drawn reports, how to move through all manner of country, and how to survive in the wild. Usually, he moved in large parties which included cooks and riflemen. Wheelock was one of 130 official surveyors in Texas during the Mexican era. They dealt with the uncertain definitions of length (varas varied from province to province), uncertain costs, uncertain safety, and uncertain pay. The frontier surveyor needed a sense of adventure and the ability to withstand the shock of seeing a "passing bison hump"[12] through his transit.

At the time of their commissioning, Wheelock and the other surveyors swore to support the (1824) Constitution of the Federal Government of Mexico and the State of Coahuila and Texas. Presumably, they were now Mexican citizens.

During January, February, and March 1835, Wheelock surveyed leagues for seventeen men and two women—Lavina Rolitson and Sarah Pillow.

Surveys were continually challenged. Wheelock was later to appear before Chief Justice Francis Slaughter to swear that Joseph Ferguson's survey had been done according to law. On February 8, 1835, Wheelock was instructed by Robertson on exactly how to draw the Jeremiah Tinnin league, about which there had been trouble. Moreover, Wheelock made his share of honest mistakes. He drew up half of Joseph Hadley's league in Burnett's Colony because (just come from a lifetime of living near large rivers, most recently the Mississippi), he did not recognize the Navasota (the colony's eastern boundary) as a river at all and described it as a little creek. Sometimes George Ripley helped his father as a chainman, but probably Mary Wheelock liked to have her almost grown son with her when her husband was absent.

Most Robertson settlers came from southern states and brought with them the traditional cordiality of that region. George B. Erath, who settled near the former Tenoxtitlan close to Wheelock Prairie, later reminisced:

I would like to express my appreciation of the people who were the early settlers of Texas. They were honest and cordial and neighborly. . . . Although with various degrees of intelligence among them, at least two-thirds could read and write. Farming and stock raising formed their chief occupation, but farming was carried on in a very primitive way except near the coast where there were slave owners. Families were very comfortably established in double log cabins with rock chimneys and plank floors.[13]

For the time being, these were the mansions of the colony.

Wheelock's Fort was a refuge not only from Indian attacks but also from the elements. What George W. Bomar calls "the peculiarities of Texas' brand of weather"[14] struck most newcomers very quickly. Among these anomalies Bomar lists hail, high winds, flash floods, hurricanes, tornadoes, thunderstorms, dust storms, droughts, and untimely freezes. The speed with which temperatures could change was amazing to newcomers.

A. Y. Kirkpatrick of the Hill County wrote,

In those days northers came very suddenly and we called them blue northers because there was not a cloud in sight and the sky looked blue when these northers were blowing. I have seen them come so suddenly that a man who was oppressively warm in his shirt sleeves would in less than fifteen minutes come near freezing to death.

I heard of a man who was driving a yoke of very fat oxen through this section of the country some years ago. The day was very warm and one of his oxen became overheated and dropped dead under the yoke while traveling along, and before the driver

could get the yoke and hide off him, a blue norther came up and
froze the other ox to death.[15]

Mr. Kirkpatrick's tall Texas tale has been widely repeated.

The residents of Robertson's Colony counted themselves
rich in their land of bountiful food, water, beauty, space, solitude, and all the other blessings of the wilderness. True, they
were living in a foreign country and under its odd laws and were
deprived of their religion. But the Mexican government was far
away and seemed content to leave them, taxless and unregu-
lated, to live life as they willed.

Nothing, however, stays the same for very long, especially
the sunny things, and already events were shaping a perilous
chapter in Texas history which would shatter the peace of
Robertson's Colony.

CHAPTER 8

THE GATHERING STORM: JANUARY–JULY 1835

A Defense of Robertson's Colony

Persons who like to give economic reasons for historic events will have no trouble in labeling the Panic of 1819 and its subsequent depression as a major cause of the Anglo immigration into Texas. There is much to commend this theory. Many early Texans and their leaders were bankrupt in the states. Most wanted only a good living for themselves and their families. Others coveted riches. No nineteenth century American deprecated such a wish, for was not prosperity a mark of God's favor? S. F. Austin, aware of the humiliation of his father's many failures, did not conceal from his intimates his desire to be a wealthy and socially prominent man. It was the drive and persistence of those who wanted something more which opened Texas for the less ambitious.

A lot of nonsense has been written about the motives of men who gave their time and money to bring immigrants into Texas, some being awarded halos and others pitchforks for what were essentially the same acts. In particular, the Texas Association of Tennessee, under its subsequent names as the Nashville

Colony and Robertson's Colony, has come in for disapprobation, labeled as a gang of speculators and crass dispensers of scrip, its colony minimized or ignored.

Did Robertson's Colony deserve to be thus singled out? As Reichstein reminds us, "Until the end of the nineteenth century land speculation was a regular line of business in the United States."[1] He continues, "All Old Texans had mixed their political aspirations, military efforts, and statesmanship with the animating pursuit of land speculation. These had sparked the westward movement which made land available to millions of people. Their motives would furnish the sinews of war for the revolution."[2]

The Mexicans wanted United States settlers to form a buffer between themselves and the United States of America, and between themselves and the Amerinds. That is why their colonization laws were written to require Texas landowners to live on their land, cultivate it, defend it, and die for it if necessary. With a few brilliant exceptions, the Mexicans had little desire to do any of these things themselves. The majority of the settlers intended to fulfill the terms of their contracts with Mexico. If a few Mexicans and foreigners exchanged leagues and labors for profit, regardless of whether anyone lived on them or ever would, that was human nature. But such activity was not approved by the serious farmers and ranchers of Robertson's Colony.

The reason was simple. Investment and speculation in Texas was only injurious if no settlers followed. Unfortunately, Mexican nationals were excepted from many of the rules of land ownership which bound Anglos. In Article XXIV of the Colonization Law of the State of Coahuila y Texas of March 24, 1825, it had been specified that Mexicans alone might buy up to eleven leagues of land. This was a lot of land. Between 1825 and 1832, 176 such parcels were sold. Inasmuch as only a few Mexicans could afford these prices, the eleven league grants were quickly sold off to interested foreigners, most of whom regarded them as investments rather than as future homes. This law-sanctioned profiteering brought in few settlers. The Tennesseans and other serious colonization efforts brought in many.

According to Dr. Malcolm McLean, Austin's huge grants to Mexican politicians during his illicit occupation of what he called his Upper Colony set back settlement in Central Texas for fifty years. But where genuine settlers were brought in, as by the Nashville Company, no one objected to reasonable profit making. Everyone who invested in schemes to settle Texas did so to make money, even S. F. Austin. Judging by results, Austin was by far the most successful (or culpable, if one disapproves of all profiteering). He arrived a pauper in debt up to his eyebrows and died the richest man in Texas.[3]

The signers of the Texas Association compact of Kentucky and Tennessee were substantial citizens whose prosperity kept many of them at home, but who provided solid (if poorer) family men to settle Texas in their places. Many of them were enthusiastic Texas boosters. Among the signers, Texas numbered some of her more prominent sons: Sam Houston, Sterling Robertson, Robert Leftwich, George Childress, William Wharton, and many others. Someone had to finance the original empresarios' long stay in Mexico while that newly independent nation sorted out its colonization policy. Austin did it on borrowed money, the repayment of which was to be long delayed. Leftwich did it largely on salary from the Texas Association.

Whether one man or seventy-four were the organizers of a colony, the results were the same. Let these visionaries be judged by their works, and the Nashville Company does not come out so badly. Through the Association, favorable ideas of Texas were funneled to Andrew Jackson and other influential Tennesseans; great men like David Crockett and hard-working men whose names few people know were inspired to immigrate. A good argument could be made that Texas would have been hard put to survive without the Tennesseans.

But for the closing of Mexican borders to Anglo immigration in 1830 (a prohibition Austin somehow exempted himself from) and Austin's grab of Robertson's Colony for himself based on perjured evidence (which caused costly delays before Robertson was able to reverse it), Robertson's Colony would have been as well-populated and successful as any, as in the long run it was. After overcoming all these obstacles, Robertson's Colony deserves to be remembered as one of the finest achievements in Texas history.

Making a good living, however respectable as it might be, was not the whole story. The men who came to Texas wanted more than financial independence. They wanted a particular kind of freedom. The Mexican government gave them "freedom from tithes and taxes, . . . cessation of customs duties, and during a crucial formative era freedom from government itself."[4] This was eden indeed. A hatred of government and government regulation, which the debt-ridden Texas colonists brought with them from their United States homes, lingers today.

While the strong lure of land ownership and freedom from governmental interference pulled colonists toward Texas, the cord binding them to their former homes was weak. They were mostly broke or hog-tied in some way by bureaucracy and they lacked the bond with central government which we take for granted today. As T. R. Fehrenbach (so often right when discussing psychological motives) points out, they had "no concepts of nationhood."[5] They did not experience much regret at leaving the United States and swearing allegiance to Mexico.

On the surface, the required oath to follow the Roman Catholic religion seems to make hypocrites of the Anglo-Celtic protestant settlers. Few (Sam Houston was a notable exception) underwent Roman Catholic baptism, although hindsight suggests that Wheelock at least was not hostile. Most had been quietly instructed beforehand that the Mexicans really did not care what religion they believed in so long as they gave lip service to the established church. There were few priests in Texas to examine the consciences of the Anglo settlers. Colonel John Hawkins summed up the feelings of many settlers when he declared, "I know I can be as good a Christian there as I can here. It is only a name anyhow."[6]

The pioneer life required a special kind of person, one who throve on solitude, who took physical courage, strength of sinew and character, and the Puritan work ethic for granted, who had tremendous self-confidence—an independence hard to imagine today. It required no organized law, no public assistance, no repairmen, no insurance companies, no hospitals, no banks, virtu-

ally no money or shops or transportation, no one imposing outside standards.

Every land holder was as important as every other land
holder in this "pure male democracy."[7] "Every Texan could en-
vision himself as a petty emperor in his mini-empire."[8]

The Troublemakers

It was those who wanted power as well as prosperity and liberty who introduced snakes into this garden of eden.

The first intimation of discord came when a hothead
named William Barret Travis along with an armed party attacked the Mexican customs inspector at Anahuac. Travis "who
basically hated and was contemptuous of Mexicans"[9] was far
from typical, but his rabble-rousing attracted attention.

The majority of Texans condemned Travis for taking the
law into his own hands, and some wrote letters of apology to
Gen. Martin Cos and to the military commander of Texas,
Domingo de Ugartechea. The Mexican government's under-
standable attitude was one of outrage.

While the recently arrived Robertson's Colony settlers were
preoccupied with surveys, houses, and plowing virgin soil,
Samuel May Williams was still scheming to console himself
for the loss of the so-called Upper Colony, which he and Austin
had illegally held from 1830 to 1834. His attempt to bring off
a large coup for himself and his friends "under the influence
of bribery"[10] evoked the first shot of the Texas War for Independence.

Because of confusion caused by Santa Anna's political
machinations in Mexico City, the province of Coahuila and
Texas "had fallen into chaos."[11] A rump state legislative group,
which could in no way be considered legally elected, passed
some laws favored by Williams and others, one setting up a
scheme involving a 400 league grant which would greatly enrich
him and his party and another reassigning Robertson's Colony
to Williams and Austin.

On March 14, 1835, this spurious state legislature passed
an additional law stipulating that the governor could dispose of

up to 400 leagues of public land "under the bases and conditions which he may consider convenient."[12] That is, without
complying with already existing immigration law.

On May 11, Anglos Samuel M. Williams, Francis W. Johnson, and Robert Peebles applied to Governor Viesca for 400
leagues of the public domain, in return for which they agreed to
raise and equip 1,000 militiamen to fight the Amerinds. This
was seen by many Mexicans as civil rebellion. General Cos did
not believe that this legislation was valid, nor that 1,000 armed
men in Texas could be trusted not to ferment a revolution.[13] No
doubt he passed his concerns on his brother-in-law Santa Anna
in Mexico City.

In the labyrinthine depths of centralist politics, President
Santa Anna, the political chameleon, was revealing himself in
his favorite self-assigned role as the Napoleon of the West.
Outraged that the state of Coahuila dared to protest his dictatorship, he sent soldiers to restore order and rescind the illegal
legislation. The arrest of Williams was ordered, along with that
of several officials and colonists who had joined with him—John
Durst, Jose Carbajal, James Bowie, Benjamin Milam, Dr. James
Grant, and Francis Johnson.[14]

Those seeking peace and justice in Texas were now in the
uncomfortable position of having to choose between the dictator Santa Anna and a crooked legislature supported by a hand-
ful of Anglo opportunists. The fugitives fled north across the Rio
Grande with their allies, Juan Seguin and the deluded Governor
Viesca. Captain Vicente Arreola warned authorities that their
purpose was "to stir up a revolution."[15] General Cos ordered
them all to be intercepted and detained. Williams was jailed in
San Antonio de Bexar.

On June 7 Williams escaped from his cell in Bexar and disappeared into the United States.

On June 28 J. B. Chance wrote reassuringly to Sterling
Robertson:

> I gladly embrace this first opportunity of communicating to you
> since my return from San Felipe. I left there on the 24 inst., the
> day after the great Sanhedran of Austin met, the result of which
> was to raise a force sufficient to go and bring the governor to San

Felipe. They got 35 volunteers. They have now abandoned the
project and they are now only going to San Antonio to seize all
the arms and military stores which belongs to that place. Times
are quite squally. There is no doubt but there is 7000 troops on
their way to Texas. 3000 coming by land and 4000 by water for
the purpose of bringing Texas in subjection to the great Dictator
Santa Anna. I did intend to have started this day to Viesca, but I
now see that it is absolutely necessary that I should go on the
above expedition to San Antonio. Old Judge Hall came by my
house yesterday and informed me that you were in a state of de-
spondency from the belief that you had lost your colony, I will
now inform you that it is all a bubble, that you now stand in the
same situation you did before the meeting of the legislature and
all you have to do is to stay at home and mind your own business
and whenever the government settles down everything will be
right. It is true that Austin's party would have done a great deal
if they could have succeeded in getting the governor to Texas to
have signed and published the laws passed by the last legislature,
but fortunately for you, not one act passed by the legislature had
yet or will it become law unless a subsequent legislature shall
think proper to pass the same laws.[16]

In other words, the actions of Williams at the illegal legislature had come to naught, except for the mischief scattered by
his fleeing cohorts among the settlers.

Misgivings

Meanwhile the settlers of Robertson's Colony were busy
with their own concerns and E.L.R. Wheelock as surveyor began
to record certain practices of Land Commissioner Steele, which
seemed to him questionable. On January 19, 1835, Wheelock
had received his deed for one league of land "and shortly after
that date, when he returned to Viesca from a surveying expedition and went into Commissioner Steele's office to pick up his
deed, he mentioned to Steele that he had heard a rumor to the
effect that Steele had no proper authority to put anybody in possession of land—except those who had signed the petition to the

government of Coahuila and Texas to have the Colony restored to the Nashville Company. When Wheelock said that, Steele became agitated and made use of harsh language, and went to a trunk and produced a writing, which he said was his commission, but Steele only held it, saying it was translated into English. Wheelock started forward to take the document, but Steele suddenly turned around and put it back into the trunk; consequently, Wheelock did not get to read it."[17] Wheelock found this perplexing.

"Wheelock said he had oral instructions to make surveys for anybody who applied, but he was restricted from surveying along the Brazos River because Steele said that area was especially reserved for members of the Nashville Company."[18] Likewise, "When Wheelock got his land grant, he presented his passport—from the State from which he had emigrated—thinking it would be necessary to record his passport with his title in order to perfect it, but Steele said that would not be necessary. In fact, Wheelock got the impression that Steele did not want applicants with passports, and that he would have refused to issue a grant to Wheelock if he had known he was going to present such a document."[19] What could this mean? Did Steele seek to exclude settlers of good character and substance who might be harder to cheat? Why was he unwilling to show his credentials? Did Sterling Robertson know what was going on?

"Wheelock also said that, when he had arrived on his first trip to the colony, he heard from Robertson, Steele, and Stone that Stone had made a contract with Robertson to introduce a considerable number of families from the United States, in consideration of certain services rendered to the other parties, which had enabled them to obtain the Colony, and that Stone was to have a preference next to the petitioners for the Colony and the Nashville Company, and even over those who had settled in the Colony under Austin and Williams. Later Steele told Wheelock that he was interested in the profits from that arrangement, and asked Wheelock to make their surveys, but Wheelock declined."[20] He was probably also scandalized, for his sense of right and wrong was Puritan rigid.

Sometime in the spring, Wheelock was invited by Primary Judge Joseph L. Hood and Land Commissioner William K.

Steele to join them in an agreement to let no newcomer have
land unless it was infertile, and to refuse land altogether unless
the newcomer let one of Steele's group clear it out on shares.
They declared that all the officers of the ayuntamiento of Viesca,
with the single exception of John Marlin, had made such an
agreement. They said that all lands thus acquired (through the
extorted shares) could be sold to advantage in the United States.
Wheelock got the impression that there was some kind of conspiracy against the rights of the people, but learned nothing
more.[21]

Finally, Steele proposed that Wheelock survey some land
for him and return the field notes with the name of the recipient left blank, in return for which Wheelock would receive seven
leagues of land for himself. Steele added that "It was no harm to
cheat the Mexicans, for all of them were guilty."[22] Wheelock refused and remained deeply troubled.

He had been continuing, of course, to act as a deputy surveyor for Robertson's Colony, and in March and April surveyed
plots for eight newcomers, including former Illinoisans James
and Silas Parker.

The Parker land, where they subsequently built their
doomed fort, was located on the Navasota River north of present day Groesbeck. Like the Wheelocks, the Parkers had come
from Illinois, where they had recruited a congregation for their
Pilgrim Predestinarian Regular Baptist Church of Jesus Christ.
Most of the faithful came with them to Texas, about forty to fifty
families, to begin a communal life.

On May 26, 1835, Sterling Robertson signed a contract
with Colonel Wheelock permitting him to select, survey, and locate fifteen leagues of land on any unappropriated vacant lands
within Robertson's Colony. It stated that "he [is] in all things
conforming to the Laws of Colonization, and he is allowed until
the first day of May next to complete his Surveys and Locations
and introduction of the settlers."[23] Thus he became, like others,
one of Robertson's sub-agents.

Some time during the summer of 1835, according to Dr.
McLean, hard feelings arose between Wheelock and Robertson
"because Wheelock did not like the way that titles were issued in
the Robertson Colony Land Office."[24] Perhaps Wheelock asked

Robertson to explain Steele's special agreement, of which he may have thought the empresario ignorant. Nevertheless, he looked forward to helping Robertson with the peaceful settlement of his colony and to earning a prosperous future for his family in Wheelock Prairie.

Enter Rumor, Full of Tongues

Robertson's Colony in general only wanted to be left alone. Most colonists, it soon became apparent, would have to be frightened into rebelling against Mexico, which enjoyed their general support. A Texas War Party appeared for just that purpose.

Reichstein wrote: "The men who wanted to separate Texas from Mexico at any price and join it to the United States . . . spread the most hair-raising rumors: several thousand soldiers were on the march to Texas, they were going to free all the slaves and, together with the Indians, they were going to subjugate Texans under the dictatorship of Santa Anna and the Catholic Church and force them to pay immensely high taxes."[25]

Benjamin Milam, when arrested, wrote to Francis Johnson, July 5, 1835, warning: "These plans of barbarity will make a wilderness of Texas and beggars of its inhabitants, if they do not unite . . . If the Federal (state) system is lost in Texas, what will be our situation? Worse than that of the most degraded slaves. . . .The people of Texas will never submit to a dictator."[26] No one knows how many colonists believed these rumors, which were quite untrue but took their toll.

The War Party consisted mostly of people who had come to Texas and failed to get land grants, disgruntled merchants, lawyers distressed by the Mexican legal system, and adventurers spoiling for a fight. The young men of the 1830s, with eagerness, even with joy, gathered from the four winds into Texas, their hearts light at the prospect of a good brawl.

An early inhabitant of Wheelock, N. C. Duncan, recalled in his later years that when he and his family immigrated from Tennessee in late 1835, they fell in with David Crockett aimed in the same direction. A traveler headed back east stopped to ask Crockett whether he had any message for his wife, left behind in Tennessee. Crockett answered, "Tell her I will send her Santa Anna's head for a soup gourd."[27] The former congressman was typical of the increasing number of immigrants into Texas who had come solely to wage war.

"Expansionists and adventurers such as Travis, Fannin, Smith, Chambers, Archer, Wharton, and Williamson understood how to use the advantage of the moment aptly."[28] If enough settlers could be made to believe that their central government had turned against them, shooting would follow.

The Peace Party was made up of the great majority of the farmers and planters, including those in Robertson's Colony, especially those who had recently received grants and were now busy with their crops and anxious to set settled in their new homes. Like his grandfather before him when New Englanders began to talk treason against the Mother Country in the 1770s, Wheelock and his ilk were placed in a most uncomfortable position. They had come to Texas to prosper by their own toil and wits and now found themselves in a pre-revolutionary cauldron.

CHAPTER 9

IGNITION:
MAY-OCTOBER 1835

The Committees of Safety and Correspondence

Did the Anglo population of Texas, now over 25,000, want a revolution? By the summer of 1835 the Peace Party, no longer sheltered by a stable central government in Mexico City, stiffened its sinews. The "outside and most exposed populations on the three rivers, Guadalupe, Colorado, and Brazos, populations ever distinguished for undaunted courage and patriotism, were the first to adopt the means looking to self-preservation . . ."[1] To this group of imperiled colonies, Robertson's Colony belonged.

Committees of Safety and Correspondence, along the lines of those used in the American Revolution, were set up first on May 8 in Mina (Bastrop) and on May 17 in Gonzales and Villa de Viesca, capital of Robertson's Colony. The members of the Viesca Committee of Safety and Correspondence were Samuel T. Allen, John Pierson, Albert G. Perry, E.L.R. Wheelock, Silas Parker, and J. L. Hood. But was it these settlers' design to separate Texas from Mexico? Probably not.

Between July 4 and August 15 similar committees were formed in nine other locations. The minutes for Villa de Viesca have been lost, but those of the other Robertson's Colony committee, Columbia, survive. The Columbia Committee resolved to continue to support the constitution and laws of Mexico, which they had so lately sworn to uphold, and (since their state government in Monclova had collapsed) to recognize J. B. Miller, their political chief, as the highest executive officer. They recommended immediate organization of a frontier militia and urged the formation of a council "with full powers to form for Texas a provisional government on the principles of the constitution, during the reign of anarchy in the state."[2] Wheelock and his committee agreed. They wanted to preserve peace pending restoration of lawful Mexican government. But the War Party had other ideas. Mexico's legitimate moves to punish wrong doers were spun into attacks on the basic freedoms of the Anglo settlers.

Of course, cooler heads knew better. On June 30 Judge Thomas Jefferson Chambers, Robertson's old lawyer, wrote to Dr. James Miller of Gonzales:

> I understand that copies of a letter written by Carbajal are circulating in your neighborhood in which he states among other things that the general government has decreed the confiscation of lands of the colonists and their expulsion from the country with a view to alarm and excite them to rise against the general government. I take this early opportunity of informing you that such statements are utterly groundless and false in fact. . . The simple facts are these "the administration of the government of this state during the present year has been of the most shameful character. Poor Viesca was completely hoodwinked and deceived by a few whose only object was to use the government for their own private use. A law was obtained for the sale of Four Hundred Leagues of vacant land and the most shameless acts of Speculation were committed against the state and the interest of Texas. The general government has passed a decree annulling these sales, and the purchasers . . . are the (source) of reports which you have heard and which I trust the colonists will pay no further attention to them and treat them with contempt. The movement of troops toward Texas is aimed only at these individuals."[3]

Robertson County sent a committee to San Felipe to make a stand for peace in Austin's belligerent colony. On June 1 a group including William Wharton wrote to Col. Domingo de Ugartechea, principal commandant of Coahuila y Texas, assuring him of the Texans' loyalty.

On July 3 the Committee for Columbia in Robertson's Colony met again and wrote General Cos and Colonel Ugartechea expressing their intense desire to avoid any collision with the established authorities.

The Committee for Gonzales in DeWitt's Colony recommended that a convention be called to make a formal investigation and place the burden squarely on the shoulders of those renegades who had originated the disturbances. They suggested that for purposes of fairness the convention should not be held in San Felipe, a War Party center. The Columbia Committee met again on July 11 and appointed a sub-committee of five to urge again their earnest desire for peace. Their effort was doomed.

On July 15 the representatives from Columbia and San Felipe met in San Felipe and signed an address to the citizens of the Department of Brazos (to which Colonel Wheelock belonged) assuring them that there was no cause for immediate alarm and that they hoped that the present commotion could be quieted without any collision with Mexican troops. All of these proceedings were published in *The Texas Republican of Brazoria* on July 18.

Most colonists agreed with sarcastic James Kerr:

To Thomas Jefferson Chambers, July 5, 1835.

I have seen the letter you wrote to Dr. Miller . . .everything corresponds to what I had believed before: . . . Williams, Johnson, Carbajal, Bowie, and other shouting "Wolf, Wolf, Condemnation, Destruction—War—War—to Arms." Williams says "I have bought some leagues of land from the Government, but if the governor is not brought to Bexar I won't be able to get title." O, what a pity!⁴

Other peace seekers wrote to Colonel de Ugartechea that since most Texans remained loyal to Mexico and took up arms only against the Indians, the only thing needed to defuse the situation was for the Mexican troops to stay out of Texas. On July 25, James Miller in San Felipe wrote to John Smith in Bexar that all was peaceful and if only the Mexicans would arrest F. W. Johnson (a notorious land speculator), Robert McAlpine Williamson (Three Legged Willie), William Barret Travis, Samuel May Williams, and Lorenzo de Zavala that peace would be restored. Williamson, like Travis, was a hot-head and trumpeter of revolution.

On July 31, William Steele wrote Sterling Robertson that "the Indian excitement is up and very great; a few days ago news reached us that the Wacos has returned to their old village (the present site of Waco) and taken possession of it and were destroying the corn &c."[5]

On July 13, Austin had been released from his prison cell in Mexico City by Santa Anna during a general amnesty and had sailed for New Orleans. His political position had taken a U-turn. He was now definitely anti-Mexican.

On July 30, William Travis wrote to his fellow hawk, James Bowie, "The peace-party, as they style themselves, I believe are the strongest and make much noise. Unless we could be united, had we not better be quiet, and settle down for a while?"[6] Perhaps his good advice came too late.

The central Mexican government wanted only the named fugitives. But a new central government was in power. Even in loyal Robertson's Colony, Santa Anna's legitimacy was suspect. On August 15, the citizens of Columbia passed a series of resolutions which continued to call for moderation and peace. This time, however, their loyalty had one reservation. "We will not give up any individual to the Military Authorities."[7] "In other words," to quote McLean, "they preferred to plunge the whole state into war, if necessary, rather than give up the less than half a dozen unconstitutional and illegal land speculators mentioned by Ugartechea in his order of July 31."[8]

Something had changed. To the citizens of Columbia Santa Anna's government was not the government they had sworn to uphold. He represented tyranny, and they were not prepared to deliver any Anglos, however guilty, into his hands. Thus "fraud was at the foundation of the whole."[9]

Stephen F. Austin now returned to San Felipe from New Orleans, where he had been advertising for troops to fight the Mexicans. Having decided on war, he warned Texans against the Mexican invading army and ignored the guilty fugitives, one of whom, Lorenzo de Zavala, he was sheltering in his house.

On September 19, Steele received a letter from James B. Miller, the political chief of the Brazos Department (taken in by the Monclova duplicity) instructing him to cease all action as commissioner of Nashville Colony and to turn in his papers. Steele wrote back courteously that such an order was illegal and he did not feel bound by it. He continued to issue titles until December 28. Robert Peebles and Spencer C. Jack were meanwhile issuing spurious titles for Austin and Williams in Robertson's grant, hoping that Williams and Austin's second illegal grab for Robertson's Colony would prevail.

On the same day the hawkish San Felipe Committee advised every district to arm. "War is our only resource." [10]

In the midst of this political unrest, tragedy again touched the Wheelock family through the death of the colonel's brother, George Woodward Wheelock, at the home of John Walker in Robertson's Colony. First little Thomas, then John, now George. Fever again. Colonel Wheelock had looked forward to welcoming George and his family to Wheelock Prairie. Now his widow, Ann, and infant daughter Louisa would take up his head right and come under the protection of their brother-in-law and uncle.

With the threat of war looming, the Indians became bolder and surveying was even more hazardous than before. That same month, Frank Brown wrote, "Surveying parties . . . were attacked by Indians while at work on the San Gabriel. Two whites were killed. The others saved themselves by flight. Numerous depredations were committed. Many small parties of frontiersman fitted out and did good service affording protection. The savages seemed ubiquitous. They were not often seen, . . . Their powers of endurance were greater than those of the whites. The savages were capable of traveling over a hundred miles though prairies and forests, without rest or food." [11] But Wheelock continued to survey.

It was about this time that pressure from Amerind raids led

to the abandonment of Sarahville de Viesco and the removal of Robertson's capital to Nashville-on-the-Brazos. Among Nashville's earliest settlers were Elijah and Catherine Powers of Tennessee, two of whose children would marry Wheelocks. Son Andrew Jackson Powers would be the second husband of Colonel Wheelock's daughter Annette, and daughter Lucinda Powers the first wife of his eldest son, George Ripley Wheelock.

While revolution simmered, Sterling Robertson was in Tennessee recruiting settlers and delivering a double message. On the one hand, in order to attract families, he advertised a peaceful Mexican colony:

> The arms of Santa Anna were victorious over the Federal Constitution in every part of the Mexican Empire except Texas. She stands alone, and aware of her danger, is easily excited by any rumors of danger, that interested partisans may set afloat to answer their own views. Such was the case just before I left Texas which caused a belief that an invasion of Texas was inevitable; but when sifted to the bottom was found to be the artful design of land speculators who had made a fraudulent bargain with the state authorities and were declared traitors by the general (central) government and fled into Texas and tried to make the impression that all Texans were included in the denunciation of the general government. . . .
>
> General Cos (who was reported to command troops destined for the invasion of Texas) had informed one or more of the political chiefs of Texas that it was not the intention of Santa Anna to invade Texas, that he wished the people to remain quiet and peaceable, and they would not be molested . . .[12]

For potential investors, Robertson painted a different picture, one of rebellion, independence, and eventual absorption by the United States of America:

> To persons wishing to invest money in a profitable speculation, I can inform them that lands can now be got there for a trifling sum, that will in a few years sell as high as the lands do now in the southern lower country. They are more productive, more healthy, and as well situated to market, and only want a settled government to give confidence to sale holders to make them rate

with the highest lands in the United States. That confidence cannot be long withheld, for it must before long come under the government of the United States and be independent, as the present
state of things cannot last long. Texas has the ability to proclaim
and maintain her independence and if no other alternative will
do she will consummate the act; and will carry her arms success-
fully, beyond her present limits.[13]

The Incident at Gonzales

Unbeknownst to Robertson, the fat was already in the fire.
The sin of Samuel May Williams in promising the rump
state legislature to arm 1,000 militiamen in return for 400
leagues of land had incited Ugartechea to call for help from
General Cos, and it was Cos who received reinforcements from
his brother-in-law, Santa Anna, to suppress any rebellion which
might be fermented by Williams and his co-conspirators.

Prudently, Cos decided to reclaim ordinance which had
been left scattered about the Anglo settlements, just in case.

On October 1, Capt. Francisco Castenada arrived in
Gonzales, the capital of DeWitt's Colony, to pick up a cannon belonging to the central Mexican government. Unable to cross the
swollen Guadalupe River, from which hostile Anglos had removed the ferry and all other boats, he camped along its banks.
On the other side, a rag-tag assembly of volunteers attracted by
the smell of gunpowder raised a flag emblazoned "Come and
Take It" and fired the cannon at the Centralist troops.

Taken aback, Castenada asked why he was being fired
upon. The reply was that the Anglos would never live under a
tyrant. The captain replied reasonably that he himself was a republican but he was also a professional soldier and had to obey
orders, which were to get the cannon if the settlers would turn it
over peacefully or, if not, to withdraw, and that he had not come
to make war on them. The Anglos opened fire.

Thus the War Party had its way, and the first shots of the
Texas Revolution exploded out of Texian guns.

Honest settlers had sincerely tried to keep the Mexican law.
They denounced the illegal acts of the madcaps and the in-

triguers. But others had arrived in Texas with the idea of a non-Mexican Texas already fixed in their minds. For them the larceny of Williams and his ilk provided a convenient excuse for revolt.

Among the newly arrived who believed that Texas was destined to be a part of the United States was Sam Houston. On October 5, he had already written to Isaac Parker in Tennessee:

> If volunteers from the U.S. will join their brethren in this section, they will receive liberal bounties of land. We have millions of acres of our best lands unchosen and unappropriated.
> Let each man come with a good rifle and 100 rounds of ammunition and come now.
> Our war cry is "Liberty or Death"! Our principles are to support the constitution and down with the Usurper![14]

Later in the month, something happened which destroyed any hope of reconciliation between the Anglo settlers and the Mexican government. The Constitution of 1824, to which all Texas immigrants had sworn allegiance and which Houston had urged them to support, was repudiated by Santa Anna, the usurper. The Peace Party was appalled. War now seemed inevitable.

BOOK THREE

INDEPENDENCE

. . . history has proven that even in Texas every man is not a hero.

—The Anonymous Buckeye

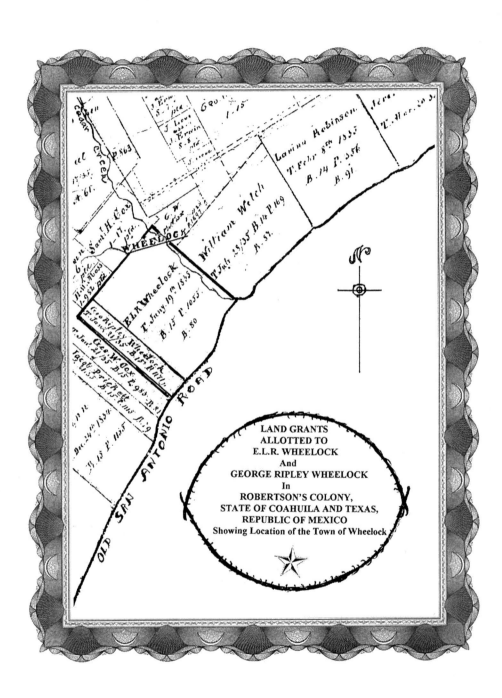

LAND GRANTS
ALLOTTED TO
E.L.R. WHEELOCK
And
GEORGE RIPLEY WHEELOCK
In
ROBERTSON'S COLONY,
STATE OF COAHUILA AND TEXAS,
REPUBLIC OF MEXICO
Showing Location of the Town of Wheelock

CHAPTER 10

REVOLUTION:
OCTOBER 1835-APRIL 1836

In Texas, the cards were almost dealt. The ace was a Virginian turned Tennessean called Sam Houston. After a turbulent political and military career, he crossed his Rubicon into Texas in early December 1832. He used the spring of 1833 to wander about the country, getting acquainted and meeting with Comanches, and confided to his mentor President Andrew Jackson that Texas was a fruit ripe for the plucking. Like many another rover, he had been captivated by the beauty and promise of Texas and declared that it could "sustain a population of ten million souls,"[1] an audacious prophecy for the time.

On September 14, 1835, the Nacogdoches Committee appointed Houston commander of its military resources, later commander in chief of the Department of Nacogdoches, and finally, under the provisional state government of Henry Smith, major general of the Texas Army. With its general in place, the revolution could now proceed.

One of the most curious things about the Texas War for Independence is that so much of it happened before the citizens of Texas decided on war, or their duly elected representatives decided on independence.

True, as Stephen Hardin pointed out, "the American colonists of Mexican Texas were no strangers to war; they were born to it. Most descended from America's first revolutionaries, and many . . . had fought in the War of 1812. Most had fought Indians."[2] But this does not mean that they preferred war to peace. Quite the contrary. The War Party, by and large, was composed of adventurers and men with grievances, not colonists.

The settlers had at first no thought of leaving Mexican authority, but the collapse of their state government of Coahuila and Texas (due to infighting between Santa Anna and his political opponents) convinced them that they did need an interim administration until Mexico City could regroup. Although peace advocates objected to meeting in Austin's hot-head capital, a consultation took place at San Felipe, with Sam Houston and Sterling Robertson as delegates.

Meanwhile, Gen. Martin Cos, on a limited mission to capture a few rebels, brought about 500 regulars into Texas and marched toward San Antonio, dropping off munitions and forty soldiers in Goliad. On October 9 a group of Texans attacked the Goliad garrison and captured the munitions. On October 11 a group of irregular volunteers assembled around Gonzales and selected S. F. Austin (oddly, for he had no military experience at all) as their commander. Austin rashly decided to lay siege to San Antonio, the strongest centralist town in Texas.

The partisan San Felipe newspaper, the *Telegraph and Texas Register*, urged any men who could fight to join Austin in San Antonio, where he had sent out a call for "help, help, help."[3] Instead the interim government authorized Silas M. Parker to gather a group of men to range and guard the frontiers between the Brazos and Trinity Rivers. They knew that the colonists were much more afraid of Indians than of Mexicans.

The "indecisive convention called the Consultation"[4] was not yet willing to declare for independence, and instead proclaimed Texas a new state within the Mexican system and elected Henry Smith its governor. It also created a co-equal governing council. Only then did it turn its thoughts to the military situation in San Antonio and its faltering chief. Hardin wrote: "Clearly Austin was uncomfortable as commander. Whenever a decision had to be made, to avoid making a fatal error, he put the matter up for a vote."[5] Texas found a tactful way to get rid of him. They sent Austin, William Wharton, and Branch Archer to the United States to solicit support for their fellow Anglos, although the U.S. government had already declared that it would do nothing to compromise the territory of its sovereign neighbor, Mexico.

The Consultation now placed Parker and his troop on firmer footing and in so doing created a legend. On November 13 it passed the "Organic Law," accompanied by a document entitled, "Of the Military," Article 9 of which stated, "There shall be a corps of Rangers . . . divided into three or more detachments and which shall compose a battalion under the Commander in Chief (of the Regular Army), when in the field."[6]

E.L.R. Wheelock was soon to become an officer in this illustrious corps.

To stem illegal land grabs, they made one more fateful decision. No one arriving in Texas after November 14, 1835, could get title to land. The land offices were closed for the duration.

The Capture of San Antonio

The San Antonio siege, under the new command of Edward Burleson, was now two months old, and the motley volunteers (who had come to fight, not wait) were getting restless. When on December 4 Burleson prudently ordered his troops to withdraw to Goliad for the winter, his men were outraged. These volunteers set little store in military discipline and almost none in their officers. Their greatest assets were their own self-confidence and their Kentucky rifles, with a range 130 yards longer than that of the Mexican carbines.

At this point, with the insubordination to be typical of the Texas soldier, Benjamin Rush Milam, whose name was on the Mexicans' wanted list, ignored orders and uttered his deathless trochees—"Who will go with old Ben Milam into San Antonio?" As Noah Smithwick later recalled, "Some were for independence, some were for the Constitution of 1824, and some were for anything just so long as it was a row."[7] Here was a chance for a good row. The unkempt army swarmed over the city, the Texians won, Milam died, and Texas had its first martyr.

Defeated, General Cos swore never to enter Texas again
and retreated south of the Rio Bravo. Everyone went home. It
seemed that the undeclared and unwanted war was over and
that Texas had won.

On December 18 Empresario Sterling Clack Robertson returned from Tennessee to a very different country from the one
he had left only a few weeks before. There were now, it seemed,
three Texases: one political, one military, and one colonial.

In political Texas, affairs approached the absurdity of an op-
eretta plot by Sir William S. Gilbert. Texas now had two authorities equal in rank, a governor and a council. The duties of neither had been defined. Soon Smith and his council were at each
other's throats and by January 1836 had succeeded in canceling
each other out, leaving Texas with no active government at all.

In military Texas, the commander of the volunteers at San
Antonio, Col. James Neill, requested reinforcements; there was
a rumor abroad that General Santa Anna himself was approach-
ing from the south with a large army, eager to avenge the defeat
of General Cos. Recognizing the superiority of Santa Anna's dis-
ciplined army, General Houston ordered Col. James Bowie to
march from Goliad to San Antonio with about thirty men, destroy fortifications there, and withdraw the troops. At the same
time Governor Smith ordered William B. Travis to San Antonio
with about thirty men to direct an evacuation. Both orders were
given by men who knew that San Antonio was no longer defen-
sible. Neither order was carried out.

On February 11 Neill turned over his skeleton command of
100 men to Travis and went on leave. The Hon. David Crockett
had arrived with about twelve Tennesseans and from February
14 on, Travis (for the regulars) and Bowie (for the volunteers)
shared an uneasy command. On February 23 Santa Anna
reached the city of San Antonio with an army of about 6,000
men, and the Texans withdrew into the fortress of the Alamo, an
abandoned mission. On February 24 Travis was still free to pen
and dispatch his immortal letter addressed to "the People of
Texas and All Americans in the World." The next day Bowie was
forced by illness to relinquish his share of command. Travis was
now in full control.

In colonial Texas, most of the settlers in Robertson's

Colony were in ignorance of these events. They were waiting for what seemed to them a minor squabble between the Texas War Party and the Mexican government to resolve itself. Settlers continued to arrive. Unable to issue land legally because of the closing of the land offices, Empresario Robertson began to keep a semi-official roll of newcomers. He had organized his own informal Ranger company to protect his settlers from Comanches. No one really expected serious trouble from the south.

While the foundations of their world were crumbling in San Antonio, life went on in its trivial way for the settlers of Wheelock Prairie and E.L.R. Wheelock got into trouble with some of his neighbors. On February 16 Niles F. Smith wrote to Empresario Robertson:

> Col. Hays has reported everywhere on the Road that things are agoing on well, and Robertson Colony is the finest place in the World, Wheelock to the contrary notwithstanding! Give my respects to Sam Allen and the Ladies![8]

Had Wheelock been so tactless as to call Illinois a finer place than Texas?

For whatever reason, Smith did not forgive Wheelock for his lack of chauvinistic pride. On February 20 Samuel J. Hays wrote to Empresario Robertson from Natchitoches, Louisiana:

> I have just been informed by Mr. Niles F. Smith who reached this place a few moments since that Col. Wheelock stated to him on his way here, that I had penned an article for publication on my arrival to the U.S. which he professed to have seen, in which I have not only denounced the colony, but impugned the integrity of yourself. . . I assure you that there is not even a shadow of truth in the statement of Wheelock. . . I do not pretend to disguise the fact that I have frequently said that I had no doubt great abuses had been practiced in your colony (in this I believe you concur with me), but have never for a moment attached blame to yourself. . . You are hereby authorized and would confer a favor by pronouncing it a base libel . . .[9]

Smith backed this accusation with his own letter to Robertson, dated February 22, which says in part, "I saw Col.

Hays who pronounced Col. Wheelock a Damd, old liar. . ." It
would be interesting to read Wheelock's reply to Robertson
when he heard about this accusation, but it has not survived.
Wheelock indeed agreed that great abuses had taken place in
Robertson Colony's land office, but he did not blame "old man
Robertson" any more than Samuel Hays did.

The citizens of Robertson's Colony were now busy electing
delegates to a convention to establish a permanent Texas government. One of the voting precincts was headquartered at the
home of James Dunn, on Wheelock Prairie. Colonel Wheelock
served as clerk as the thirty-six eligible voters chose George C.
Childress and Sterling C. Robertson, both of Nashville, Tennessee, to represent the Colony at the new capital, Washington-on-
the-Brazos. Among those voting were Francis Slaughter, George
Ripley Wheelock, E.L.R. Wheelock, James Dunn, and Sterling
Clack Robertson. The other precincts agreed with them, and the
uncle and nephew were duly gazetted.

Remember the Alamo, Remember Goliad

On March 1 thirty-one men from Gonzales joined the defenders of the Alamo, increasing their number to 187. Until the
last minute, Travis hoped for massive reinforcements from
Goliad. When they didn't arrive, he may have decided to surrender, but if so he had waited too long.

On March 6 at four in the morning Santa Anna attacked
the Texian position and in two and a half hours the battle was
over. Undoubtedly almost to the last the Alamo defenders could
have retreated honorably. Indeed, their commander in chief had
ordered them to do so. Some deep sense of decorum almost
opaque today held them in their hopeless position. Like
Achilles, the defenders of the Alamo chose glory before length
of days.

Meanwhile, in Washington-on-the-Brazos, fifty-nine elected
delegates, faced with the fact that reconciliation with Mexico
now seemed impossible, met to set up their independent government. They had two goals. The first was to issue a
Declaration of Independence, without which, they were assured,

no loans, money, or material help could be expected from American citizens. The second was to write a constitution. The first was easy. George Campbell Childress of Nashville, Tennessee, a nephew of Sterling Clack Robertson, arrived with the document already written, read it aloud on March 2, and saw it approved without comment. Thus the birthday of Sam Houston and the birthday of the Texas Association also became the birthday of the Republic of Texas.

On March 4 the convention affirmed Sam Houston, present in Washington as a delegate, as commander in chief of both the regular army and the militia.

While Empresario Robertson was serving at the convention, he became alarmed by news of Santa Anna's advancing army and wrote to his son Elijah asking him to move the Robertson Colony Papers to a place of safety. The dismayed convention had just been advised by General Houston of the fall of the Alamo. As soon as Elijah had taken the papers to a haven in San Augustine, he wrote to his father assuring him that the documents were safe, adding:

> Your mares when I went away were let out to the following persons: Mr. Webb got Rockser. . . Capt. Friar the bay bogy had. Mare that . . . colt Mrs. Wheelock the . . . little bay . . .[10]

It is not clear which horse was entrusted to Mary Wheelock, but Robertson was later to breed fine horses, and his horse flesh was very dear to him, so the favor must have been a great one. McLean enters this letter under the date of May 5, but the date when Elijah farmed out the horse or horses to Mrs. Wheelock must have been earlier, because the Wheelocks participated in the Runaway Scrape in early and mid-April.

More Texas Ranger companies were needed to contain the rising Indian danger, and on March 3 the convention passed a resolution authorizing Jesse H. Benton and Lt. Col. Griffin Bane to raise a new regiment of Rangers, drawing the same pay as the Regular Army and subject at all times to the orders of the commander in chief of the public forces. Wheelock was with his family on Wheelock Prairie. No longer in his first youth, he nevertheless felt an obligation to place his military experience at the service of his new nation. On March 16 he was appointed a second lieutenant of Rangers, where he served until May 7, with pay of $50 a month plus an allowance for feed for his horse.

The lieges had finally been aroused.

On March 17 at Washington-on-the-Brazos, interim Republic of Texas President David Gouverneur Burnet and interim Vice-President Lorenzo de Zavala were sworn into office at the desperate hour of 4:00 A.M.

General Houston had a hard row to hoe. Few Texians, as the old settlers were called, wanted to join a formal army and few wanted to obey orders either from friends or strangers. But it was obvious to Houston that someone had to take hold and stop the impetuous settlers from running into any more debacles such as had already been suffered in San Antonio. On March 14 he ordered Fannin to withdraw from Goliad. But again as at the Alamo the men in the field thought they knew better than the commander in chief. Fannin stayed put. On March 19 Goliad was surrounded by the army of Gen. Jose Urrea and captured, with 340 Texians soldiers surrendering to become (as they thought) prisoners of war.

But Santa Anna had made it quite clear that rebels would be treated like common criminals. On Palm Sunday, March 27, 340 of the 417 Texans were shot as outlaws. One of the dead was Henry Dearborn Ripley, son of erstwhile Texas President and U.S. Major General Eleazar Wheelock Ripley of Louisiana, first cousin of Colonel E.L.R. Wheelock. For the Wheelocks, the war was touching home.

Anglos love lost causes. News of Texas's two defeats resonated across the continent in a way that nothing else could have done. "Santa Anna's brutal and in no way justifiable measures brought support for Texas from many parts of the United States, and with one blow legitimated the war against Mexico, putting the Texans into such a rage that they were able in the end to carry off the victory against a Mexican army that was far superior to them in numbers," Reichstein wrote.[11]

The men who fell at the Alamo and Goliad were primarily newcomers from the United States recruited to fight. The remainder of the Texas Army, under General Houston, included many settlers. Originally about 1,200 in strength, it shrank to about 800 when news of the fall of the Alamo sent men rushing home to protect their families from the advancing Mexicans. In consequence, many missed the decisive Battle of San Jacinto in which Texas finally won her freedom. "Taken up with the sacred duties of husband and father, the old Texian would not and could not be present on the memorable 21st of April to show his devotion to the cause of Revolution."[12]

The Runaway Scrape

In the previous May 1835, when Mexican states-rights advocates had rebelled in the State of Zacatecas, Santa Anna had "crushed them with a ruthlessness that was to become his trademark. Upon defeating the rebels, Santa Anna rewarded his Centralist soldiers by allowing them two days of rape and pillage in Zacatecas; more than two thousand defenseless noncombatants were killed during that orgy. Texians received reports of the rape of Zecatecas with dismay and foreboding."[13] News of the fall of the Alamo and the Goliad massacre re-activated these anxieties. When the settlers received word that their government had decamped from Washington-on-the-Brazos to Galveston Island, they remembered Zacatecas and fled.

Some forgotten Paul Revere brought the perilous news to Robertson's Colony; one of Santa Anna's armies had orders to march up the O.S.R. all the way to Nacogdoches. Such a route lay directly athwart Wheelock Prairie. General Houston had authorized one Ranger as escort for each fleeing family. This was enough for Colonel Wheelock, who gathered his community together and headed pell mell toward the safety of Louisiana.

Ranger Noah Smithwick left a description of this terror-stricken flight. He and eight other Rangers were stationed on the O.S.R. beyond Plum Creek to watch for the enemy, but after a few days returned to their headquarters in Mina (present-day Bastrop). From there their whole company traveled south along the Colorado to join General Houston. Smithwick noted:

> The desolation of the country through which we passed beggars description. Houses were standing open, the beds unmade, the

breakfast things still on the tables, pans of milk moulding in the
dairies . . . And as if the arch fiend had broken loose, there were
men—or devils rather—bent on plunder, galloping up behind
the fugitives, telling them the Mexicans were just behind, thus
causing the hapless victims to abandon what few valuables they
had tried to save.[14]

Families in colonies closer to the scenes of battle and farther away from the United States border had even more trouble.
Dilue Rose Harris, living near present-day Sugar Land, was only
ten years old at the time of the Runaway Scrape, but fear makes
vivid memories. She later wrote:

> . . . the people of San Patricio and other western settlements were
> fleeing for their lives. Every family in our neighborhood was
> preparing to go to the United States. Wagons and other vehicles
> were scarce . . . Father hauled away a part of our household fur-
> niture and other things and hid them in the bottom . . . On the
> 12th of March came the news of the fall of the Alamo. A courier
> brought a dispatch from General Houston for the people to
> leave . . . We left home at sunset, hauling clothes, bedding and
> provisions on the sleigh with one yoke of oxen . . . We camped the
> first night at Harrisburg. Next day we crossed Vince's Bridge and
> arrived at San Jacinto in the night. There were fully five thousand
> people at the ferry. . . . We waited for three days before we
> crossed. . . At the Trinity River men from the Army began to join
> their families. I know they have been blamed for this, but what
> else could they have done?[15]

I. T. Taylor of present-day Jackson County wrote that panic
"flamed like a wild prairie fire when Santa Anna crossed Texas
while Sam Houston and the Texas Army retreated. Tight lipped
women, squalling children, frightened slaves, the aged and in-
firm all were fleeing, many were thinking their days were numbered . . ."[16]

Jeff Parsons, a slave belonging to Maj. George Sutherland,
recalled the situation clearly:

> We had hardly settled down before trouble with Texas and
> Mexico. I remember the runaway well as we went ahead of
> General Houston's army. The women, children, slaves and a few

old men reached the Sabine before the Battle of San Jacinto. There was a lot of scared folks in the runaway crowd. Some went on sleds, some on contrivances made with truck wheels, some on wagons, some on horseback, some on foot, or any way they could get there. I can't begin to describe the scene on the Sabine. People and things were all mixed and in confusion. The children were crying, the women were praying, and the men cursing. I tell you it was a serious time.[17]

"The settlements from the Colorado to the Nueces . . . Victoria, San Patricio, Goliad, and Refugio, were in a great measure broken up during the war and but few of the inhabitants have yet returned," the Anonymous Buckeye was to write in the spring of 1837.[18] Many never returned to Texas, and some of those who did faced scorched earth and hunger. The crops and food supplies were gone. All the survivors mention the near-starvation they endured until another crop could be planted and harvested. Taylor likens it to the starving times endured by the English at Jamestown in 1619, stating that many went without bread for almost a year.[19]

Annette Wheelock remembered that before her party left Wheelock Prairie, Samuel A. Kimble had buried "a small trunk wrapped in a cow hide." Into it he packed "carpenters tools, set of dishes (a Moss Rose design), and other things. . . He told Annette that if he never got back that they would never find that trunk."[20] They never did.

Kimble joined with Wheelock, Mary Wheelock, and the Wheelock children in their bolt to Louisiana, but the two men together with young George stayed only long enough to see the women and children comfortable and safe before turning their horses back towards Houston's army. Like many of the other Rangers coming from the northern colonies, they arrived a day after the Battle of San Jacinto. Only Robert Williamson and two others, galloping ahead, were able to arrive in time to take part in the battle.

Victory

Now Texas was beginning to wake up to reality. Houston at

last had an army under his personal command, and could plan his campaign. The Texians were fighters, but they were ill-equipped and untrained. Their officers were ready to run pellmell into danger, but like bad chess players could not see three or four moves ahead. Everyone hounded General Houston, including his political bosses. He was dirty, he was drunk, he was a coward.

He kept his own counsel, a lifelong habit which was maddening to many. On March 29 he had written to Rusk, "had I consulted the wishes of all, I should have been like the ass between two stacks of hay . . . I consulted none—I held no councils of war. If I err, the blame is mine."[21]

The bitter voices continued to taunt him and would do so all his life and beyond. But Houston knew what he was doing. As Hardin stated, "Houston was the first commander with the ability to plan beyond the next battle."[22] He retreated, waiting for the wily Napoleon of the West to make a mistake. It came. Santa Anna divided his army, leaving half in the south. Then, in mid April, wishing to finish off the rebels, he force-marched almost 1,000 men to a spot near General Houston's future namesake city, hoping to catch up with the Texians, who had been resting at a nearby plantation.

On April 18 Houston reached Harrisburg where, under a small guard, he left the army's baggage and 248 men who were too ill to march. What was left of the Texian Army pressed forward and camped on Buffalo Bayou.

On April 21 Santa Anna was reinforced by 500 soldiers under the command of General Cos, whom he had absolved of his promise not to return to Texas. Exhausted, they rested on the shores of the San Jacinto River, named by the Spanish to honor Saint Hyacinth, a Christian martyr in imperial Rome. At four in the afternoon Houston attacked on his huge white stallion, Saracen, and in twenty minutes routed the Mexican army of 1,300. The battle was decisive. Texas was free.

The terrified Mexicans ran into Peggy Lake, where neither General Houston nor any other officer was able to prevent a blood bath. The Texian soldiers were remembering the Alamo and Goliad.

CHAPTER 11

THE TEXAS RANGERS: MAY-JUNE 1836

Men on Horseback

If history is entitled to any credit, no people ever suffered more than the first settlers of Texas. The whole country was filled with savages who understood the fatal consequences of permitting the white man to get a foothold in their country. Contending for their homes, upon both sides it was a war of extermination.[1]

So wrote the Anonymous Buckeye. Against this backdrop, the legend of the Texas Rangers was born.

"The title Ranger was already old in Anglo-America,"[2] used during the French and Indian War to describe groups of mounted, mobile soldiers who fought Amerinds on their own ground using Amerind tactics. Celtic settlers seemed to have brought the word and the concept of the ranger from the Scottish borderlands. But the Texas Rangers were unique. They amounted to a paramilitary force countenanced by government and supported by government when money was available, but mainly recruited by frontier communities and supported by them.

111

Map showing area of Wheelock's career as surveyor between Brazos and Navasota Rivers. Excerpt from "Map of Texas, compiled from surveys . . . in General Land Office" by Richard S. Hunt and Jesse F. Randel (New York: Sherman and Smith, 1845). Reproduced in McLean, Papers, *XVII, 72.*

According to T. R. Fehrenbach:

They were . . . one of the most colorful, efficient, and deadly band of irregular partisans on the side of law and order that the world has ever seen. . . . The Ranger captains were unusual men—not merely brave but officers who showed an utter absence of fear. This breed of captain was called forth both by the rough nature of the men he led and the incredibly perilous situation of the tiny Ranger bands on the war frontier.[3]
   The Ranger captains had to be not only field generals but superb psychologists, understanding the enemy and their own men. . . They had to learn something of cultural differences. Human torture was an abomination to the Anglo-Celt, and he had to learn that he could not surrender with honor to either Mexican or Amerind, whose cultures permitted it. One factor in the success of all great frontier captains was that they never made the "fundamental and possibly fatal error of believing their enemies were, or thought like, Anglo-Americans in red or brown skins."[4]

The Rangers were all volunteers. They found that their best defense was a reputation for implacable fierceness. This fierceness was largely directed against the Comanches and their allies.

The Adversaries

The rise of the Comanche started with the dispersal of the Spanish pony over North America, Barb and Arab, chosen for their toughness, resilience, and speed. By 1750 mounted Amerinds were common as far north as Canada. About the same time out of the Rocky Mountains came a poor tribe, primitive hunters and gatherers, speaking Shoshone, calling themselves, like most Amerinds, "the Human Beings" (everyone else, by implication, being not quite human). Plains Indians called them "Snake People," but the Spanish called them Comanches, a prophetic Ute word meaning "always my enemy."
   The horse completely revolutionized the life of the Comanches, leading them to abandon their icy mountain home for the open plains to create a new horse-centered culture. They

became the most efficient light cavalry the world had ever seen, and the greatest horse thieves of all time. The horse gave them a deep sense of pride and superiority, as it had the mounted man, the knight or the caballero of Europe. Like Moors and Spanish, they boarded their horses from the right; on their own, they invented a thong by which a warrior could drop over the side of his horse for safety while thundering in a circling charge.

Settlers who witnessed the Indians' preparation for a raid never forgot the circle of fire, the clever, intense riders, as skillful as modern rodeo performers whose predecessors they were, the painted faces, the cries of the warriors seeking the Comanche Valhalla.

The lightly built Comanche moved down into Texas about 1725 like Genghis Khan. They were the finest horsemen ever known. Their long plains lance reminded Europeans of the Crusader lance; their bison hide shield was hard enough to turn a musket ball. They fashioned their bows of the Bois d'Arc branch and believed that "mutilation on a corpse was endured by its spirit in the afterlife."[5] Even the Apache had fixed homes, but the Comanche lived everywhere and nowhere. Fehrenbach wrote: "Comanches rode to war by the light of the moon; their favorite tactic was to strike deep into enemy territory, two or even three hundred miles or more away, kill, despoil, take prisoners, and gallop back to the trackless plains."[6]

The Comanches, driving out the Apache, now had for their own "the highest concentration of large game on the continent."[7] Plundering and horse stealing was their way of life.

At first the more friendly Wacos and Tawakonis stood between the Texans and the Comanches, but as the colonies grew, spreading farms began to encroach on Comanche hunting grounds in East Texas. In 1834, the year Wheelock Prairie was established, raids of the settlements began, which were to continue for a generation before the warrior tribes were finally banished from Texas after the Civil War.

Wheelock was to have an adversarial relationship (he was captured by Indians five times) and later a paternal relationship with Texas Amerinds for the next decade. During and since his grandfather's mission to the Indians of New England his family had enjoyed a history of sympathy with Amerinds. Now his experience was nearer that of more remote ancestors in early Massachusetts during King Philip's War when Amerinds raided the settlements directly and put Europeans to fire and blade. Texas was not his first pioneering experience, but it was his first experience where blood was still flowing.

Wheelock's Rangers

At the time E.L.R. Wheelock became a captain of Rangers on May 8, 1836, it was the raiding Amerind that Robertson Colony settlers feared, not the defeated Mexican. Common practice when traveling was to stop at dark, build a fire, eat, and sneak away to spend the night at another spot eight or ten miles distant. Camping three to four miles on one side or the other of the trail with plenty of sentries was also advised. The Indians were not fooled very often.

Nerves were raw. Rumors flew, some true, some exaggerated, all believed. In March Col. James Morgan had reported to Interim President Burnet that some Negro slaves high up on the Trinity were trying to get some Coshutti Indians to help them in a revolt. Another report that Mexican agents were among the Cherokees in Northeast Texas inspired Burnet to write to U.S. General Gaines on the Louisiana border asking him to send troops into Texas to protect the settlers. Gaines subsequently sent 324 men into Nacogdoches, where they found neither Indians nor settlers, but did get in trouble with Washington City, which was attempting to maintain neutrality during the Mexico-Texas conflict.

Farther south, the fear of the Mexicans was greater than the fear of Amerinds. During the period after the Battle of San Jacinto, the interim Texian government was by no means sure that hostilities had ceased. Having moved for safety from Washington-on-the-Brazos to Galveston, they were daily confronted with rumors that new Mexican armies were forming south of the Rio Grande to redeem Santa Anna's humiliation. As a logical outgrowth of this fear, more men were put under arms. Wheelock had served as a lieutenant in a Ranger company for seven weeks. Now it was time for him to organize his own company, recruited at Fort Wheelock and including many home town boys. His son George signed up, as did his future sons-in-law Andrew Jackson Powers and Samuel A. Kimble.

Here is a list, taken from his private papers, of Wheelock's first Company of Rangers, serving under Col. Jesse Benton:

Captain—E.L.R. Wheelock

1st. Lt.—Cantwell, Thomas	1st Sgt.—Kimble, S. A.
3rd Sgt.—Lyons, G. W.	2nd Corp.—Allen, Elijah
2nd Lt.—Cary, Seth	2nd Sgt.—Archer, John
4th Sgt.—Williams, John	3rd Corp.—Garner, Isaac
3rd Lt.—Doyle, F. M.	
1st Corp.—Towsend, J.	

Privates

Adams, John	Barrow, P. R.
Davis, G. W.	Witcher
Lyons, DeWitt	Davis, John
Pride, Alfred	Arthur, Wm. H.
Smith, W. D.	Williams, Samuel
Thompson. N. B.	Lagrone, W. A.
Williams, Jackson	Vaughn, Willis (Barker)
Bell, Joseph F.	Barrow, Levi
Teer	Crabtree, Wm.
Rhea, J. R.	Limney, H.
Wheelock, George	Murrey, James
Rodgers, G.	Ryams
Rial, John W.	Mower
Butler	Walker
Bloodgood, Wm.	Clark
Finch, I. M.	Barrow, Solomon
Lawrens, John	Roark, W.
Rush, Joseph	Rodgers, Robert
Springanneur, J.	
Taylor, Joseph	

It was a proud assembly. When George W. Davis died, his grave marker recorded as one of the great events of his life that he had ridden with Captain Wheelock's Rangers.

Another version of this list (at the Texas General Land Office) adds the names of William H. Altree, Edward Jackson, Chester Gorbet, William Morse, and John Williams.

The oath they signed was similar to the one below, dated the following September:

> We the undersigned do hereby enroll ourselves as permanent volunteer Rangers in the service of the Republic of Texas to be subject for duty at all times. . . to the military laws of the Republic and to be attached as a part of the force ordered to be raised by Col. Wheelock acting under orders of the Commanding General and in all things conform to the rules and articles of WAR and in all things that are lawful obey the order of such officers that are appointed to command us. All of which (we) voluntarily subscribe to this 14th day of September 1836.

The recruits were "sworn to support the Republic of Texas by me, E.L.R. Wheelock, Capt. Commanding R. Rangers on Recruit Service, Texas Army." Names not on the muster roll but appearing on the oath were A. J., Elijah, Lewis B., and . . . Powers, William and Francis Winans, John Edmondson, and five Spillars brothers. Many, like seventeen-year-old George Ripley Wheelock, were very young, but having been brought up on the frontier were well on their way to being as purposeful as their fathers. Their commanding officer at forty-three was one of the more elderly Ranger captains, but obviously still able to ride and shoot with the best of them.

With his wife and four youngest children safe (as he thought) in Louisiana, Wheelock was able to concentrate along with the other colonists on making sure the Mexicans were beaten, bringing order out of the chaos of revolution, and keeping the frontier safe from the Amerinds.

A Ranger captain's first duty was to see his men equipped, usually with strouding, "a coarse woolen cloth, blanket, or garment, formerly used by the British in bartering with the North American Indians (named for the village of Stroud in Gloucestershire, England, where they were woven). The usual length received by each Ranger was from two to two and a half yards, mostly red although some Rangers received blue." [8] This strouding was reminiscent of the Scottish plaid which the Highlander slept in at night and wore as a garment by day, although the cold weather original was much longer.

They also were "charged with plugs of tobacco, pantaloons, shoes (from sizes 6 to 10), gun locks, guns, shirts, a coffee boiler, and lawn (a thin or sheer linen or cotton fabric), either plain or printed."[9]

Third Corporal Isaac Garner, helping in 1874 with a compilation of veterans' records, stated that he was born in Louisiana, immigrated to Texas in 1834, and served under Capt. E.L.R. Wheelock in the Rangers until his discharge between the 8th and 15th of August 1836, on the Aransas between Goliad on the Sanantone River and San Patricio on the Nueces River. He stated that he had never been in a proper battle, having only reached the Texas Army on May 8 because of being detained by high waters.[10] Raiding was different.

The Raid on Fort Parker

In May 1836 the most celebrated of all Texas Indian raids occurred near present-day Groesbeck in Robertson's Colony. The victims were the extended Parker family, which had arrived from Illinois in 1833 with 136 members of the Baptist church of which Elder John Parker was patriarch and pastor.

Like several other associations pioneering in Texas, they planned to establish a utopian community dedicated to their strict way of life. The heads of families and single men received their headrights in 1834 (some surveyed by E.L.R. Wheelock) and in 1835 built a substantial fort on the Navasota River, at first known as Fort Sterling (probably to honor Major Robertson), and later as Fort Parker. They were on the exposed northern rim of Anglo settlement.

The Indians may have targeted Fort Parker because of Silas Parker's special status as an Indian fighter. Early in 1835 settlers had assembled at this fort to form an informal company of Rangers to guard against Amerinds. On October 17, 1835, the General Council had authorized Silas Parker to employ twenty-five Rangers to control the Indians between the Brazos and the Trinity Rivers. The following spring, on May 19, 1836, about 600 Comanches, Tawakonis, Caddos, Wacos, and other tribes attacked the almost deserted fort while all but five of the men were cultivating distant fields. Two Parker brothers, Benjamin and Silas, tried to parley with their visitors, but were killed by Comanche lances, as were two Frosts, one perhaps the boy prophet who had told the Fort Parker saints that Texas had won the Battle of San Jacinto before earthly messengers arrived with the news.

Now free to enter the fort, the invaders stabbed Elder John Parker, scalped him, and cut off his private parts. His elderly wife was stripped, pinned to the ground by a lance and repeatedly raped. The other women met a similar fate; two of these died.

Hearing the return of the farming contingent, which had been alerted by gunfire, the Comanches and their friends now rode away taking five captives: Rachel Parker Plummer and her small son James, Elizabeth Kellogg, John Parker aged six, and Cynthia Ann Parker, aged nine. It has become popular recently to romanticize this kidnaping and its subsequent history. There was nothing romantic about it.

After the Indians had celebrated their victory dance and thoroughly raped all the women, torturing the two adults, they split up. Rachel was taken to the Rockies where she became a Comanche slave and never saw her son again. The child she bore to her captor was killed by the Indians by being thrown onto the ice. She was ransomed in Santa Fe eighteen months after her ordeal began, but she did not live long after her repatriation.

The more fortunate Elizabeth Kellogg was allotted to a Caddo tribe, which took her to their lands near the Red River. During a pow-wow with the Caddos in December 1836, Sam Houston was able to buy her freedom for $150. In 1842, after six years as Comanches, John Parker and James Plummer were also ransomed. John was unable to readjust to Anglo life and returned to the tribes, looking for his sister, Cynthia Ann. Eventually he married a Mexican girl who had been a Comanche slave and went to live with her in Mexico, where the two survivors of a savage captivity made a life for themselves.

Blond and blue-eyed Cynthia Ann Parker fell to the lot of the most remote and warlike of the Comanches, who took her hundreds of miles away into the Staked Plains. Fehrenbach reported: "Although she was seen or heard of a number of times, all efforts to ransom her failed. In 1846, a U.S. Army colonel at a council of Indians saw her briefly. He said she refused to speak, wept incessantly, and ran away."[11] Later she painted the insides of her ears red according to the custom of Comanche women and became the wife of Peta Nocona, a Comanche Chief, and the mother of Quanah Parker, last chief of the Comanche. When she was eventually rescued, it was much too late for her to reclaim her Anglo life.

Fehrenbach said: "The Parker raid was not unusual. It was to be repeated in various ways many hundred of times."[12] These raids evoked a virulent hatred of the Comanche because the raiding was directed against farming families, not hunters and frontiersmen.

> For forty years this bleeding ground was filled with men and boys, wives and sons, who had kinfolk carried off, never to be heard from again or to be ransomed and returned in shamed disgrace. Thousands of frontier families were to see the results of Comanche raids: men staked out naked to die under the blazing sun, eyelids and genitals removed; women and children impaled on fence poles and burned; captives found still writhing, dying, with burned-out coals heaped on scrota and armpits; ransomed teen-aged girls and women returned to their relatives with demented stares.
>
> These were insults and injuries the Anglo-Celt stock would not forgive or bear.[13]

Captain of Rangers E.L.R. Wheelock, whose Fort Wheelock troop was the nearest available, may have pursued the Comanches who devastated Fort Parker, but by the time he and his men arrived in the vicinity, the Amerinds would have been long gone. As was so often the case, the rescue party became a burial party. All the grim-faced Rangers were of course personally acquainted with the victims.

Wheelock's Rangers were now directed to help feed the hungry Texan Army by protecting cattle running wild (after their owners had abandoned them during the Runaway Scrape) from becoming the prey of rustlers.

May 25, 1836
Republic of Texas
Jurisdiction of Liberty
To Col. E.L.R. Wheelock

Sir:
Having been informed that a number of persons are at present
engaged in removing from this jurisdiction stock which justice required should not be removed, this is therefore to authorize you
to detain and prevent any cattle from being crossed over the river
Trinity until a sufficient time shall have elapsed to consult the
proper authority now located at the town of Velasco in the jurisdiction of Columbia - after which you will receive further orders.

Given under my hand in the town of Liberty this 23 of May 1836.
William Carding

It was taken for granted that the Rangers should also be com-
petent cow hands.

Yet while patrolling, recruiting, equipping, and drilling the
Rangers were going on, so was everyday life. Wheelock was still
headquartered in his own exposed community and new settlers,
having heard of the Texas victory at San Jacinto, were once
more pouring into Robertson's Colony. Among the many
Wheelock did business with during this period was John
Darrington, to whom he sold several headrights, possibly some
of those allotted to him as sub-agent of Empresario Robertson.
Colonel Darrington's family and the Wheelock family were together during the Runaway Scrape, and Darrington had afforded the Wheelocks favors and protection during that perilous time.

This was the same Colonel Darrington who informed U.S.
Gen. Alexander McComb in New Orleans that the Caddo
Indians could not be concerned in attacking the Texians, as was
being rumored, because they were but few in number and quite
insignificant. But General McComb believed less well-informed
sources and writing to U.S. Secretary of War Lewis Cass asked for
a force of 20,000 to shield Louisianans from possible Indian attacks during the Texas Revolution.

In a manner typical of the confusion of the time, Wheelock's orders to contain stray cattle were soon countermanded.

Mr. Clark Beach
Dear Sir:
In reply to the verbal message which you bring me from Col. Wheelock that he has been ordered by Judge League to assist the Sheriff in taking certain cattle into his possession, you will please state to him that he must desist from the execution of said order and proceed without delay to the army where he will report himself to the commander.
                              Yours, M. B. Lamar, Sect. of War.

With the frontier on fire, Wheelock must now turn his back on Indian problems and focus his attention on the south, where new-born Texas was still in neo-natal critical care.

June 15, 1836, Velasco
Executive Department
To Capt. E.L.R. Wheelock
Sir:
You are requested to put your company in condition for active service and as soon as possible to join this command of Brevet Brig. General F. Huston from whom you will receive orders for future operations.
                              Your Obt. Servant
                              David G. Burnet

A more personal message followed:

To Capt. E.L.R. Wheelock
George Ripley Wheelock, a private in Capt. Wheelock's Rangers, Texas Army, is hereby furloughed for three months to take care of the family of Capt. Wheelock, now in the field, and is requested to (depart) June 22, 1836.

George Ripley's support was needed at home. Mary Wheelock

had returned to Texas from Louisiana without her youngest child, Thomas Ford Wheelock, who is believed to have died there of yellow fever at the age of three. The remaining brothers and the teenaged Annette now joined to support their mother in her mourning as the family tried to restore order to their home place after its abandonment during the Runaway.

The father of the family, sick at heart at the loss of his youngest child, rode south on a war footing.

CHAPTER 12

THE VELASCO REBELLION: JULY-SEPTEMBER 1836

David Burnet

In the minds of the Texians and their interim government the War for Independence was far from over. No one knew how Mexico City would react to the news of the capture of her dictator or whether she would honor his treaties.

The Treaty of Velasco, signed on May 4, 1836, by Interim President of the Republic David Gouverneur Burnet and Generalissimo Antonio Lopez de Santa Anna, was a two-fold document. The public portion proclaimed an end to hostilities, promising that Mexico would never make war on Texas again and that her army would stay south of the Rio Grande. A secret codicil traded Santa Anna's quick release for Mexico's recognition of the independence of the Republic of Texas.

The repatriation of Santa Anna was by no means a popular idea; many Texians wanted him hanged. And many Mexicans agreed with them. As Michael Meyer characterized him, "Often clever, never wise, he set an example of dishonesty and complete failure to adhere to any set of principles."[1] Santa Anna's safety was by no means assured.

The sudden responsibility of running an independent nation was overwhelming to Burnet and his instant bureaucracy. Food for the swelling army (now consisting of 2,000 volunteers from the United States, who had been promised free land) was becoming a serious problem. Many wealthy and prominent Texans had managed to dodge military service for one reason or another (Samuel May Williams, Henry Austin, the Groces, Charles S. Taylor, Thorn and Haden Edwards, to name only a few) and had little sympathy for military problems. The out-raged army, having borne the heat of the day, refused to abdi-cate their interests in favor of well-placed dodgers.

Before taking ship to New Orleans for surgery on his leg, which had been shattered at the Battle of San Jacinto, Gen. Sam Houston had appointed Thomas Rusk as his successor as com-mander in chief of the Texian Army. The appointment was not a success, and Rusk was soon losing control. On June 1 Burnet put Santa Anna on board the *Invincible* at Velasco (at the mouth of the Brazos River) for his voyage home, as provided by the se-cret treaty. At once a mob surrounded the temporary capital building, "as feeling against both Burnet and Santa Anna in-creased."[2] The ship did not sail.

In early June the army addressed Interim President Burnet and by inference Interim Secretary of War Lamar, accusing them of failure to provide food and supplies for the army and "ne-glecting to strengthen the military in the wake of those who had deserted or been honorably discharged."[3] Opposing repatria-tion of Santa Anna, they wanted to let the soon-to-be-elected First Texas Congress decide his fate and the fate of the Treaty of Velasco. Burnet's reply was a general reprimand, cold to the army's plight. The Texian Army became restless, dissatisfied, hungry, and indignant.[4]

Revolt

At a secret meeting, "it was decided to arrest Burnet, seize the government, and put Santa Anna on trial for his life."[5] Lt. Col. Henry Millard was delegated to go to Velasco, where the in-terim government was meeting, to take Burnet into custody and to bring him into camp for trial as an enemy of the country.[6]

This high-handed action was the brainchild of certain general officers who wished to remain in the background until
Burnet was safely in custody. Their delegate, Colonel Millard,
more naive than they and perhaps having more courage of his
convictions, was a veteran of the Battle of San Jacinto, where he
commanded the right flank of the infantry. Millard was the kind
of officer who took the welfare of his men much to heart, and
had become a friend of Captain-of-Rangers E.L.R. Wheelock,
who shared both his indignation at the neglect of the army and
his anti-Austin political stance.

A pathetic letter which Wheelock received from one of his
own men the following summer illustrates the level of poverty
which evoked the protest to Burnet.

> Victoria
> To Capt. E.L.R. Wheelock
> Sir:
> I hope to be fit for duty in [a short time] and should be glad to
> go to the [company] as soon as possible but I have nothing to ride
> as my mule has been shot [since] I saw you. I wish you to get me
> a good horse if you can and if not a shirt and pantaloons for me
> if you can, . . . your humble servant, Charles L. Lorbet

The civilian population, recovering from the Runaway
Scrape, had little food or clothing to share. Still, the army considered that it had delivered victory to these civilians. It wanted
a say in the fate of the defeated Mexican general and it wanted
to be fed and clothed. A shirt and pantaloons did not seem too
much to ask. After setting forth its privations and want of provisions, army representatives wrote to Burnet:

> And to whom are we to charge these injuries? Surely to you, as the
> President of the Republic! It was your duty to have paid particu-
> lar attention to the army, to have inquired out their wants, and
> relieved them. It was surely your duty to have caused provisions
> at least to have been furnished. . . In conclusion we repeat to you,
> General Santa Anna must be safely secured, and placed at the dis-
> position of the coming Congress.[7]

Wheelock may very well have aided in drawing up these

charges and specifications, with which, as a former United States regular officer and militia officer in two wars, he agreed.

On June 3 the unfortunate David Burnet had already disembarked Santa Anna and handed him over to fiery late-comer Gen. Thomas Jefferson Green, who had received his post-war commission for recruiting troops in the United States.

When Millard was ordered to present this ultimatum to Burnet by those in the rebellion of higher rank than himself (whose names were never discovered, although Gen. Felix Huston and Gen. T. J. Green were probably among them), he turned this duty over to a volunteer, Capt. Amasa Turner. Dorothy Fields wrote that "Captain Turner was a friend and admirer of the president, and feeling that Millard's order was treasonable, quietly went to Burnet's home . . . and gave him Millard's order for the arrest. President Burnet advised Turner to report to Millard that the president was not subject to the army's control and therefore would not submit to their arrest, but that he would answer to Congress for his conduct."[8]

Once the attempt to arrest Burnet became public, it died a natural death. A divided cabinet offered to resign, but Burnet refused to accept their resignations. He tried to get rid of his gadfly, Secretary of War Mirabeau B. Lamar, by making him commander in chief in place of Rusk, but the army would have nothing of it. Lamar had fought well at the Battle of San Jacinto but had only arrived in Texas in March 1836, just in time to join Sam Houston, and the army blandly informed him that he lacked the qualifications of a commander in chief.

The Quartermaster General

Exasperated by inefficient Texas government, Wheelock did what he could to repair the deficiencies of army supplies, although it would not be until statehood that he was to be repaid $60 for eight hogs, $40 for corn and bacon, $30 for providing transportation for the army, and $250 for various other expenses incurred by him on its behalf. This was a hardship for Wheelock, not a wealthy man. However, he had served in the Quartermaster Department of the U.S. Army during the War of

1812 and felt it his duty to share his expertise with the Quartermaster General's Office. His suggestions were well received and
endorsed by Millard.

> I most sincerely approve the views of Col. [Wheelock] [and am]
> induced to believe that some arrangement of the [sort] is the only
> remedy for the present defects which magnify themselves every
> day in practice.
>
> Henry Millard
> Lt. Col. Commanding.

On July 19 the QMG wrote to Rusk that "the proceedings
of Col. Millard has had so far a most excellent effect . . . The
President has acceded to Millard's propositions and says he is
desirous to do all in his power for the army."[9] But underneath,
affairs remained much as they had been before.

The office of quartermaster general was held by Almanzon
Huston, a New Yorker turned innkeeper in San Augustine.
Almanzon retained his native Yankee efficiency, but he struggled
constantly with inadequate staff, the bickering of the government, and countermanding of his lawful orders.

About this time, Texas received the unsettling word that
Mexico had repudiated both Velasco treaties. General Urrea was
rumored to be gathering a force at Matamoros with which to
carry on the war.

General Felix Huston (not to be confused with Almanzon
Huston, the QMG) was Wheelock's commanding officer, another Texan who had not arrived in Texas until one month after
the Battle of San Jacinto. Having talked himself into the military, he "had used his influence to prevent Santa Anna from
being returned to Mexico. He had also helped to prevent
Mirabeau B. Lamar from being accepted by the army when he
sought to take command under an appointment by President
Burnet in early July."[10]

Typical of a certain type of aggressive incomer, his over-
weening personal ambition would later lead him into serious
trouble. The Anonymous Buckeye, writing the following year
about events in 1836, declared that about one-half to three-
fourths of the men in Texas were old settlers "differing little

from solid citizens of the U.S. south." A few were speculators who had brought about the revolution for gain. The other quarter to half came after the revolution had started. Of the 3,685 men who fought in the Texas Revolution, forty per cent were United States volunteers. "Some were men of desperate fortunes, some were cast off by society, . . . some came to seek a theatre for their ambition, some for love of adventure, and some from genuine sympathy to relieve the sufferings of the oppressed," according to Andrew Muir.[11] It was becoming apparent to Wheelock and other old hands that these newcomers were slowly but surely taking control of Texas.

Crumbling temporary President Burnet, his government near collapse, now prudently decided that the time had come to call a general election. He named September 5, 1836, as election day.

Wheelock was in Columbia, where Santa Anna was being held by the army. In July John R. Jones wrote to his son in St. Louis:

> Brazos
>
> My dear children:
>
> . . . Genl. Santa Anna is still under guard near Columbia and is likely to remain until our independence is recognized by the Mexican govt. Cols. Menard and Wheelock and our Mexican friend Don Juan Placedo (arrived) a few days ago, just from our army on Guadaloupe and say our forces are 1700 and daily increasing—that the Mexicans are embodying a considerable army at Matamoros and other points on the Rio Grande and General Urrea declares his intention of waging a war of extermination putting to death men, women and children, but if we get the assistance we expect from the U.S. it is more than probable he will not for a second time have the pleasure of seeing the Colorado, for almost every man in the whole country is turning out.[12]

On July 18 a letter passed from President Burnet to General Rusk asking him to put into effect Col. Millard's recommendations for the Quartermaster Corps (which were largely Wheelock's suggestions) and praising them highly.

Wheelock continued to urge the government to clothe its

army, and the quartermaster general was confident that Millard and Wheelock would between them be able to persuade the temporary president to better ways as indicated in this letter:

> To Brevet Brig. Genl. F. Huston:
> Dear Sir:
> At the request of Col. Wheelock, I have sent for your command six pieces of cotton drilling for suits, it being all we have or all that could be gotten at this place. Colonels Millard and Wheelock leave here today for Galveston and I am in hopes affairs will soon be in a better state; their mission to this place has had a most excellent effect on the Govt. and they have shown themselves worthy the trust committed to their charge . . . My hands have been completely tied, it would seem that the Government were determined to put down the army at all hazards.
> > I have the honor to be Sir Your Ob. St. etc.
> > A. Huston, Qr. Mr. Genl.[13]

And to feed the army, he wrote:

> To Theo S. Lee, Asst. QMG
> Sir:
> You will forthwith proceed to Liberty and as far as lies in your power collect or cause to be collected all the cattle that were donated also those that were seized for the use of the Govt. You are also authorized to purchase to the amt of 500 head of beeves giving Govt. paper for same. Taking care to take and keep duplicate accounts of your purchases. In collecting the Beeves donated and seized upon you will be governed by Col. Wheelock's order. You will have all the Beeves you can procure driven west of the Brazos River between that and the Colorado and there herded until further ordered.
> > I have the honor to be Sir Your ob St. etc.
> > A. Huston, Qr Mr. Genl[14]

But higher authority had other uses for those beeves, and A. Huston found another order countermanded. No one in the government seemed to care whether the army ate or not.

Wheelock was now asked by the beleaguered quartermaster

general to become his second assistant, the first assistantship already being occupied by R. B. Irvine. As noted in the following letter, Wheelock's experience, Huston believed, would be of enormous help to the embattled department:

Office of the Qr Mr Genl
Quintana July 24, 1836
To Brig Gen Thos J. Rusk, Comdg the Texian Army
Dear Sir:
From the little knowledge I have of Colonel Wheelock's enterprising spirit and energetic manner of doing business, I have endeavored to get him into my department. The Government have refused to commission him; they have also refused to commission me an Asst Qr Mr Genl. I have been much troubled to get energetic men into this Department: consequently nothing can be done. Every branch of operations is completely tied up.
    Col. Millard will inform you Col. Wheelock has shown much spirit and anxiety in getting matters arranged to facilitate the movements of the army and is worthy the gratitude of his Comdg Genl.
    I have the Honor to be with much respect Yr ob St etc.
    A Huston, Qr Mr Genl[15]

But alas, Lamar was not able to grant Gen. Almanzon Huston this help. One assistant was all that was authorized and one assistant was all he got.

Re-enlistment

Meanwhile, the ordinary business of Wheelock's Rangers continued. In August their term of enlistment expired, but with war clouds still threatening most signed up for a second term and a new muster roll was drawn up.
    This new Muster Roll of Capt. E.L.R. Wheelock's Company of the Regiment was ordered to be raised by the convention of Texas Rangers under command of Lt. Col. Griffin Bane but came under the immediate command of Brig. Gen. Felix Huston from the day of enrollment.

This group was essentially the same company recruited in May. T. F. M. Doyle had been promoted to 2nd Lt., S. A. Kimble reduced to 2nd Sergeant, and Alfred Pride is identified as a musician. New names include Barton Baker and Reuben Barlow. Samuel Williams had been detached and ordered to take care of Wheelock's family, and his pay became the responsibility of Colonel Wheelock. Washington Krash had transferred to another company. Stephen Rogers had left sick. Willis Vaughn and Edward Jackson had been added. On June 1 G. S. Gorbitt, W. L. Morse, John Williams, Peter Hynes, and John Hynes signed on. At the bottom of this document are the words: "We agree to serve the Republic of Texas Three Months longer than our term of enrollment in Wheelock's Company of Rangers." Signed at Camp. Cibolo on August 23, 1836.

Others listed were:
Milo Mower—6 mos.
N. B. Thompson—6 mos. but discharged after three months.
Joseph Walker—duration of war
G. S. Gorbett—six months
A. Carlin—duration of war
Joseph, an Indian—duration of the war
Charles Baker—duration of the war.

The Rangers were ranging, on patrol in the coastal regions.

Headquarters Colletta
August 2, 1836
Col. Wheelock:
Will be allowed to pass to Linn's Landing (on Lavaca Bay) free of molestation or hindrance.
    By order of Thomas Rusk
    Brig Gen Commanding
    by Sam Austin, Aide de Camp

Meanwhile, neither the army nor Interim President Burnet considered Texas's quarrel with Mexico at an end. Wheelock was still in and out of Velasco, where affairs seemed to be going from bad to worse. Early in August his friend Henry Millard wrote frankly to Thomas B. Huling that he believed the neglect of the army had a political motive:

Headquarters Colletta August 2, 1836
Thos. B. Huling Esqr.
Dear sir:
    . . . I have just returned from Velasco where I have been in company with Col. Wheelock on a mission from the army to the Government whom I found imbecile, inactive, and incapable of performing the high duties assigned to them, a complete disorganization of every department that could or ought to be rendered. (NO) efficient aid to the army and people for whom they were delegated to act.
    . . . The waste of military stores, clothing, provisions, and in fact everything that passed through their hands has been shameful beyond calculation, while the army have suffered severely for the want of a Little energy or honesty on their part. But I left them fully employed in devising ways and means of perpetuating their power, that and speculation being their only employment for the last 2 months.
    Their primary object is now to elevate Stephen F. Austin to the presidency and no stone will be left unturned by them to effect their object that they may again come into power under his patronage. Genl Austin is with them hand and glove and their ostensible object in my opinion is to throw us back under the Mexican Dynasty by the release of Santa Anna who will confirm their power in Texas with all their fraudulent claims of 1,300 leagues and powers to perpetuate their authority. They have tried hard to destroy the army of Texas, the only barrier between them and their nefarious views.

                                                        an old Servt
                                                        Henry Millard[16]

Denouement

    Finally, in the first week of August, Burnet seemed to have identified two names, Millard and Wheelock, among the rebels of Velasco who tried to oust him from office in June. He was determined that Millard at least should bear the full thrust of his displeasure, as noted:

Executive Department
Velasco 5 August 1836
To Brig. Gen. T. J. Rusk Commg.

Sir:
. . . If the Order of which you send me a copy was the only one,
as I presume it was, under which Lt. Col. Millard acted, on his
late eventful visit to Velasco, then that Officer has been guilty of
a high misdemeanor for which his expulsion from the Army is a
mild and lenient retribution.

The Order was followed by a long tissue of charges and
specifications subscribed by a certain Mr. Wheelock, a personage
whom I have never yet had the honor of seeing. . .

For these reasons I have ordered and do hereby Order with
the consent of the Cabinet that Lieutenant Colonel Henry
Millard be stricken from the Rolls of the Army and that his
Commission be null and void from this date.

Mr. Wheelock I do not know as an officer of this
Government. If he is exercising any Command in the Army I require to be informed on what authority he does so.

Respectfully, Your Obt Servt, David G. Burnet[17]

This last paragraph was disingenuous. Burnet knew perfectly well that Wheelock was a captain of Rangers. Rusk (who although he swore that he was not involved in the Velasco
Rebellion was known to be sympathetic with its aims) waited a
while for the interim president to calm down and then found a
very clever way to answer Burnet in his wrath while protecting
Colonel Millard. At the end of the following letter he reminds
Burnet that he himself had addressed E.L.R. Wheelock as a captain of the Texas Rangers in letters on several occasions and
must be aware of his military position.

Headquarters Victoria
2 Sept. 1836
To His Excellency D. G. Burnet, President
Sir:
. . . I informed Col. Millard of the facts and he prefers an investigation. It will therefore be necessary that charges and specifications be made out and sent on and that proof be forwarded.

Upon the subject of Captn Wheelock, he reported to me as a Captn of Rangers under Col. Bane or Burton . . . He was at the time he visited Velasco recognized as a Captn of Rangers on the authority of a communication from yourself relating to the Indian expedition upon which Genrls Green and Houston were ordered some time since.

If there are any Books or authorities at Velasco on the subject of courts martial I will thank you to send them out at the same time you do the charges and proofs as we are destitute of Books here and in a case of this kind it is important that our proceedings be based upon correct legal principles. . .

Thomas J. Rusk
Brig. Gen. Commg.[18]

Both Millard and Wheelock continued with their commands as if nothing had ever happened, so presumably they were protected by higher-ups who had sparked the Velasco Rebellion and did not wish that fact to come out in a court martial. By the end of September, what direct action had failed to achieve for the Velasco rebels the general election won: the expulsion of the incompetent interim government of David G. Burnet.

Meanwhile, Indian alerts continued to come out from the north. In September John B. Harvey, his wife, and son were found scalped and dead at their farmhouse twenty-five miles north of Tenoxtitlan. This was too close to Wheelock Prairie for comfort. Wheelock must have been very worried.

Several routine orders to Captain Wheelock of Wheelock's Rangers are dated August of this year, when he is known to have been in Victoria, Galveston, Coletta, and (briefly) New Orleans:

August 1836
Headquarters Texas Army
Captain E.L.R. Wheelock is authorized to call upon two men to value all such property as is necessary for his command in purchasing, transferring or otherwise as the case is, reporting to me or my superior all such acts, holding himself accountable to the government for his conduct.

J. Brant

Headquarters Texian Army
Coletto August 18, 1836
By Order
Captain E.L.R. Wheelock of the Ranging Corps will without any
delay obey the orders of the Commanding General and Sec. of
War using discretion in all things for the honor of the corps. He
will observe a strict impartiality as to Public Property and keep up
a perfect respect to the interest of private individuals as well as
Public good. The instructions of the Govt. must be paramount to
all others. In case of issuing orders he will nominate such officers
as may be necessary and report frequently.

By order of Genl Bane.

On August 19, 1836, Millard sent Wheelock a flattering
commission:

Headquarters
You are authorized to recruit for my regiment for a period of not
more than two years or during the war five thousand good and
effective men at any point you may think advisable promising the
bounty pay and emoluments provided by Law for the 1st
Regiment of Texas Infantry. For the purpose of recruiting an em-
ulation with patriotic young men, you will nominate such young
men as you are satisfied will do honor to the corps for Lt., who
upon enlisting and producing 28 men shall be commissioned as
such. If these young men can raise 84 men and can agree with
themselves as to rank, upon your recommendation they shall be
commissioned as the officers of a company. The object is to augment the army by an efficient regular force. You will be cautious
as to the materials you obtain.

Upon your coming within the limits of this government you
will organize and report by a regular muster roll and descriptive
list upon which you will draw rations for them as part of my regiment from the proper department. You are authorized to administer the oath of allegiance as faithful service as much as if
you were an officer of my regiment. Placing confidence in your
honor and fidelity to promote the justice of our country I give
you a Latitudinal Discretion. Hoping that you will be able to assist me in performing my duties to a beloved country,

Very Respectfully
Your ob. srt
Henry Millard, Lt. Col. commanding
1st Regiment Reg. Texas Infantry

But Millard's plans were doomed by the election of new officials, as on September 5 all eligible voters of Texas gathered at their polling places to choose their first government. The candidates for president were Sam Houston, S. F. Austin, Henry Smith, T. J. Green, T. J. Rusk, and Thomas Archer. Sam Houston won by a landslide.

Texians no longer trusted Austin, indeed had not done so since the Monclova affair. The other candidates received only token votes. Mirabeau B. Lamar became vice-president, and in a referendum Texas declared herself heavily in favor of annexation by the United States of America.

BOOK FOUR

THE REPUBLIC

Vox clamantis in deserto.
> —Motto of Dartmouth College

CHAPTER 13

PRIVATE LIFE:
NOVEMBER 1836–APRIL 1837

Land Title Lawyer

Now that peace had been declared and the Republic of Texas had a stable government, the settlers of Robertson's Colony resumed their interrupted private lives. E.L.R. Wheelock remained at the head of his Ranger troop in South Texas but spent increasing increments of time establishing his private future in real estate, business, and the practice of law. Although his license to practice in the Republic of Texas was not granted until March 1837, he began accumulating clients somewhat earlier. Like most attorneys of his time, he never attended a formal law school but had learned his profession in the office of an older practitioner, in Wheelock's case in Kentucky.

He concentrated on helping settlers who had arrived in Texas after the closing of the land offices in November 1835 to receive the grants to which they ought to have been entitled. Mexican law now no longer obtained, he awaited new land law from the first Texas Congress.

"The affairs of the land office were the subject which most entirely engaged the feelings and attention of the people."[1] So wrote the Anonymous Buckeye, adding ". . . those who had a large number of floating claims upon the domain of the country, in their anxiety to locate them, overlooked policy, prudence, and the Constitution."[2] An eye witness, he wrote of the Congress, "I have heard more expressions of regret from the really patriotic part of the community that there should be so little talent of any kind among the various officers of government . . . than upon all other subjects of complaint put together."[3]

Even by so wrong-headed a body, some steps had to be taken at once to establish local government. On December 16 Massilon Farley became chief justice of the area (now known as the Municipality of Milam) which contained Wheelock Prairie. But all eyes were directed toward the new Texas government as it struggled with land law.

Wheelock and his clients, along with other old colonists, were at first impatient and then aghast as they realized that Texas was now run by men who did not intend to live by accepted land rules. Accustomed to the idea that any decent citizen who settled in good faith, built his cabin, and tilled his fields was entitled to own those fields, they now heard non-resident claimants wrangling over conflicting titles. In the long run, Texas law came down on the side of established residents, but those non-resident claims frayed the fabric of Texas land law for three generations.

Because of S. F. Austin's double attempted grab, Robertson's Colony titles were among those most disputed. The congressional committee in charge recommended that claims of people who had received illegal Austin and Williams grants in Robertson's Colony would have to be decided in the courts along with the claims of legitimate immigrants. No one wanted to evict the few honest families who had been established by Austin during the so-called Upper Colony days. But Austin had also granted enormous areas to non-residents. That they should receive the same consideration in the courts as legitimate settlers seemed outrageous.

Austin was not the only target of Wheelock's wrath. As soon as the new Congress met in Columbia in December, Wheelock had petitioned on behalf of his clients for redress in the matter of the notorious Jose Maria Nixon grant, a twelve-league grant issued by Sterling Clack Robertson to a prominent Mexican.

Because it opens a window onto the feelings of these embattled homesteaders, his petition is worth quoting in full:

> To the Honorable Senate and House of Representatives in Congress Assembled:
>
> Your memorialists, citizens and residents of the County of Milam as aforesaid, would most respectfully represent that they settled within said county under the colonization laws of the late State of Coahuila and Texas and that they brought with them all the requisites required by that law from the place they last resided and were legally admitted colonizers of the aforesaid state, with all the privileges and immunities of Citizens under the aforesaid Laws of Colonization of the Republic of Mexico;
>
> And at great Expense, Trouble and fatigue your memorialists traveled the country to find homes for themselves and families, and finally selected, tilled, and improved their modest residences from the fall of the year 1829 until 1834, upon entirely vacant and unimproved land, and at the time a part of your memorialists settled there was no legal municipal authority of government in force claiming jurisdiction of the residences of your memorialists, nor was any until the latter part of the summer of 1834, and that was organized by the Commission of the Nashville Colony;
>
> [When they sought titles] they were utterly refused upon the ground that the Empresario had sold and (desired) their lands, and that they would not have lands in the Colony.
>
> Your memorialists then appealed to the Empresario or contractor for him to exert his influence and authority to have your memorialists put in possession of the quantity of land designated by law together with their domiciles and improvements, which he refused, saying that he was compelled to dispose of the same to Jose M. Nixon while he was in Monclova as a bonus or bribe to assist him in getting his colony, which sale was after your memorialists were in [possession] of their labors, and your Memorialists, knowing that the ayuntamiento was probably a tool used by the Empresario, (be)came suspicious (and that) they had found a conspiracy to hold up all land from the colonists until they would relinquish their head rights by employing them or one of them (the Robertson officials) to pay the due fees and give him one half of the lands they were entitled to.
>
> And afterward to wit in the months of January and February

1835 Joseph B. Chase, a surveyor of the Commissioner of the Nashville Colony, surveyed in the name of Jose Maria Nixon twelve leagues running around the dwellings and improvements of your Memorialists without their knowledge and consent, upon which your memorialists are informed said Commissioner has made a deed or deeds to said Jose M. Nixon in the name of the late State of Cohuila and Texas, thereby under the cover of his office attempted to deprive your memorialists of their legal and vested rights.

All of which are but a small amount of the many difficulties and obstacles which have been thrown in the way of your memorialists and other citizens of this county by the Commissioner of the Nashville Colony and other officers under the color of their offices.

Your Memorialists, trusting in the wisdom, magnanimity and humanity of the Congress of the Republic of Texas, do most respectfully ask them to return and exercise their authority in a serving way that may be constitutional without compelling them to resort to the long and tedious course of judicial investigation and not compel your memorialist to litigate with the wealthy and opulent.

That they are on the frontier and have been so continually hampered and jeopardized by the inroads of the savages and internal enemies that they have not been able to acquire property or means to carry on a law suit to defend their homes, and if it were decided by fraud or chicanery against them, they would not have an opportunity [to] select and locate [other] land except it be immediately on the frontier, compelling them to duplicate the privations of former times, which rather than do they would prefer leaving the beautiful country of their adoption.

We therefore conjure and implore your honorable body to act in some way, either by actual Settlement Law or appointing commissions to adjust land claims in this colony or some other way that in your wisdom you may devise, to settle and give ample justice to your memorialists and other injured citizens of this colony.

And your petitioners as in duty bound, etc.[4]

This petition would bear fruit, but not until 1841, five years in the future. Meanwhile, legitimate settlers' claims twisted in the wind.

Wheelock now began to collect newcomer clients who had not yet received grants in Texas and were willing to exchange his expertise as an old Texas hand for money or a share in land grants obtained through his assistance. Wheelock's fee bought his skill in obtaining legal documentation attesting the client's eligibility for the land grant, in selecting suitable land, in conducting the survey, and finally, in obtaining legal title for the client. Some of the later agreements stipulate that the client can elect to deed Wheelock up to half the land obtained through his offices in lieu of payment, and according to the Anonymous Buckeye, "Those . . . who contracted to take such claims through all the legal steps necessary to procure a title from the government when the land office is opened for the one half and pay all attendant expenses made the safest and more profitable speculation."[5]

Wheelock thus made a clear distinction between families who sought title to land they were already settled on and new settlers arriving in the Republic, who needed expert help to select land and obtain title. He assisted the former for a small fee or pro bono, the latter for larger pre-arranged fees.

In September Wheelock received a letter from Bard Chambers, brother of T. J. Chambers, evidently written in Kentucky, assuring him of his family's comfort and safety on Wheelock Prairie, and expressing fear that Texas heat and fevers might dampen immigration. It reads:

Dear Friend:

. . . I left Mrs. Wheelock and all your friends in good health. The neighborhood generally was unusually healthy for the season.

I feel anxious to hear from you whether your health is better, how you stood traveling, how you are succeeding in your arrangements, and negotiations toward effecting your great object in the west. I fear the Mexican War will be prolonged longer than we expected. I expect you are well informed. . . you should enable the Company to transact business as soon as the war closes, whether it be this fall or the ensuing. There's no analyzing the results. I cannot but think, however, that the present war will be a disadvantage to the Company and to Texas. Men being drawn from all parts of the United States to make a camping out in a southern

climate in the hot and sickly season with poor horsemanship and sickness which disgusts them will all no doubt transmit their disgust to the whole country and their description be believed accordingly. But the course of Texas is something that cannot be stayed.
With best wishes for your health and success I remain,
                                        Very Respectfully, Your ob. svt
                                        Bard I. Chambers

Bard Chambers's prediction that "Texas is something that cannot be stayed" proved true beyond his dreams.
Wheelock's great object in the west must refer to his plans for a land company, a scheme which had been in the back of his mind for several years. Plans for such a company would be formalized the following April.

Family Life

Wheelock's personal life now began to occupy more of his time. His children were growing up.
Even after the ravages of a lifetime spent on the frontier, photographs of Colonel Wheelock's only daughter, Annette, taken when she was in her sixties, show a face still full of charm and vivacity. As a young girl, she must have been a knock-out. Like many frontier women, she was married three times, two tragic alliances followed by a final one, which brought her great happiness.
The circumstances of Annette's first nuptial were both perilous and heroic. In November 1836 the colonel and his lady gave permission for Annette to marry Samuel A. Kimble, the family friend who had helped them to escape to Louisiana earlier that year and fought with the colonel as one of Wheelock's Rangers. There is a family tradition that Kimble, knowing that he was fatally stricken with yellow fever and fearing to die alone, persuaded Annette's mother to let her marry him and nurse him until the end in return for his league and labor of land and other property she would receive as his widow. For this act of charity, Annette would later be allowed to marry the man she loved,

Andrew Jackson Powers, son of Wheelock's friend and business partner Elijah Powers.

If the story is true, Annette's fortitude must have been great for one just fifteen years old. The course of yellow fever, this mosquito-borne viral hemorrhagic fever in its malignant form, was and is horrific. Three to six days after being infected, the patient experiences sudden high fever, chills, and flu-like aches lasting about three days. He is anxious, has a red-tipped tongue and foul-smelling breath. Nausea and vomiting develop along with minor hemorrhages. Remission follows for twenty-four hours.

The symptoms then return in a more intense form along with an appearance of jaundice. Black vomit is a characteristic and frightening sign. Next comes generalized bleeding through the mucous membranes, renal damage, delirium, stupor, and coma, with death occurring on the seventh to tenth day of illness.[6]

Only a few days after the marriage vows had been pronounced, Kimble was dead and Annette a shaken young widow.

For the Wheelocks the year 1836, so filled with terror, joy, and history-making, ended on a sad note. Sometime in December Mary's eldest brother, Abraham Prickett, fell ill and died in Natchitoches, Louisiana, where he had been engaged on a contract to dredge the raft-packed Red River. E.L.R. and Mary had now each lost a brother to Texas fever.

In January 1837 another Wheelock wedding was celebrated. Eighteen-year-old George Ripley Wheelock, the colonel's eldest son, was united in marriage to Lucinda Powers, the sister of Annette's fiancé, Andrew Jackson Powers. Both of these unions were to come to tragic ends, prey to the hazards of frontier life.

On November 7 Wheelock's captainship in the Rangers came to an end. The disbandment of Wheelock's Rangers anticipated President Houston's solution to the problem of feeding and clothing the Texas Army by only two months. Early in the new year the chief executive furloughed all except 600 soldiers and sent the surplus home to care for themselves. Thus was cut the Gordian Knot which sparked the Velasco Rebellion.

Spring brought an especially gratifying official document to Colonel Wheelock's hand. On March 8 he was admitted to the Milam County Bar:

County Court
Term 1837
To all whom it may concern: Be it known that E.L.R. Wheelock
Esq. having petitioned the county court of the county aforesaid
giving evidence of his good moral character and also of his legal
qualifications to be admitted to the bar;
Be it therefore resolved that we grant to said Wheelock the rights
and privileges of practicing as an Attorney at law in the courts of
this County.
Signed . . . Massilon Farley
    Chief Justice

On June 3 the *Telegraph and Texas Register* printed this brief
notice: "Married, in Milam County by the Hon. Judge Farley,
Mr. Andrew Jackson Powers to Mrs. Annette Kimble, daughter of
Col. E.L.R. Wheelock." The bride was still two months shy of her
sixteenth birthday.

The Towns of Precinct Three

The Municipality of Milam jutted out into Indian country,
where President Houston was loath to interfere with tribal custom. As Houston stalled, the Comanches raided. In April James
Coryell was killed by an unidentified tribe near Viesca while out
with a little band of men to cut a bee tree. This and other depredations caused the so-called Second Runaway Scrape, during
which families on the exposed north and west refugeed at
Wheelock.
    One of the small boys jammed together at the fort with his
parents was A. C. Duncan of Wheelock. As an old man he remembered:

Of course there were numbers of boys in these families who had
nothing to do and no way to occupy their time, only in fighting
with each other, so Capt. Barron detailed Mr. Fitch to teach a
school for these children. He had a small school house and a very
few pupils who were advanced enough to cipher as we called it
then.

Those who could were stationed out under the trees to cipher and watch for Indians, and incidentally, squirrels. The squirrels migrated that year, moving west in countless numbers. When the boys outside would report the squirrels coming, the teacher would say "Put down your books boys and let's kill the squirrels." So they would all go out and the teacher was left handed but he used a bat and killed them like batting a ball. We hear much now about free school, but that was the very first school I ever saw—a free school in every sense of the word.[7]

This small schoolhouse on Wheelock Prairie, in which the younger Wheelock children and their friends were pupils, was one of the first in its area.[8]

At the same time Colonel Wheelock must have realized that a town was growing up on his prairie. Why not attract attention to this new village by giving it the name of a prominent Texan? Houston's name was already spoken for, so he decided to call his town Lamar, after Texas's vice-president. It was to be a singularly unfortunate choice.

As the first stop in his campaign to establish a land company, Colonel Wheelock set up two business partnerships, first between himself, Elijah Powers, Richard Jarmon, and William Moore, and later, when Moore returned to the states, among the first three.

These ambitious gentlemen had plenty of rivals. As the Anonymous Buckeye declared during his visit to Texas, "A mania for towns is characteristic of all new countries and is especially so here."[9]

The list of ghost towns in the third precinct of Robertson County to which Wheelock Prairie belonged is a long one, considering its small size. Each town was born of hope. There was Tinninville, which came into existence in 1836 and vanished in 1838. There were Holly, Acorn, and Lake. There were Shiloh, Eaton, Curry, Morgan, and Ridge. There were Coal Branch, Henry Prairie, Camp Creek, and Devil's Jump. There were Hayes Church, Easterly, and New Baden. But no one will find them on any twentieth century maps or most nineteenth century maps either.

In the summer of 1837 Tennessee immigrant Francis Slaughter laid out the town of Old Franklin, the first county seat of Robertson County and named in his honor, at the headwaters of Mud Creek ten miles north of Wheelock Prairie.

J. W. Baker wrote: "Old Franklin, the outpost of surveyors and rangers, that braved both a wilderness and savage Indians in the decade of the Republic, must be considered one of the truly great little towns in early Texas. None but brave men chose to live there and the account of battles fought and lives lost is an epochal tragedy that deserves a place in Texas history by the side of the Alamo and other places of great sacrifice." [10]

Slaughter chose his site well. Mud Creek, in spite of its name, was spring fed and "the sloping hills were covered with great trees. The land, once red clay, had been cut and nurtured by overflows and the strip of alluvial soil was rich. To the west were rolling hills and creeks, inhabited by Indians, and to the north the endless wilderness stretched across the face of Central Texas." [11]

Soon Old Franklin's vacant public square was surrounded by little shops and offices. Wheelock client Leander Harl got a contract to build a courthouse and jail. The two-storied courthouse was to be twenty feet wide and twenty-five feet long, with eight-foot ceilings, built eighteen inches off the ground, "boarded all around to prevent the admission of hogs and other small animals." [12]

Later Old Franklin died, and the inhabitants moved a few miles away to Morgan, which changed its name to Franklin and became the county seat in 1841. It is again the county seat of Robertson County today, laid out on Francis Slaughter's head right and his legacy to his county.

The Village of Wheelock/Lamar was located in 1834 on a 300-square-mile area between the Navasota and the Brazos Rivers, which became Precinct Three, in the southeastern part of present day Robertson County. The precinct includes the exact center of the county and "the lush prairies that parallel the O.S.R." [13]

The E.L.R. Wheelock residence and fort was at the intersecting roads that ran through the community across State Street. The prairie was never entirely safe from Indian attack during Colonel Wheelock's lifetime, and the women must always have lived with one eye on the rifle hanging over the fireplace and the other eye on the stockade.

In late 1834 James and Isabella Dunn, Ulster Scot settlers

from Staggers Point, moved to Wheelock Prairie. The Dunns had arrived in America from Belfast in 1820. Mrs. Dunn's passage was paid in tobacco based on her weight, which was ninety-six pounds including her clothes and a babe in arms.[14] Dunn purchased land a short distance to the south of the site of Lamar village.

The children of the Dunns and the Wheelocks worked together in the fields, danced their reels and contra dances together to the fire-lit fiddle, and became good neighbors. The area developed into a huge unfenced cattle range and the Dunns proprietors of one of the largest cattle enterprises in the state. Later Mary Dunn, daughter of James, would marry Felix Robertson, a cousin of the empresario, and their son would take for a wife Nancy Killough, a granddaughter of the Wheelocks. So the families intertwined through marriage.

The Cavitts were another early Wheelock family of note. Andrew Cavitt and his wife Ann were engulfed by the Runaway Scrape, during which Andrew became one of many who died of yellow fever in Louisiana. He left his widow, seven children, sixteen slaves, and a headright in Coryell County. Ann moved her family to Independence and hired E.L.R. Wheelock as her attorney to settle Andrew's estate.

Her friendship with the Wheelock family led her to relocate on Wheelock Prairie, where in 1836 her slaves and her seven sons built a cabin which still stands. Its cedar logs encompass a 25 x 30 foot central room, with a loft area, lean-to, and cellar. During her first year this intrepid woman farmed sixty acres of Colonel Wheelock's land, selling corn, sometimes to the Texas Rangers, and hiring out her slaves for a livelihood.

Mrs. Cavitt shared Colonel Wheelock's ambition for the new town, which was no less than to be chosen as the capital of the Texas Republic. "So certain were Colonel Wheelock and Ann Cavitt that Wheelock (then Lamar) would be the capital, they laid out the town in the grand manner of a newly emerging town being planned for the capital. Signing the town papers with a quill pen, they named the street in front of the Cavitt cabin State Street, which it remains today."[15] In a few months this formidable woman was able to purchase the 300 acres she had been farming for Colonel Wheelock.

In 1837 citizens of the town of Wheelock/Lamar stood on tip-toe, in full expectation of a sunny future. They had their freedom from Mexico. They had their republic. They were determined to create an American idyll of their own on land of their own. It was precious not only because it was beautiful or because they had fought for it and some had died for it. It was precious because they owned it, because it was theirs.

CHAPTER 14

THE TEXAS UNIVERSITY COMPANY: MAY–DECEMBER 1837

Erudition on the Frontier

When a copy of the Constitution of the Republic of Texas finally reached Colonel E.L.R. Wheelock in printed form, he must have read one clause with particular interest. Section Five of the General Provisions stated that it would be "the duty of Congress as soon as circumstances will permit, to provide by law a general system of education."[1]

His grandfather, the Rev. Dr. Eleazar Wheelock, had been a pioneer in American education, running a school for Indians which developed into Dartmouth College. The nebulous dream of his boyhood, set aside for so long, had been to follow in these illustrious footsteps and now began to take solid form. Creating a school in a wilderness ran in his blood, and here was a wilderness indeed and a chance indeed. It seemed that he had only to put out his hand and grasp the opportunity.

In the first days of May 1837, Colonel Wheelock and several friends met in his double log cabin in the town he had decided to call Lamar in honor of Mirabeau Buonaparte Lamar, first elected vice-president of the Republic of Texas. The choice of name was in some ways an odd one. Unless Lamar's basic sympathy had been with the Velasco Rebellion, an attempt to oust Interim President Burnet in which Wheelock had been associated with Lt. Col. Henry Millard, the colonel could not have been sure of Lamar's good will.

Lamar was one of a large group of latecomers to Texas who had seemingly arrived just in time to take over the infant republic without having borne any of the angst of frontiering. He arrived in early April 1836, caught up with Gen. Sam Houston's army at Groce's plantation, and enlisted as a private. During a skirmish the day before the Battle of San Jacinto, he caught the eye of General Houston, who promoted Lamar to command his cavalry on the spot. From lightning promotion to military victory, it was only a nimble step to political power.

As the Anonymous Buckeye put it, "It was from these adventurers that the Army of Texas was principally supplied, and they in a short time took upon themselves the management of the whole affairs of the nation."[2]

Technically, Lamar was not eligible to stand for election as vice-president of Texas because he did not meet the residential requirements, but no one else signed up, and he won by default. Few men could have been more unsuited to be Houston's second in command, and during their statutory two years in office the two men became bitter enemies, differing over the question of Santa Anna as well as over the Indian question.

In this vice-president, Colonel Wheelock now put his hopes of becoming the founder of a university.

Rules and Regulations of the Texas University Company Adopted by the Stockholders the 10th Day of May, 1837

Republic of Texas
County of Milam
For the purpose of establishing an Institution of Learning in the county aforesaid, and also to promote the growth of a village with inhabitants of a sober and orderly character, we, E.L.R. Wheelock, R. B. Jarmon, Elijah Powers, Massilon Farley, William D. Moore, and A. G. Perry, all of the county aforesaid, do enter into and agree upon the following articles of Co-partnership:
Article 1st: The name and style of said parties in copartnership shall be the Texas University Company.

Art 2nd: The said Wheelock grants and conveys to the said Texas University Company all his rights, title, and interest in and to that part of his League of Land which he holds as a headright known and called the Town of Lamar; said Town of Lamar containing One Hundred and Seventy-Seven acres of land and situated in the County aforesaid; provided however it is understood and agreed that there be and is hereby reserved from the above conveyance thirty-five lots, which said lots the said Wheelock agrees and contracts to sell and convey unto the members of said company severally and respectively, viz—

Here the thirty-five reserved lots are distributed among Powers, Jarmon, Farley, and Moore for services rendered. Article 3 goes on to provide for open records. Articles 4 through 9 set forth rules concerning the land management of the campus and the town.

In order that the town of Lamar grow as intended, the stock holders were required to improve at least one of their lots within two years, and a failure to do so would forfeit their lots to the university, although they could redeem them by paying $100 to the treasurer.

Fifteen acres of land were set apart for the Male Institution and two acres of land for the Female Institution for the purpose of erecting suitable buildings, including professors' residences.

Provision for the education of women at the university reflected Colonel Wheelock's high regard for the perspicacity of his wife, Mary.

Thirty-three lots were to be donated to create a "Publick Square." No tippling, dram shops or gambling house, billiard tables or disorderly establishments could be erected since these activities were strictly prohibited. It was to be the duty of the officers to make these prohibitions part of the contract in conveying all deeds, whether by purchase or donation, excepting that the keeper of the hotel serving travelers could have his own tavern or barroom.

Such caveats were necessary to keep out "gambling, the besetting sin . . . everywhere in Texas . . ."[3] and their houses where "[i]t appeared to be the business of the great mass of people to collect around these centers of vice and hold their drunken orgies."[4]

The president, secretary, treasurer, and trustees were "re-quested to use great precaution in donating lots to an orderly, correct, and industrious people, that it may have an influence in laying good examples to the students."

Wheelock's Puritan background was very much in evidence.

Another document dated the same day states that Wheelock, Farley, Jarmon, Powers, Perry, and Moore had each deeded one labor of land to the Texas University Company solely for the purpose of promoting education and disseminat-ing knowledge upon correct and liberal principles entirely re-publican.

It is not known who presented these documents to the Congress of Texas, who may have received them and failed to act upon them, who may have rejected them, or whether any of these things took place. Lamar certainly received a copy. "Vice President Lamar may have been flattered by the naming of the 'Village of Lamar,' but Sam Houston's antipathy toward Lamar may have proved an obstacle in getting Congress to give Col. Wheelock a charter in 1837."[5]

During the Second Congress, a man named Kelsey H. Douglas introduced a bill to incorporate a "University of Texas," the first recorded congressional mention of such an institution.[6] This bill may have been a reworked version of Wheelock's pro-posal. It was soundly defeated.

Why did the Republic of Texas Congress resist the estab-lishment of a state university? One strong factor was that Texans felt by inheritance that education was not the business of gov-ernment but of home and church. During the entire period of the republic only one town, Houston, established a public school system, although these had been authorized in 1839.

The Texas government was now meeting in the new town of Houston where the Anonymous Buckeye, an attorney, was spending much time in the visitors' galleries of the Congress. He was not impressed. "If there was anything like statesman-ship or business faculties among the members of Congress of the session of which I speak, it surely escaped the observation of myself as well as all others."[7] ". . . the greatest subject of re-gret and fear is that Texas cannot hope much from the talents of the men who have taken her destiny into their hands."[8] So concluded the Anonymous Buckeye. Wheelock would not have disagreed.

Texas in 1837 had to face some hard facts. Money was almost non-existent. Crops and property were still recovering from the devastation of the Runaway Scrape. When Congress endowed early education with land, it was making an almost empty gesture. It did not dream of Santa Rita. University founding must have seemed like a frill which could be added later, after Texas was eating well again.

And of course Lamar and the Congress may have wanted the national university in the national capital. No one quite knew where that would be.

When Lamar became president of Texas in 1839, he revived Wheelock's university plan but not its location. Perhaps Wheelock Prairie was considered too exposed to Indian attack to house a university town, yet Waterloo (now Austin), the site eventually selected, was even more vulnerable.

Eventually, nineteen private colleges were chartered by the Republic of Texas, of which nine actually opened their doors to students. None has survived at its original site. Southwestern University in Georgetown considers itself descended from Methodist Rutersville College, originally established near LaGrange. Baptist Baylor University, chartered at Independence in 1845, has moved to Waco. But it was not until almost fifty years after Colonel Wheelock's proposal that Texas University began classes.

Whistle Blowing

In his quest for congressional approval of his dearest dream, Wheelock was unlikely to have placed much dependence upon his senator, Sterling Robertson. The two had had differences already in regard to the way the former empresario's staff had distributed land in his colony. An unsent petition to Congress which Wheelock composed late in 1837 lays out his feelings.

This petition accused officials of Robertson's Colony of attempting to destroy the archives of the colony, altering and defacing public records, granting leagues to persons who had drawn lands in other colonies (which was illegal), antedating deeds, issuing deeds since the closing of the land office, and issuing deeds for full leagues to young or unmarried men, who were only allowed one labor. (One of the latter may have been S. C. Robertson's son Elijah.)

Everyone was waiting to see whether the United States would honor Texas's request for statehood made in the referendum of 1836. On March 3, 1837, on his last day in office, President Andrew Jackson of the United States of America recognized the Republic of Texas, of which his protégé, Sam Houston, was president. It must have been with great satisfaction that Jackson toasted this land he had long hoped to make part of the United States. True, it was not in the Union yet, but he had faith that it soon would be, as the will of its own people had decreed. The population of Texas was now 45,000 Europeans, 5,000 slaves, 3,000 to 3,500 Tejanos, and 12,000 Amerinds.

Why was Texas not received into the Union until almost ten years later? The political hot potato was slavery, legal within her borders. Opposition to the acceptance of an additional slave state was strong enough in Washington City to forbid the bans.

This interval was, of course, not without its benefits. The ten-year delay gave Texas time to learn to think of herself as a sovereign nation. On April 21, 1837, a delirious celebration broke out in the Texas capital on the first anniversary of the Battle of San Jacinto. Sam Houston, "dressed in a rich velvet suit, moved among the throng with a gallantry and grace which have always distinguished him when he chose to assume them."[9]

For the remainder of 1837 Wheelock continued to practice law, to sell land on commission, and try to obtain titles for newcomers. Mary Wheelock's brother, the Hon. David Prickett, continued to prosper as state attorney for the Judicial District of Illinois. And on Wheelock Prairie James Dunn built its first gristmill.

Most of the papers and receipts Wheelock left behind him cast light only on business, but occasionally a personal paper surfaces.

May 23, 1837,

1 Piece of Domestics	$11.00
9 Yards of ditt	5.50
7 yards of calico	3.50
3½ yds domestic	1.60
1½ yard fine line	2.25
4 yds. calico	4.00
7 yards calico	3.50
7 yds. ditto	3.50
6 yds. silk	16.00

TOTAL $ 50.00
   Paid in Full
      G. Ward

Perhaps this represented Annette Wheelock Kimball Powers' trousseau for her marriage two months before.

Amerinds continued to raid sporadically. Two Rangers had been killed in a pitched battle earlier in the year at Elm Creek, eight miles northeast of present-day Cameron. The Post Oak Massacre of 1837 had left five Rangers dead in Milam County. On May 15 James Dunn wrote Senator Robertson complaining of raids in the vicinity of Wheelock Prairie, and on June 12 President Houston reluctantly signed into law a Bill for the Better Protection of the Northern Frontier. The Indians paid little heed.

In spite of the fact that Wheelock was no longer a captain of Rangers, military orders occasionally still came his way as ex-officio head of an Indian fort, probably as a result of Houston's Protection of the Northern Frontier bill.

August 17
War Department
Houston
Sir:
You are authorized to deliver to Col. Wheelock twenty muskets for the use on the frontier, to be deposited at Fort Lamar. (Wheelock)
   J. Snively
      Acting Sec. of War.

On the 25th of September, the Second Texas Congress convened in Houston, Milam County continuing to be represented by Sen. Sterling Clack Robertson with Samuel T. Allen as representative. A bill to open the badly needed new land office was vetoed by Sam Houston. Torn by his sympathy for the Indians, he was not wholly in accord with the land-absorbing aims of the frontier or with its effort to protect itself from indigenous resistance. "Some time early in Sam Houston's first term as President of Texas, Sterling C. Robertson went to the City of Houston, then the national capital, to request the government to assist in protecting the frontier from the Indians. President Houston is alleged to have replied,—'God eternally d—n you, I wish the Indians had the whole of your scalps'."

Also in the fall of 1837, as a reminder of Wheelock's activities as a rancher he wrote:

The mark and brand given by Col. E.L.R. Wheelock for record as being that by which he designates his stock from other peoples is a crop off each ear and an under bit in the right and his brand (at this time some of his stock is marked with two sawtooth crops.) The above mark and brand were given and recorded this 30th day of September, 1837. The above is a true copy of the original on record—

M. D. Thomson, County Recorder.

Later a similar brand was used by the famous King Ranch.

Congress, still struggling with the land laws, ordered all the former empresarios to hand over their records. "Some supposed that the empresarios refused to comply with the law making such demand from an unwillingness to expose the true condition of their several colonies."[10]

Nevertheless, Senator Robertson made an effort to gather up his colonial papers which had been taken from Nashville for safekeeping during the Runaway Scrape. On October 29 Ann Cavitt turned over to Robert Henry the documents relating to Robertson's Colony she had been holding, consisting of surveys done by Dr. Felix Robertson when he visited the future site of Nashville on the Brazos in 1824, a list of titles issued by Wm. H. Steele, a second Steele list, and a list of the colonists who had arrived in Robertson's Colony after the passage of the Organic Law. These probably constituted some of the evidence Colonel Wheelock gathered to support his unsent petition.

No mention of the town of Lamar has been found after November, 1837; presumably the colonel had decided to abandon the unfruitful patronage of the vice-president. The fort reverted to its original name, Fort Wheelock, and the town to Town of Wheelock. So it remains today.

Personal Problems

In November, E.L.R. received a letter from his brother-in-law, George Prickett Jr., shedding light on the continuing desire of Illinois residents to move to Texas.

November 15, 1837
Springfield, Illinois
Dear Brother:
Yours to David of the 5th of September is before me and I assure you that it gives me much pleasure to hear from you and family, but I am sorry that you have not given some account of the country as I have had for some time considerable anxiety to see that country. If there is a probability of doing as well or better there than here I should like to make exchange. You must give the health and in short all the particulars as it will assist me very much in my decision in the case. We have heard of the decease of Jacob, but it has been contradicted. Let us know the facts. Abraham we have also heard is dead which we have no doubt is fact.

There are a great many persons in this place who would like to remove south if they believe it to be as healthy as this state. Some very good young men and some with families have spoken to me on the subject of Texas. People are much dissatisfied with this climate and will come to Texas if they are sure of no difficulty with the Mexicans. What is the state of society with you? Some have the idea that they are all cut-throats. We have no news here except that there is a great revival of religion pretty much throughout the state. Abraham's twin boys have obtained religion and joined the Methodist Church a few weeks since. . .

There is great pressure in the money markets and times are hard quite as much as they were in 1819-20. There have been a great many failures of merchants. The seat of government of this state is removed from Vandalia and located at this place. They have commenced a fine state house of stone.

Write to me at this place without delay.

> Your brother,
> George Prickett, Jr.

Later on George Jr. did immigrate to Texas to be near his sister Mary and her family.

In the last month of the year 1837 Congress further modified the political division in which Wheelock was located by creating Robertson County out of that portion of Milam County lying east of the Brazos River. Francis Slaughter had already been appointed interim chief justice to get the county organized, and was now confirmed as its first chief justice. His town of Old Franklin was selected as the county seat.

Meanwhile Colonel Wheelock had reduced his day-to-day responsibilities on his plantation by leasing his home place out to Charles G. Plummer, with "free use of fire wood and timber for farming purposes to be cut on said league. Said Wheelock reserving to himself the use only of the cabin he occupies, the crib his corn is now in, one stable, and liberty to use water from the well . . . and said Wheelock agrees that in case he should take his family to the states said Plummer shall continue to cultivate and preserve the said home plantation."

Disappointed in his schemes to found a university and make his home a capitol, Wheelock was considering leaving Texas. He did not go, but it would not be the last time the idea occurred to him. After these sacrifices and struggles during the Texas revolution, it must have been galling for him and his ilk to watch the country being taken over by newcomers unsympathetic with their aims. Still, that same winter Wheelock thought better of abandoning his town and built a house for Mary and their two sons still at home, William and David, a real house such as he remembered from New Hampshire with columns and porches and second stories.

Wheelock had no background in architecture or fine building, but his neighbor, Ann Cavitt, did. Some time in late 1837 or early 1838 a New England architect named Charleton passed through Texas and was hired by the Widow Cavitt to design a house reminiscent of the plantation houses she had grown up in back in Tennessee. "He gave the house some of the feeling of their section of the country, taking into consideration the climate . . . and making an imposing home."[11] The Cavitt house was ten years in the making and turned into the principal inn of the neighborhood.

The Wheelock place was more modest, having no commercial intent, but it seems likely that Wheelock rented out the expertise of Mrs. Cavitt's slaves for the making of hand-hewn pine and cypress boards, hand-carved doorways, and native ironstone mantlepieces, hand-forged nails, latches, keys, and hinges, hand-made pink brick, and home-made glass panes contrived "using special sands from the local river bottoms."[12]

Mary Wheelock must have rejoiced. William, her second son, was to inherit this fine two-story house and live in it during his life as a member of the state legislature, county sheriff, and successful cattle rancher.[13] Alas, it did not survive the ravages of time, but the Cavitt house has been restored and stands sturdily in Wheelock today, looking much as it did when Sam Houston stayed the night.

CHAPTER 15

GROWING PAINS: 1838-1839

Red Men

In the political background (so far as President Sam Houston was concerned), but in the foreground as perceived by Robertson's Colony and the other colonists on the northern frontier, lay the continuing Amerind problem. In the south, as usual, anxious eyes still turned towards the Rio Bravo. Sometime in the spring of 1838 these two fears united when Texas Rangers killed Manuel Flores, a Mexican Indian working out of Matamoros, and discovered documents on his body linking the Cherokees and other tribes with the Mexican government. Secretary of War Albert Sidney Johnston wrote to Cherokee Chief Bowles confronting him with this proof. Bowles denied involvement.

The citizens of Robertson County sent another petition to Congress:

Memorial From citizens of Robertson's Colony to the Senate and House of Representatives of the Republic of Texas
Republic of Texas, Entered under April 23, 1838

County of Robertson
To the Senate and House of Representatives in Congress assembled: Your memorialists residing high upon the Brazos and Navasota Rivers, from sad experience deeply feel the neglect of our government in not providing some means to protect the exposed frontier—therefore your memorialists pray your honorable body to afford them some means of protection as speedily as the nature of the case will admit of, for your memorialists are daily and hourly exposed to the mercy of the merciless Savages. Our surveyors have been murdered together with their hands and within the last two days one of our neighbors was inhumanly butchered and his scalp torn off in triumph by the Indians, and they not meeting with opposition are daily becoming more insolent and bold and your memorialists are generally in moderate circumstances and unprepared to follow the Indians and retake the booty that they are carrying off together with the scalps of our relatives and friends. Therefore your memorialists pray your honorable body to send some means to protect the frontier and drive back the Indians, so as to enable your memorialists to complete their crops, and your memorialists would respectfully suggest to your honorable body the vast importance of sending up a few pieces of artillery, one at least to each dense settlement, together with some of the munitions of war. With great reluctance your memorialists will be compelled to leave their homes and crops unless some speedy and efficient means of protection is awarded to them by your honorable body, and if for want of the necessary protection your memorialists have to leave their homes, many of them no doubt will continue on to the land that gave them birth, and thereby Texas itself will become weakened and the frontier become entirely depopulated. Whereas on the other hand let the means of defense be afforded and your memorialists will as in duty bound ever pray &c.

Among the 155 signatures to this petition were E.L.R. Wheelock, George R. Wheelock, Andrew Jackson Powers, Cavitt Armstrong, Francis Slaughter, James Dunn Sr. and Jr., and J. C. Duncan.

This was not what Houston wanted to hear. He was in the midst of appealing to Congress (in vain) to ratify a treaty which he had negotiated between Texas and the Cherokee Nation, of which he was an honorary citizen. But since the Flores incident, the civilized tribes such as the Cherokees were indistinguishable to the legislature from the Comanche and other wild Amerinds. Another Mexican courier had been killed by Texas Rangers and found to be carrying documents suggesting a Mexican-Indians plot. Houston was hard pressed to defuse an increasingly incendiary situation. When a Mexican band of plundering malcontents led by Vincinte Cordoba were joined by a small band of Indians, Texas appeared "about to explode."[1]

This explosion targeted the accessible tribes, not the elusive Comanche. In the Cherokee War of July 1838, Chief Bowles, 83, was killed and barbarously skinned and 100 other braves died. An outraged Houston declared, perhaps with some foundation, that Bowes was a better man than his murderers. In another Trail of Tears, the Cherokee moved north of the Red River into Oklahoma. They were soon followed by the Shawnee, then by the smallpox-devastated Kiowa.

None of these tragic events deterred the Comanche, who embodied most of the settlers' actual danger. Wheelock continued surveying, and surveying continued to be life-threatening. In the fall of 1838 at Spring Hill twenty-four surveyors were ambushed, and in the ensuing battle twenty braves and twelve surveyors lost their lives. Near Larissa, eighteen settlers were slaughtered.

Dejected, Houston ordered a force led by General Rusk to Nacogdoches and on October 16 Rusk defeated Cordoba and his men in a major battle. Still, nothing really changed for the settlers.

On December 1 a newspaper reported that a Mexican officer had gone into Comanche country offering to pay "five dollars for each scalp they may take from the Texians."[2] Siege conditions continued in the settlements.

Home Folks

Within this context Colonel Wheelock and his community, which had now risen to the dignity of a post office, carried on daily life. On January 9 he received Bounty Warrant 1686 for 640 acres for his military service from 16 March to 7 November 1836. His eldest son George was also entitled to bounty land and received 320 acres for service from 8 May to 8 August 1836. Both of these grants had already been patented to others. Land was plentiful and money scarce.

On February 16 Wheelock signed a lease with Ann Cavitt for a portion of his head-right rent free for five years in return for her opening and improving this land.

Wheelock took time to obtain a letter of introduction to a citizen of LaGrange, with a view of buying some lots in that town.

> My dear brother:
> I have one moment to introduce to you E.L.R. Wheelock, a cousin of Gen. Ripley. He is a young gentleman of liberal education and has been uncommonly friendly to us. It will please you to pay him every attention. Peace be with you through Jesus Christ.
>
> > Pastor of Church W. L. Hacola
> > LaGrange, Fayette County
> > Republic of Texas.

On April 30, 1838, Colonel Wheelock bought two prime lots in the town of LaGrange from John Henry Moore, first settler of the Upper Colorado, paying $200.00 for the pair. Bounded by LaFayette, Fannin, Franklin, and Madison Streets, they occupy a city block near the center of the town, and may have formed the nucleus of a plan to move his home to Fayette County, which however was never carried out. Perhaps he had read the congressional report recommending LaGrange as the Texas capital. Either way, it was a good investment.

At this time Robertson County was an enormous area stretching from the O.S.R. north to include some of present-day Dallas. Old Franklin, its county seat, was growing. On July 27 Chief Justice Francis Slaughter deeded land there for a school, Franklin Academy, which operated until Old Franklin disappeared in 1842. The Wheelock School having disbanded at the end of the Second Runaway Scrape, Franklin Academy was now

the only school in a county with 100 children in a white population of 300. Unfortunately, only twenty youngsters were able to
afford an education. Baker asserts that "80% of the children who
grew up in Robertson County between 1835 and 1850 were destined to sign their names with an X."[3]

Ambitious Franklin Academy taught law and medicine in
addition to reading, writing, and arithmetic. Tuition was $28 per
term with room and board extra. Among the first boys in atten-
dance were Josephus, Sheridan, Andrew, and James Alexander
Cavitt of Wheelock. Colonel Wheelock elected to educate his
younger sons, David, 8, and William, 12, privately at home and
paid a tutor, O. R. Powell, $24.00 for five months' instruction.
On September 3 the colonel paid R. Powell $25 for a saddle and
$20 for ten volumes of books, meant for the education of his
sons. That he was able to expend these sums marks him as a successful businessman for his time and place. His 1837 national
and county taxes amounted to $7.82.

Education having been provided for, law now followed. On
October 1 Robertson County, as member of the Third Judicial
District, established a schedule of court sessions in Old Franklin.
The quality of the justice there dispensed was still somewhat wild
and wooly.

"If he will keep in mind that the lawyers of the country are
admirably qualified to make darkness visible, he may form some
idea of the Judiciary of Texas," so opined the Anonymous Buckeye.[4]

The first court session in Robertson County ". . .was a jolt-
ing experience for its citizens. The famous Three-legged Willie
Williamson, who had progressed from fugitive to judge,
presided. Williamson's reputation preceded his arrival.
According to Sam Houston, he had tamed Shelby County in
prior months and impressed on the frontiersmen the importance of respect for Texas law."[5]

On the first tour of his jurisdiction, Three-Legged Willie
was welcomed with the information that the inhabitants desired
none of Sam Houston's courts there. Judge Williamson un-
packed his saddlebags, established himself behind a table,
placed a rifle at one elbow and a pistol at the other, and an-

nounced, "Hear ye, Hear ye, court for the Third District is either now in session or by God somebody's going to get killed."[6]

On another occasion a drunken lawyer was arguing a case before Williamson when the judge interrupted him to ask, "Where is the law to support your point?" The inebriated attorney drew his Bowie knife, drove it into the top of the desk, and proclaimed, "There is the law!" Judge Williamson eyed the ruffian, drew his pistol, and pointed it at the attorney and said, "Yes, that knife may be the law here, but this pistol is the Constitution of Texas."[7]

The list of the first veniremen included Ripley Wheelock, but whether father or son was called is not clear.

Acquiring a new house now enabled Wheelock to place the family of Mordicai Boone, who worked some of his land, in the original family cabins. Provision was made to dissolve their contract in the event of Mexican invasion, still a real possibility to the Texians.

Lamar's Term

On December 10, in the city of Houston, Mirabeau Buonaparte Lamar was inaugurated as second president of the Republic of Texas. Departing President Sam Houston, who was prevented by law from succeeding himself and whose candidate had been defeated, was not a gracious loser. At the inaugural, the "outgoing president, dressed in the style of George Washington, complete with powdered wig, literally and figuratively towered over the diminutive Lamar."[8] Looming over the assembled guests, Houston delivered a three-hour speech lauding his administration and so exhausted the crowd that Lamar retired from the rostrum, leaving his secretary to read his own short inaugural address.

The two men were natural enemies. Houston favored annexation and amity with the Indian tribes. Lamar denounced annexation and envisioned an all-Anglo Republic of Texas which would one day reach the Pacific Ocean. Houston had lived simply on a salary of $1,000 per year. Luxury-loving Lamar presented a budget which included a salary of $10,000 for himself plus generous allowances.

Lamar appointed anti-Amerind Hugh McLeod, a business associate of Colonel Wheelock, as commander in chief of the Republic of Texas Army. "In the wings stood Felix Huston, back in Texas and writing Lamar that he would like to locate on the Rio Grande . . . 5,000 military colonists"[9] But Lamar wished to settle the Indian question first.

Fehrenbach cautions us not to be too hard on Lamar for his anti-Amerind stance: "The Indians Lamar considered merely trespassing vermin on Texas soil. . . . The notion that Indians were tenants at will, without inherent title to American soil and that white men might dispossess them without formal legal action was already imbedded in American thought and practice. They were policies that had already acquired the legitimacy of two hundred years . . . Lamar merely enunciated them without hypocrisy."[10]

It had been established again and again in American history that the government had no power to prevent white encroachment on Indian lands, and that if the Indians resisted the government owed the settlers protection. Sam Houston was one of the few great Americans who tried not to give the Amerinds a reservation or treaty lands but a legal title to their soil under Anglo-Saxon common law. The attitudes of the majority of Texans who violently opposed this were essentially no different from the attitudes of the men who earlier conquered Virginia and Massachusetts.[11]

Lamar hoped to build a great empire in Texas and sought to promote the supremacy of the state. Although he did not admit it publicly, he was obviously well aware of the self-serving of previous congresses, and appealed to his congress to direct their views to general rather than individual interests. He used the word Texian to represent those who had been in Texas before the end of the revolution, a definition which only barely included himself and made no distinction between early settlers and American hot-heads arriving on the eve of the Battle of San Jacinto.

Lamar's Congress obediently passed bills appropriating large sums of money for Indian fighting and authorizing large numbers of fighting men. To pay for all this, they issued promissory notes. Lamar called for volunteers to fight as Minute Men along American Revolutionary lines in the outlying settlements between the Brazos and the Navasota. One of the first to volunteer was young George Ripley Wheelock, already a veteran of the Texas War for Independence. Each Minute Man was obligated to keep a horse ready at all times, together with saddle, bridle, arms, blanket, and buckskins. These, together with supplies of coffee, salt, and sugar, were to be "ready at any time to start on fifteen minutes warning."[12] Dr. Anson Jones, the defeated candidate for president on the Houstonian ticket, commented that "Texas is overwhelmed with army and navy officers. There are enough for Russia."[13]

Dr. Jones was also articulate concerning his opinion of the Lamar government.

On April 10, 1939, he wrote, "It will take about one year for the present Admin. of Texas to demonstrate its weakness and corruption. Every honest and tried friend of the country has been removed out of the way to give place to a few newly imported knaves who intend to reap the profits of others' toil and sufferings."[14] And on April 13 he added, "It is strong evidence of the poverty of worth or talent in a country when such a man as Lamar is selected for the head. He is a very weak man and governed by petty passions which he cannot control and prejudices which are the result of ignorance."[15]

By the end of Lamar's administration, finances were at "the lowest possible ebb."[16] Texas circulated over $2,000,000 in paper money. Each dollar was worth 16.66 cents.

Bryant's Defeat

On New Year's Day 1839, the home of George Morgan, six miles above Marlin, in Robertson's Colony, was attacked by Indians who rushed in, tomahawked, scalped, and killed George Morgan, Mrs. George Morgan, their grandson Jackson Jones, Mrs. Jackson Morgan, and Adeline Morgan, aged fifteen.

The Rev. A. B. Lawrence, traveling in the vicinity in 1840, ran into members of the surviving family. Upon being asked whether they had had trouble with the Indians, "our hostess, whose thin and pale countenance, her shining and unsteady dark eyes, grizzled and disheveled hair, rendered her appearance almost haggard, remarked with great bitterness, 'I am afraid these cursed Indians will never give me peace more. I was in hopes I had heard the last of them. My family has been butchered, and I been driven about by them until my soul is sick of life.'"[17] She had lost a son, two sisters, and her father and mother on that New Year's Day of 1839.

The bereaved families packed up and moved down to the lower settlements for safety, and forty men under Benjamin Franklin Bryant took off after the Indians. One of these would-be avengers was Annette Wheelock's second husband, Andrew Jackson Powers.

On January 10, 1839, seventy Indians attacked John Morgan's house near Bucksnort. The Indians were repulsed and seven of their number slain.

Bryant's little army of Robertson County men found the Indians led by Chief Jose Maria on January 16 and charged. Withering fire from the Indians drove them backward, killing three settlers. Shortly thereafter Andrew Jackson Powers fell dead after making a courageous but futile foray. The surviving settlers were then ordered to form a line on the open prairie, but the order was misinterpreted as a command to retreat. As the Texans withdrew, Jose Maria's men charged from the woods, firing their guns and screaming a fierce battle cry. The Texans became disorganized and scattered through the area. Still, the savages advanced. Bryant's men, reduced to panic, ran for their lives.

Wilson Reed fell from his horse and was clubbed to death. Hugh Henry and William Fullerton stood back-to-back fighting with guns and knives until they were shot and killed. Washington McCree, Alfred Eaton, and A. J. Webb also died. Six others, including two more Powers boys, were wounded. When darkness came, the remainder, about twenty-six in all, escaped. When Jose Maria retired, Francis Slaughter sent men from Old Franklin to bury the dead.[18]

The fallen came from Staggers Point, Old Franklin, and Wheelock. The people at Staggers Point always called this en-

counter the Battle of Horn Hill, the people from Wheelock
called it Morgan's Defeat, but most called it Bryant's Defeat.

In her old age Annette remembered the events of her second widowhood clearly. The couple's only child, Thomas
Washington Powers, had recently died at the age of three weeks.
She was informed that the chief of the victorious Indian tribe
had cut out her husband's heart and eaten it, hoping thereby to
inherit his brave spirit.

She was not consoled.

Later, when this same chief was captured, he offered to
shake hands with Annette, as the widow of a worthy opponent.
Annette refused. The chief then gave her as a gift of honor a
horn full of gun powder, cautioning her always to keep it full to
ensure prosperity. Evidently, Annette made a lasting impression
on this tribe. At a subsequent date her father had to rescue her
from admirers who wanted her as a wife for their chief.[19]

It is no wonder that on March 2 Senator John A. Greer
wrote Attorney General John C. Watrous:

> The frontier in this section (Robertson County) is in a miserable
> condition. They have been and are now on the eve of breaking
> up, at least those who are able to get away, a great many are wid-
> ows who are unable to get off, others have had their horses stolen
> and are left without the means of moving . . . You must try and
> have them protected. Indeed if they had not hoped the Comms.
> would locate the seat of Govt. at the falls they would have broken
> up long since.[20]

In late March Colonel Wheelock received news of the death
on March 1 of his cousin and mentor, Maj. Gen. Eleazar
Wheelock Ripley, in West Feliciana, Louisiana. It was the end of
an era. General Ripley had led young Lieutenant Wheelock during the War of 1812 at the Battle of Lundy's Lane, had invested
in his real estate ventures, had served briefly on paper as president of Texas, lost a son at Goliad, and been honored in the
name of his cousin's first established town, Ripley, Illinois. He
would be sorely missed.

While the frontier waited, Colonel Wheelock continued
various other business activities. Next to Indian raids, land title

continued to be the dominant issue in Robertson County. The land offices had finally been reopened in February of 1838, and again the people of Robertson County petitioned Congress to untangle their title disputes.

Evidence of fraud by Robertson Colony officials was still surfacing. Sometime in 1839, when Colonel Wheelock was at the Falls of the Brazos, James Martin, knowing his interest in fighting chicanery, handed him a fraudulent deed for a league of land in blank, supposedly issued by Steele. Wheelock handed it on to Dr. George Washington Hill, representative to Congress from Robertson County and member of the House Standing Committee on Public Lands, to enable the government to "detect such frauds." Hill handed it back to Martin for safe keeping. Martin remarked that Captain Monroe had a similar document. Wheelock believed that both Martin and Monroe had come by the documents innocently "and only retained them for the public good." Wheelock added that he believed that the Robertson Colony officials "were in the habit of doing their business loosely."[21]

But appeals to Congress for the settlement of land disputes were as vain as appeals for the defeat of the Comanche.

CHAPTER 16

POLITICS AND PROVOCATION: 1840-1841

Frontier Troubles

The tragedy of Bryant's Defeat on January 16, 1839, where one of the fallen was E.L.R. Wheelock's son-in-law and men from all parts of Robertson County died, added to the misery of the frontier families. Peace did not come, and the people of Robertson County continued to struggle. Indians raided, ripened fields were burned, horses were stolen. In spite of bills and oratory no substantial help came from Texas's national government.[1]

On the land law front, men of good will continued to seek clear titles for those who were legally qualified to receive them. On January 15, 1840, an Act to Quiet Land Titles in the Nashville Colony was passed by Congress, under the auspices of Dr. George Washington Hill, representative from Robertson County.

And still immigrants continued to arrive from the United States. By 1840 the town of Wheelock housed many prominent citizens as its organized program for selling land drew settlers to

Map showing original size of Robertson County as created on December 14, 1837, by the Republic of Texas. Author's sketch is based on WPA map from McLean, Papers, *XVI, 66-67.*

the surrounding prairie. If there was plenty of misery, there was also plenty of hope.

Money Troubles

The national officers of Texas tried hard to correct her grave financial situation by negotiating foreign loans, but no one wanted to risk capital in such a precarious semi-nation as Texas, perhaps poised to be retaken by the Mexicans, or absorbed by the United States, or to choke on its own audacity. Recognition of the republic by major powers in Europe would help, but the most sought Great Britain foundered on the slavery question. France was more easy-going. Early in 1840 Count Alphonse de Saligny moved to Waterloo, the new Texas capital (now denominated Austin), paid his teamsters with counterfeit money, and bought a lot from Dr. Anson Jones.

President Lamar then provoked a new extremity of violence by inviting the Comanche chief Muguara to an ill-fated peace conference in San Antonio. Maguara agreed to bring in his white captives as a gesture of good will, but in the event, brought only one, fifteen-year-old Matilda Lockhart, emaciated, covered with bruises, and disfigured for life. Her nose had been burned off.

Colonel William Fisher, in charge of keeping order, posted three companies of Rangers around the council chamber. Whether by design or mischance, shots rang out, leaving thirty Comanche dead (including Maguara) and seven dead Rangers. Twenty-seven Indian women and children and two very old Indian men were captured. The women were parceled out to Austin families as servants.

Back at the Comanche camp, a horrified passer-by witnessed their grief. "Women shrieked and howled and cut off fingers in mourning. The men gave the guttural moans of the dead. Horses were sacrificed for two days. Then thirteen (Anglo) captives were roasted to death or killed in lingering, revolting ways."[2] After this debacle, the Comanche nation entered into a full state of war with Texas, which was to last a generation. Putting a thousand warriors in the field, it ravaged

Victoria, razed Linville, and raided ranches and farms everywhere.

Robertson County was not neglected. The Minute Men were called out and a new company of Rangers was formed under Captain Chandler. At the new moon (now becoming known as the Comanche Moon), there was a fierce Indian fight at Englewood, two miles east of Old Franklin.

During this bloody time a band of Comanches sortied into the settlements, killing members of several families along Big Cedar Creek. They were pursued by a company of Minute Men who overtook them at Horn Hill in present Limestone County. Six Texans and twenty Indians were killed.

Colonel Wheelock wrote to Judge King:

> On return home I found my eldest son absent on an excursion after Indians. It appears that the neighborhood of Bryants Fort on Little River has been alarmed by a large body of Indians from 100 to 150 as supposed. My son, who returned last night, said that there was tallied when he left 35 men at the fort and at Mr. Wilson's. They intended to act entirely upon the defense. Their spies expected that the Indians were disposed into seven parties, with the (total) of each squad larger than the whites. They are supposed to be the war party of Wacos, etc.

Leaving Indian fighting more and more to the younger generation, Colonel Wheelock's own attention was focused on political affairs. He had his eye on public office again, and wrote a long letter to Judge King laying out his ideas for a national bank, similar to those of Ashbel Smith, who said, "If we obtain the (French) loan and it be proposed to be made on the basis of a bank, the President, you know, will recommend a purely national bank. The country is clearly in favor of one which shall be partly owned by the nation and partly by individual stockholders."[3]

But in the end the question was moot, because the French loan never materialized. The French Minister, affronted by Lamar's opposition to a French immigration scheme and insulted by the actions of Austin boardinghouse keeper Richard Bullock in the so-called Pig War, asked for his passport and huffed back to Paris.

Land Troubles

About this time Wheelock published a closely written three-column broadside to further his candidacy for the Senate. Addressed to "The Voters of the Senatorial District of the Counties of Milam and Robertson," it set forth his political stance on a variety of subjects, including, of course, the land issue.

On the land title front, many embattled settlers caught in the eleven-league trap were being forced to the final recourse of costly court battles. With cash so scarce, it was necessary to pass the hat. In April Sterling C. Robertson raised $605 for a court test, of which $30 came from Colonel Wheelock. Also in this month, land-grabbers Morehouse and Watrous had filed a suit against James Lane because he had settled on one of the eleven-league grants claimed by them. A collection was taken up to finance Lane's defense. Among the forty contributors were Sterling C. Robertson ($50) and E.L.R. Wheelock ($30).

In answer to a petition to Congress written by Wheelock, Dr. Hill, on the Standing Committee for Public Lands, continued to help his Robertson County constituents to sort out their land title disputes. To the settlers' great joy, he was instrumental in blocking Three-Legged Willie Williamson's bid to validate the illegally obtained Austin and Williams eleven-league grants in Robertson's Colony.

Sterling C. Robertson admitted to the standing committee that he had issued one of these dreaded giant grants (to Jose Maria Nixon), and that unfortunately the location was already occupied by four families of colonists. But Robertson testified that the point was moot because his grant was issued only on condition that Nixon settle one family on each of the leagues, which Nixon never did, and that the Nixon grant was therefore void.

Other land besides the Robertson Colony grants was in dispute. President Lamar continued to promote his grandiose scheme to extend Texas to the Pacific coast. His vice-president, David Burnet, declared belligerently, "If the sword must decide the controversy, let the decision be prompt and final. . . . Texas proper is bounded by the Rio Grande. Texas, as defined by the sword, may comprehend the Sierra Madre. Let the sword do its proper work."[4] Congress declined to go along with Lamar's rash proposal to send an armed expedition to capture Santa Fe, which he considered part of Texas. They dismissed the army and the navy, which they could no longer afford.

There was doubt about Texas's ability to survive as an independent nation.

In the year 1840, Colonel Wheelock's state and county taxes went up to $74.79 as he grew in prosperity.

Town Troubles

There was scandal on the home front as well as in Austin. Sometime in 1840 Ann Cavitt married her husband's nephew, Cavitt Armstrong, who had come from Tennessee to check up on her family. The ladies of Wheelock were no doubt aware that union with one's husband's nephew fell within the prohibited degrees of relationship barred from marriage according to the Church of England and presumably most churches of the time. Oblivious, the ecclesiastically illicit couple moved into their six bedroom-hostelry, now known as the Armstrong, or Stagecoach Inn, and continued to build onto it until 1854.

Wheelock pursued his campaign for the Senate. His speeches at political gatherings during this period reflected on the slave question as well as Texas's continued rejection by the United States of America. "Ladies and Gentlemen," one begins, "It appears more than probable that our American Mother will literally kick her Texian Children out of doors. I, as one, am willing to forgive her with more than Christian Charity, for she knows not what she does. If such should be the case, then we must rely upon our own prudence, patriotism, and prowess for national existence." He points out that "As a Christian people, we deplore and should the evils of Slavery," but was it not "enacted upon us by the American folly of our ancestors?" The address continues to discuss the practical consequences of putting an end to slavery, not a popular position in Texas.

Wheelock did not confine his campaigning to his own district, but often was found in Austin keeping abreast with governmental activities there. A vivid account of the danger presented by travel in the Republic is preserved in the diaries of Adolphus Sterne.

On Saturday, December 5, 1840, Sterne was traveling towards Austin and "stopped at Jones's all day to recruit our force, for the purpose of going through the stretch 75 miles Indian country without a house. Five persons arrived from Nashville on the Brazos to go on with us (Capt. Red, Col. Wheelock, Major Porter, Mr. Murray and Mr. Wilson)."

> Sunday the 6th. Fine weather. Left early this morning, some fine country. Saw many herds of buffalo but did not stop to kill any. Stopped near night at a place called the Hole in the Rock from a peculiar basin of water formed in a solid rock, in the bed of a bayou. Here we took our supper, but our horses were very uneasy and we supposed that Indians were in the neighborhood, so at eight o'clock we saddled up and went 15 miles further to the Post Oak Grove and camped for the night.
>
> Monday the 7th—Left early. Prairie all the way to Austin 30 miles. Arrived 3 pm. Was met by all my friends, and some old acquaintances, was invited by my friend Kaufman to a Ball which was given in honor of the French and American ministers. Put up at Bullock's." [5]

This juxtaposition of dangerous travel and diplomatic ball was typical of early Republic life.

Towards the end of the year 1840, Colonel Wheelock reviewed the land controversy in Robertson's Colony from its beginnings, as he understood it, for the benefit of Dr. George Washington Hill and expressed his distress at the continuing land disputes. He no longer held back from condemning William Steele, whose behavior had been suspect from Robertson County's beginnings:

> The depraved and unprincipled conduct of Commissioner Steele resulted in a combination of all the officers of the new municipality excepting John Marlin to subvert the rights of the people under the colonization laws and that no individuals but those who would answer their purpose would have land unless they chose it outside what was good. A county which could not be settled because of a savage foe has been the result.

. . . I believe, from the circumstances of these being made public, emigration stopped and they finally resorted to a more speedy way of making money, to wit the manufacture of deeds by wholesale as they could find purchasers in the United States. To support this position, I will relate a conversation which took place at my house between Jack Moore and myself in 1837. He said he was at the Falls after the closing of the land offices in 1835-1836 and that the office for writing was closed and he took occasion to ask Steele why it was so; he said that he could make but three deeds a day when the doors were open, but with them closed he could make eight or ten or more. Now mark this was after the official closing of the office. He stated that each title took a period of thirty days. Now take 30 days and multiply it by 10 and it gives 300, which is more than there have been sellers in this colony.

I am so tired of so base a subject but will only remark to you that Poor old man Robertson has been more the dupe of his own credulity than innately dishonest.

Accept my best wishes
Which are yours truly
E.L.R. Wheelock

By 1841 the town of Wheelock had twenty business establishments: general merchants, land offices, freight offices, a race track, and cock fighting pits. State Street was a busy place. A hall was available for gospel meetings, political gatherings, parties, dances, and other celebrations. The citizens did their hunting in the area now built over by the modern town of Franklin.

Times were happier for Colonel Wheelock at home. Twice widowed Annette Wheelock Kimble Powers had a new beau, Samuel Blackburn Killough. This time, Annette's marriage would last for thirty-five years and produce ten children, six of whom lived to maturity. The Killough home on the road to Dunn's Fort became a show place, surrounded by crepe myrtle and fruit trees, which bloomed entrancingly in the spring. The Dunn family built a big house nearby called The Groves. The frontier town of Wheelock was becoming a home.

Even religion had come to Wheelock Prairie. Sometime in 1841 a Methodist camp meeting was held on the banks of Cedar Creek. Hundreds of settlers attended and fifty were converted during this affair, which was remembered for half a century.

Harrison Owen remarked, "The new county will never be the same again. Some of the ruffians of Robertson County had all hell scared out of them. Never have I heard such preaching and I'm sure no one else has . . . I kept thinking of John the Baptist in the wilderness of Bible times, and I think the Methodist preachers were just as impressive."[6] But E.L.R. Wheelock's religious feelings were not aroused by Protestant eloquence. He still dreamed of the Tampico cathedral. It is unlikely that he attended.

The Lamar presidency now reached its nadir. Ignoring the fact that the Texas Congress had already refused to countenance such a scheme and using public money he had no right to take, Lamar provisioned the Santa Fe expedition and sent it freebooting west on June 21 to claim Santa Fe for Texas. The group had no reliable map and believed Santa Fe to be only 450 miles away, instead of almost 1,000. After marching some 1,300 random miles, the exhausted expedition surrendered to the Mexican Army without firing a shot, less than sixty miles from its target. As soon as it became generally known, this debacle did real damage to Texas's reputation on the world scene.

In a sweltering July, Wheelock received pay and recognition for his work as a local land commissioner in helping to untangle land titles in Robertson County, and towards the end of the summer his attempts to re-establish communications with his pious sister bore fruit. Physical separation of families, unreliable mail service, and often lack of proper addresses produced real suffering among many branches of severed families such as the Wheelocks, as seen in the following:

> Petersburgh, Pike County, Indiana, September 5, 1841
> My Dear Brother;
> I cannot express the real gratification we all enjoyed at the receipt of your kind letter of last June, and which we received in two months from the date. It appeared like one written from the dead as we had relinquished all hope of hearing from you again . . .
> When I reflect that eight long years have passed since that period I am lost in wonder, yet adore the goodness of that Providence who has protected us until the present moment.
> You write nothing of our brother George; where is he? Is he yet living? I have not heard from him for seven years, when he

wrote from the Mississippi State. I heard from William near a year ago. He was then at Alton much as usual. Remember me very affectionately to Sister Wheelock and family. Tell them sometimes of their distant aunt, who frequently thinks of them and sometimes imagines she can almost behold them in person. Adieu, dear brother, adieu. May the best blessings attend you in the fervent prayers of your sister, Nancy M. Hillman.

The enclosure from Wheelock's nephew read:

I cannot express the emotions of joy our family felt to the Divine Being for the receipt of your kind letter. I can inform you that we all enjoy good health and all other blessings that we could ask from the Great Giver of all good. I have been employed at School teaching for the last eighteen months and shall continue until next summer. I have been at New Orleans once or twice since your visit in 1833, and would have come to see you and your country had I known where to find you . . .

I remain your most affectionate kinsman,
French E. W. Hillman

Wheelock's brother-in-law added:

Dear Col.:
As my wife and French will tell you all about the little concerns of the family, I will tell you something about politics. I need not tell you of the election and death of General Harrison, nor of the accession to the Presidential chair of Mr. Tyler. It is extremely doubtful whether this President does not disappoint the expectations and the wishes of the Whigs, who elevated him to the high office he now fills. General Harrison called a special meeting of the Congress for the purpose of establishing a fiscal bank for the government and to repeal the sub treasury and distribute the proceeds of the public lands among the different states in proportion to the number of representatives from each and to raise the tariff upon certain articles. Congress has passed a bank-bill which has been met by the President's veto. Another has passed the lower house of Congress, and will probably meet the same fate, which will produce great consternation among the Whigs.

Money matters in this country are so deranged that there is scarcely a dollar in circulation, and should the president apply his veto again the whole country will be almost ruined. I remain dear sir your very respectful and obedient servant, James Hillman

Political Troubles

The United States of America was not the only country in disarray. Lamar's Indian campaign, although effective in some ways, had aroused the Comanches to greater fury against the outlying settlements. His red bank notes had fallen to a dime on the dollar. His dream of a Texas stretching from the Gulf of Mexico to the Pacific lay in ruins.

In September Sam Houston had little trouble being re-elected to the presidency with Burleson as his vice-president. The citizens of Texas wanted the Raven back.

Houston brought with him a planter Sixth Congress, which immediately stopped spending, issued new money, and signed treaties with the Wacos, Tawakonis, and southern Comanches.

Colonel Wheelock was not one of the new senators. He was defeated in the local election by one tie-breaking vote cast by Francis Slaughter (in his capacity as chief justice) for Wheelock's opponent, James Shaw. Since Slaughter had already cast one vote for Shaw in his capacity as a citizen, Wheelock not unnaturally cried foul, as in the following letter:

October 25, 1841
To James Shaw Esq.
Dear Sir:
My views as to the course in the present Political controversy:
First, I am convinced that neither of us is elected because Slaughter polled Two votes.

Second, If the certificate (of election) had been given to me I could not have accepted it . . . .Third, Since I believe this election to be illegal, I know of no better remedy than to throw it back to the people to correct the evil, . . .

I am willing to bear my proportion of the expenses. If you should prefer to do so you can write me next mail.

Yours truly, E.L.R. Wheelock.

With perfect courtesy, Shaw replied,

Sir:

I received your very polite and frank letter on Yesterday by the hand of Mr. David Dawson, in which you say that you do not consider either of us elected 'because Judge Slaughter had polled two votes.' . . .

I have a certificate of election that tells me that I am 'duly and constitutionally elected senator in the District comprised of Robertson and Milam Counties.' Am I to judge of the certificate whether it is a good or bad one?

You say that I am not elected because Judge Slaughter voted previously in the election. I admit that he did. The law regulating elections says 'that in case of a tie the Chief Justice shall decide, etc.' . . . If the Judge voted in the election previously, I consider that vote an illegal one and if he voted for me you would have been elected by one vote, if for you I would have been elected by one vote.

I shall start over to Austin on Friday. If you intend going over I hope you will come to my house on Thursday evening and we will both go together.

I remain your very respectfully, James Shaw.

But Wheelock did not go to Austin to contest this election. His contest in Illinois had been denied. He was a thin-skinned man, and no doubt recoiled from the possibility of a second rejection. As was said of Burleson, "he spoke his mind with a candor that impaired his political influence"[7] and perhaps had not the elasticity to overcome this handicap. His Puritan morality and anti-slavery opinions did not endear him to many of his opportunistic neighbors. In addition to his amour propre, his sense of justice, always strong, had been outraged.

On December 13, 1841, Sam Houston, wearing his buckskins, was inaugurated for the second time as president of Texas.

CHAPTER 17

HEADING HOME: 1842-1844

Sam Houston on the Move

As Houston began his second term as president, Texas's Sixth Congress turned off the public tap, repealing all of Lamar's currency and banking laws. The country was still impoverished. In striking metaphor, Dr. Anson Jones, the new secretary of state, described the Republic at the start of Houston's second term as marooned on a island of quicksand in the middle of a swollen and rising river. The granite banks on one side led to annexation. On the other side similar granite banks led to secure independence and to the Pacific. "Texas would have to place herself upon one of those roads before the flood waters of bankruptcy, insubordination, and reconquest overwhelmed her," wrote Gambrell.[1]

As a former diplomat, Jones disagreed with Houston on the importance of international relations, which the president denigrated but Jones now sought to improve. He sent Maj. James Reilly to represent Texas in Washington City and summoned back the miffed de Saligny to mend bridges with France.

Texas needed the illusive French loan more than ever.

Congress, revealing its knowledge both of the Scriptures and the *Book of Common Prayer*, declared, "For six long years the prospect of this loan has gone before us as a cloud by day and a pillar of fire by night . . . It has induced us to do things we ought not to do and leave undone the things we ought to have done . . . The pending of this negotiation has been a curse."[2] Dr. Ashbel Smith, who had studied medicine at the Sorbonne and spoke fluent French, was sent to Paris as ambassador of the Republic. Further negotiations with England had finally led to recognition by Her Britannic Majesty, an important step up for the infant nation.

In February 1842, keen-eyed Englishman William Bollaert landed in Galveston to replace the Anonymous Buckeye (this Ohioan has never been identified) as Texas's principal foreign observer. His entertaining journal gives a tough-minded but cheerful picture of a country with 75,000 inhabitants, almost bankrupt but doing a brisk cotton business with Bollaert's home-land.

In Robertson County an era came to an end on March 4 with the death of former Empresario Sterling Clack Robertson, who succumbed to pneumonia and was buried in Nashville Cemetery, two miles below the mouth of Little River on the west bank of the Brazos, the same lyrically beautiful spot in which Dr. Felix Robertson had camped out during his exploratory tour of Texas in 1825.

Major Robertson's will, dated April 20, 1840, raised local eyebrows. Elijah, his eldest son, was sole heir. His second son, James, received nothing, nor did either of Robertson's wives. Elijah's mother, Fanny King of Tennessee, was a Texas resident. Of James's mother, Rachel Smith, perhaps a campaign wife, lit-tle is known. Both of Robertson's marriages are shadowed with mystery because of his having taken the extraordinary step of having both his sons declared legitimate by a special act of the Texas Congress. This legislation might make sense in the case of Rachel's son. But if his union with Fanny King was legal, why did Elijah, the older son and sole heir, have to be cleared of bas-tardy? Tongues wagged.

The citizens still feared Mexican invasion. When Colonel Wheelock and his wife made a contract for the sale of lumber in

March of 1842, it contained a clause stating that the agreement was valid only if "they were not driven off by the enemy."

President Houston moved the peripatetic Texas government back to his city of Houston. Although inhabitants of Austin, seeing their livelihood disappearing, refused to relinquish the State Archives, Houston had his way, and for several years (while its official papers reposed under the shadow of the Balcones Escarpment), Texas government business was conducted in the bayou city.

Colonel Wheelock wrote to President Houston offering his services in case hostilities with Mexico broke out again, and in May he received the following reply:

> Private to Col. E.L.R. Wheelock
> Dear Sir:
> Your favor by the politeness of Mr. Raymond reached me in due season; and I avail myself of his return to offer you my thanks for the interest and solicitude you express for the success of our country in the struggle in which we are now very soon to be involved. None of us, who reflect upon the present and the future with the light of experience before us, but must feel much concern for the result of the great and final effort we shall make for the permanent independence and welfare of the Republic.
>
> When the time arrives (and you may rely upon its being near at hand) you will receive due notice. When the summons comes, those who now think themselves well prepared will find that they have yet much to do. Therefore, let all prepare thoroughly for the work. March!
>
> In Haste, Accept the best wishes of Your friend and servant,
>
> Sam Houston.[3]

Answering the call to arms, on July 25 William Hillman Wheelock, the Colonel's second son, was commissioned as acting midshipman in the Texas Navy. Alas, William's career as a sailor was short lived. Four months later Congress abolished the Texas Navy as an economy measure.

On September 11 the Texans' greatest fears were realized when Mexican Gen. Adrian Woll invaded their domain and recaptured San Antonio, holding the town for nine days and taking fifty prominent Texans hostage. Attacked as they tried to withdraw, the Mexicans (in the Goliad tradition) killed forty Anglo prisoners.

Cool as usual, Houston authorized a force to deploy on the Mexican border in a deterrent posture. Out-of-control, part of this force invaded Mexico on their own initiative, capturing the village of Mier. The Mexican Army soon reclaimed their territory, and this disaster led to the death of many rash Texans. The misadventure was savagely condemned by President Houston, and put an end to Texan invasions of Mexico.

The government now perambulated again. President Houston decided to move the capital back to its original site at Washington-on-the-Brazos because of lack of space in Houston, perhaps, as the British chargé declared, "driven away by some of those springs of local politics, feuds, and jealousies, which run into such long streams of talk and knavishness on this side of the Atlantic."[4]

About this time Colonel Wheelock asked a friend to approach the Texas government (to which he could not gain access by election) for an appointive post. His desire for public service was a complicated one, but certainly included of a real impulse to be of use to the Republic. His friend wrote:

October 22,
Hon. George W. Hockley
Secretary of War and Marine
Col. Geo., W. Hockley: This is to introduce to you Col. Wheelock, a man of sober habits, and whom I believe from years knowledge of him to be honest. He had some military training, having been at Lundy's Lane in the Canadas.

His business, habits, and disposition would I think be best employed in the War Department Office or the Land Office. We and others were discouraged on the Frontier.

If possible I wish you to give him a trial as a business man—
Your friend, Major Joseph Moody.

But Wheelock's bad luck held. Hockley was soon out of office and unable to extend favors.

In late 1842 Mary Wheelock's nephew, George W. Prickett, whose mother and father had died somewhere along the Red

River, wrote to her sadly to say that he longed to visit Texas to search for their missing portraits. Alas, the precious portraits were never found, nor were those of E.L.R. and Mary Wheelock, casualties, perhaps, of the Runaway Scrape. Their likenesses may have been burnt for fuel or otherwise destroyed, or they may hang anonymously today on the wall of some stranger who collects American primitives.

In a proclamation seriously at odds with his personal style, President Houston was now persuaded to create the Order of San Jacinto so that his diplomatic corps serving in Europe could equal other diplomats in the matter of protocol and ceremonial dress. Sir William Henry Daingerfield, serving in the Low Countries, and Sir Ashbel Smith, in London, became the first (and perhaps the last) Texas knights.

Sam Houston and the Amerinds

On March 28, 1843, Texas signed a widely-based treaty with most of her Indian tribes; only the Comanche and Kiowa remained hostile. Houston's favorable attitude toward the Amerinds and a general lessening of Comanche raids in Robertson County now enabled Colonel Wheelock to resume his old occupation of Indian trading, which had financed his trek across Texas in 1824 almost twenty years earlier. On May 1, 1843, he furnished one hundred and fifty pounds of pork at four cents per pound for the use of the Delaware and Waco Indians. Later in the year Indian Commissioner G. W. Terrell certified that he paid Wheelock $6 for the pork. Other receipts state that Wheelock furnished one hog weighing one hundred and fifty pounds at four cents per pound for use of the Delaware Indians on their route to the falls by order of the Government of Texas. Through his Indian trading, Wheelock became closely associated with Indian Agent Ethan Stroud and his brother Beden.

Considering the many accounts of death and torture endured by others, it is surely worthy of comment that Wheelock was five times a captive or detainee of the Indians and five times came home safely. Other men's daughters were ravaged and mistreated. When Annette Wheelock was captured, her father brought her home unharmed. Most of Wheelock's personal problems in Texas were Anglo, not Amerind.

This argues a community of sentiment with Sam Houston, the Cherokee citizen. In July Colonel Wheelock heard again from the president. The letter reads:

July 1, 1843, To Col. E.L.R. Wheelock:
Your favor of the 29th ultima is at hand and in reply I have time only to say that your proceedings in relation to the Indians meet my approbation.

We learn here that a group of men from the upper Colorado River have gone into the Indian Country toward the San Saba River for the ostensible purpose of mining. We very much fear mischief of the most unfortunate and fatal character to the frontier may be produced by it. It is certainly to be deplored that there are to be found in any part of the country people so far lost to every proper sentiment as thus to jeapardize the lives of the exposed and in many cases defenseless inhabitants of the border. What can one man do when so many combine to thwart his efforts, disregard the laws and bring ruin and distress upon our citizens? They imagine that by thus (counseling) themselves they will bring mortification and odium upon me. They may succeed in the first but not in the latter. If the people do not now, they will ere long understand my policy and do me justice. I do not submit my acts to the judgement of faction (any) more than I am governed by the jargon and discord of public clamor. May God save us from the poison and blight of faction, that prolific source of so many evils.

Our Mexican relations have assumed a more promising and hopeful aspect. Let us never despair of the Republic, but like true citizens obey the laws, love order, be industrious, live economically, and all will soon be well. Noisy, non-productive, and disappointed men, who hate labor and aspire to live upon the people's substance, have already done us great injury abroad. At home, they are too well known to be feared.

Let every good citizen on the frontier interest himself to protect and conciliate the Indians. If the whites do their simple duty to themselves, they need have no further difficulties with their red neighbors.

Within the last few days I have received reports from the commissioners which have gone to the Comanches, under date of

2nd and 11 June. They are both favorable, and the most gratifying disposition is evinced by the various tribes met with to consummate a general and permanent peace. A-cah-quash, the Waco chief, has proved himself a true and efficient friend, and will no doubt do much to aid the commissioners in their object.

In haste, I am, very truly, yours,
Sam Houston.[5]

Shortly afterwards, a letter arrived from Houston's private secretary, urging Wheelock's candidacy for Congress once more:

July 21, 1843, Washington (on the Brazos)
Private
My Dear Colonel:
The contents of your letter were well received by His Excellency, from their justness and appropriateness. You will, I am sure, have it in your power to do much good for the country by lending a cordial support to the government authorities in this trying and important crisis. Public confidence will stay the arms of our political Moses during the conflict of the day. Your course has been such as challenges the approval and praise of every good citizen. You say that your candidates for Congress are all opposition men. How does this happen? Can't you manage to have things properly adjusted? Why is it that no administration man will run? How it is with yourself that you cannot present yourself to the people and do something for the cause? Think of it. I would like to see you in our Congress. You ought to be there. I say again, think of it and act immediately.

I am, my dear Colonel, very sincerely, Your friend and servant.
W. D. Miller (Private Sec. to the President)

Wheelock cannot but have been flattered, but he did not run.

Meanwhile, Wheelock had been advertising for sober settlers and receiving inquiries not only from strangers but also from old friends in Illinois and long-lost cousins in New Hampshire. He, the exile, must have been very gratified to find that respected people from both places wished to change their lot for his.

Late in the year Wheelock received another letter from an old friend, Colonel Darrington, asking for help in reclaiming some property lost during the Runaway Scrape. Wheelock answered:

Col. J. Darrington
My Dear Sir:
Nothing for some time has afforded me more pleasure than the receipt of your favor of the 22nd of last month which came to hand eight days ago of my friend Dr. Seely. I assure you that I am truly gratified to have it in my power to reciprocate any service for your kind attention to myself and family in 1836. Services that are remembered with lively emotions of gratitude and can only be obliterated when life ceases to exist.

I had the opportunity a few days ago of seeing John Marlin, who yet resides at the Falls of the Brazos. I enquired of him the situation of your Indian goods or claims thereof, etc. Marlin declares that on the last of April 1836 the settlement at the Falls, known as Sarahville de Viesca, first heard of the fall of the Alamo and immediately all made preparations for a retreat. On the first day they moved forward to Big Creek, about three miles, and encamped for the night; that when he started he left the goods in his house, precisely in the situation they were in when deposited. [Somehow Andrew Cavitt obtained possession of Darrington's goods.] After Cavitt's death . . . his widow returned to the Falls bringing a part of your goods; a part she had sold. Some she had used to clothe her Negroes, etc. and for the truth of his assertions referred me to several witnesses. Today I called upon her to ascertain what she was willing to do for you, in presence of her son (I think a fine, good young man). She equivocated, denied, acknowledged, and finally agreed to return all of the goods taken, knowing she had sold or used the greater part of them. I discovered several empty boxes marked Darrington, and a few butcher knives. She exonerated Mr. John Marlin from any participation in the embezzlement and at last requested me to write to you for the invoices and she would do justice. They are wealthy and should pay you.

I shall make no comments upon the depravity of the human heart, but will observe that woman's tears are their strongest weapons. Will you pardon me for this long scrawl and believe it to have emanated from an anxious wish to serve your interest.

> I am with sentiments of respect yours truly,
> E.L.R. Wheelock

We have no news that is strange. The Indians frequently visit the Falls and we hope times are gradually changing for the better. Some emigrants are coming into the country above me. Society is improving slowly, but virtue will finally triumph over vice which heretofore ruled.

Sam Houston Steps Down

Politically, Texas was anything but settled. What would she become? She had four options:

1. Annexation by the United States of America.
2. Independence within its present borders supported by recognition by Mexico and protection by Britain;
3. Union with Oregon, California, and Santa Fe to become a great transcontinental power;
4. Absorption of the underpopulated area of northern Mexico.

From 1836 Texas had favored the first solution, but the political climate in the United States of America continued unfavorable. On May 16, 1844, Houston's private secretary wrote to Wheelock from Washington City:

Private
My dear Colonel:
Our affairs have reached that point here which enables us to judge pretty correctly as to their final result. I am sorry to say that our most sanguine anticipations are doomed to be disappointed. It is now universally agreed by all parties that annexation cannot possibly take place.
Upon the rejection of the treaty by the Senate, a bill will

probably be introduced into Congress to accomplish the same thing by enactment. But this also will fail. The Senate will defeat it. I have made up my mind to the worst. We have nothing to hope from this country and must rely upon our own prudence, patriotism, and prowess for support in the hour of need. I write in haste and therefore must be brief. My regards to the family. Faithfully your friend. W. D. Miller.

Miller knew whereof he wrote. On June 8 the Texas Annexation treaty was rejected by the U.S. Senate, with, according to John Quincy Adams, "the special intervention of Almighty God."[6]

In Mexico City Santa Anna seized this opportunity to announce that he was resuming hostilities against Texas.

Colonel Wheelock now expressed his respect and confidence in his wife in a material way by giving her the right to arrange her own financial affairs, as follows:

January 4, 1844: I approve and allow my wife Mary P. to make such deposition of her property as she thinks proper.
E.L.R. Wheelock
Wheelock, Robertson County

Wheelock's land business continued to flourish. In the town of Wheelock, Hiram Hanover's Academy was now thriving and was the meeting place of the Kappa Lambda Society, to which Colonel Wheelock gave lectures on several occasions. On June 7, 1944, his subject was undesirable and deceitful immigrants. It was a subject he knew well.

Regarded also as something of an expert in Indian affairs, from 1836 until 1846 Wheelock was either advisor or the leader of all the expeditions that went out from Robertson and Milam Counties to treat with the Indians. Unfortunately, details of most of these encounters have not survived, but in July of 1844 he forwarded the following touching letter to Sam Houston from Chief Louis of the Delaware Nation, clearly showing the degree of confidence the Amerinds placed in the Colonel. It reads:

Wheelock, July 9, 1844
General Houston:
Brother:
The great spirit is good and does not die. I found my path with which I left the Council Fire to go to my Peoples. I have found 20 since. No white man has stopped it; all show a white hand. You told me so and it was true. Brother, I wish to see at the Council Fire all of my Brothers and my White Father in the front place. Our Red Brothers have a great deal to say to him. He alone can satisfy and make the Path of Peace straight to all his Red Children. They must make bread for their little ones or perish. There is not Buffalo for all. Some must have cows, and raise horses, not steal. The Great Spirit speaks in my ear and tells me that the Earth was made for the Red and the White Man. Brother, we must make corn. We must know where to put it in the ground, not crop the path which is made with a dark dust. You must come and see face to face your brothers. All will be glad. And you can tell them for good. You will not lie. May the Great Spirit be good to you, until we speak.

Louis. By my friend, Wheelock.

On September 2 the man Sam Houston had selected to bring Texas home to the United States was elected the last president of the Republic. The 125,000 people now in Texas had no trouble in choosing Dr. Anson Jones. But Dr. Jones was much under the spell of British Minister Elliott, who was godfather to one of his children. England was against annexation, and Elliott was very persuasive. Still, the last chapter in the saga of the Republic was now in the hands of Anson Jones.

BOOK FIVE

THE 28TH STATE

O Cruel road to Texas, how many hearts you broke . . .
—Berta Hart Nance

Map of Mercer Colony, from article by Nancy Eagleton in
Southwestern Historical Quarterly, *vol. 39, 275.*

CHAPTER 18

THE MERCER COLONY PART I: 1845

Although the Mercer Colony "was a source of friction from its beginning, it played an important role in peopling the Republic and State and in the annexation of Texas," wrote Nancy Eagleton.[1] Diplomacy, local politics, economics, Indian affairs, legislative battles, and judicial history all came into play during its turbulent life. His association with it was to do Colonel Wheelock irreparable harm. It cost him his post as Indian Commissioner of the Republic of Texas and shattered his confidence in his neighbors and theirs in him. If he had lived long enough, it would have separated him from his own creation, the flourishing town of Wheelock, together with all his associates and association with Robertson County.

Land Policy in the Republic

On November 13, 1835, as the Republic of Texas was being born, all empresario contracts issued by the Mexican government became invalid. Settlers who were caught in the resulting crack between signing with an empresario and issuance of an actual title faced years of grief trying to obtain justice from the new nation, and E.L.R. Wheelock was one of their most vocal advocates. Much of his law practice was involved in fighting their battles.

In spite of the grandiose declaration in the Texas Constitution that every family already in Texas was entitled to more than 4,000 acres, while those arriving between independence day (March 2, 1836) and October 1837 were to receive 1,280 acres, the Republic's stance on immigration and the distribution of land never really crystallized. She dealt grants out to military veterans and ultimately to creditors because she had no other wealth. She mandated surveys in imitation of the orderly United States system, but never had the money to pay the surveyors.

The Republic eventually did set up a method for issuing land grants which passed on most of the responsibility to local government. In an attempt to regularize the position of squatters, many of whom had been illegally in place for years, the Republic allowed them to keep up to 320 acres where they were already settled by paying fifty cents an acre.

From the beginnings, empresarios and certain land speculators, both Mexican and Anglo, had reserved the best land for themselves. An example can be found in Robertson Colony where in 1825 Dr. Felix Robertson set aside some of the most beautiful and best watered land for Texas Association members long before settlers arrived. To reward investors was natural enough, and did no harm so long as the owners came to live on the land. Huge eleven-league parcels awarded to men such as Jose Maria Nixon and never lived on by the owners resulted in strife which lasted into the twentieth century.

To this witches' brew the Republic of Texas added buyers of land scrip she had desperately issued to raise ready cash. This scrip was resold all over the United States, producing an unknown body of foreigners not even resident in the country with rights to Texas land. When one of these arrived in Texas to claim land, he was allowed to locate where he wished.

The results were predictable. A single site might be claimed under a Mexican grant, an American empresario grant, by a squatter's rights, or by a scrip owner who just liked the lie of that particular piece of land. Violence and adjudication were inevitable.

The New Age Empresarios

Bitter as the mixture already was, the Texas government under the direction of President Lamar, increasingly pressed for money, reopened empresario contracting through the Congressional Act of February 4, 1841. This act had the double purpose of securing money for the Republic and populating lands which, threatened by hostile Mexicans and Amerinds, had so far been shunned. The new-day empresarios were to receive ten premium sections for every one hundred families settled. On August 20, 1841, the first of these new empresario contracts was signed, opening the Peters Colony in North Texas. A man named Charles Fenton Mercer acted as its agent to recruit British subjects for the colony, but, as it became apparent that Texas would not abolish slavery, the British interests withdrew. On January 23, 1844, General Mercer and President Sam Houston signed a contract giving Mercer his own colony. Houston reserved alternate sections within the grant for the Republic, hoping to make a big profit by selling them as soon as the new empresario had brought in enough settlers to make the area boom.

At first Houston's idea was greeted with cheers by the frontiersmen, who were tired of looking over their shoulders for invading Mexicans or raiding Amerinds. A year later they would be leveling their sights at Mercer's men. What happened?

Charles Fenton Mercer was an exemplary human being and an exemplary public official. He came from a distinguished family and added to its luster by graduating with honors from Princeton College, serving as a major in the War of 1812, and becoming a U.S. Congressman and first president of the Chesapeake and Ohio Canal Company. John Marshall, Chief Justice of the Supreme Court, was his close friend, as was the saintly Episcopal Bishop John Henry Hobart, his fellow student at Princeton.

When he retired from Congress at the age of sixty, Mercer was hailed as "A Christian gentleman of captivating manners and address, possessed of a vast fund of information . . . He was a gentleman of the Virginia Old School, of eminently spotless character."[2]

Experienced and respected, he seemed ideal for Houston's purpose, as Eagleton described: "He had a vision of a colony in the Republic of Texas where he might realize his political, social, and economic ideals and where he might enjoy a degree of quiet and security in his declining years."[3]

Without regard for the feelings of future historians, Mercer called his joint stock company for the development of the Mercer Colony the Texas Association, in unconscious and confusing imitation of the Texas Association formed in Nashville, Tennessee, in 1821.

Mercer was honorable, enthusiastic, and energetic, and wholly within the law. But by 1944 conditions had changed on the northern frontier where his colony was located. As annexation by the United States appeared more probable, threats from Mexico and Indians waned. Rough elements on the border decided they wanted the Mercer Colony lands for themselves, never mind Sam Houston. In addition, Mercer's abolitionist sentiments did nothing to further his cause. Still, the storm of protest which met Mercer's attempt to settle his families was a total surprise to the general, a law-abider from a law-abiding culture.

At first the Texan government appeared ready to stand by its contract, but on February 4, 1845, the House of Representatives passed a joint resolution requiring Mercer to have the surveying of the outer limits of his colony completed by April 1, on penalty of forfeiture. This hostile act enabled those opposed to the colony to void Mercer's contract by preventing a survey.

Mercer had been informed that his sub-agent, Dr. Daniel Rowlett, had already caused the external lines of the Mercer Colony to be run and had placed several families near present-day Dallas. By the end of 1844 certificates had been issued to more than 100 families.

Following injuries caused by a fall from a mule, E.L.R. Wheelock had been confined to bed for much of the winter. In the spring of 1845, probably in March, Mercer asked him to undertake the office of sub-agent for that part of the Mercer Colony lying west of the Trinity River. Dr. Rowlett would continue to act for lands east of the Trinity.

Wheelock and Mercer took to each other at once and speedily exchanged contracts. Wheelock was to set out as soon as possible to locate and survey his part of the colony. Each family would have one half section, to be claimed by July 1 next, for the total sum of eight dollars. The settlers were asked to abstain from waste on the adjacent lands belonging to the Republic or to the company. Each family agreed to pay five dollars to help erect a public building to be used as a school house, church, and meeting house for the neighborhood.

Later in the month Mercer wrote to Wheelock: "I rely on your discretion to confine such contracts to lands free from encumbrance and fitted for immediate settlement with advantages of good soil, wood, and water."

Wheelock was aware that some Texans opposed the Mercer Colony, but being principled himself had no idea of the depth and strength of the resistance his fellow-citizens would bring to bear. Mercer had been welcomed when his North Texas grant was considered uninhabitable. Now that the Indians had been in great part pacified, less ethical frontiersmen needed him no more and saw a once-in-a-lifetime chance to enrich themselves. But Wheelock was not at first unduly alarmed. The frontier was his familiar ranging ground, where he knew the settlers, the climate, the terrain, and the Indians. Backed by law and right, he was full of confidence in his own ability to manage his affairs and Mercer's in this milieu.

Wheelock had for some time been waiting for the day when pacification of the Indians would be possible, opening up opportunities for peaceful trading and settlement on the northern frontier. Early in 1845 he had approached Maj. Thomas G. Western, a fellow Mason and current Superintendent of Indian Affairs, in regards to obtaining a concession from the government for a trading post on or near the Indian line.

Western had immigrated to Texas in 1831, settling in Goliad. Wheelock knew him from his association in 1835 with the Texas Army Commissary. Western was also a former member of the Consultation, Texas Ranger, officer in the Texas Army, commissioner to the Karankawa Indians, and a charter member of the Masonic Grand Lodge of the Republic of Texas.

Treachery

Wheelock began his Mercer work by writing to the County Surveyor of Robertson County:

May 5, 1845, Wheelock, Robertson County
To C. C. Taylor Esq.
County Surveyor of Robertson County
Sir: Will you have the goodness to make out a map of that portion of Mercer's Colony west of the Trinity River as is known to
you from actual surveys or by entry for the Texas Advocate. You
will please to accompany it by a Book of Reference numbering
each survey according to the date of the survey or entry, with the
name of certificate, date, No., or kind, and also the agent of location, name, his place of residence when known . . . all of which
I wish to be made formal and certified.
    I shall be able to draw dollars for funds of the Association
by the first of July now in New Orleans to pay your charges.
            Your obd. servant, E.L.R. Wheelock,
            Subagent of the Texas Association West of the T.R.

Trouble with the county surveyor of Robertson County was
not new. He had already claimed that the Mercer contract had
been forwarded to him without name or attestation, and therefore could not be recognized. Now that Mercer needed a good
map showing the boundaries of occupied lands and lands recently granted to the Cherokee so that these could be avoided by
Mercer settlers, the county surveyor saw a way to block the
Mercer Colony.

No documents were forthcoming from Taylor. Wheelock
now wrote again to the county surveyor, asking for the public
documents he needed and to which he had a legal right in order
to lay out his portion of Mercer's Colony.

On May 12, Wheelock received a warning letter from a
friend in Franklin:

Dear Friend,
Doubtless you have heard of a meeting of the citizens of this
place and have perhaps been presented with a duplicate of the

resolutions adopted by the same. You will know (if you have not known) that all this was done by the same person and should any future blame attach to it you will be much troubled to find the guilty person. Therefore to save busy men from the trouble of presenting the nuts and bolts of this, I take this early opportunity of letting yourself and the firm know that I am the man who proposed and assisted in getting up the meeting attended to. Upon what authority the thing was founded I know not. But it was loudly announced that the colony was preparing immediately to commence surveying and would not respect the citizens' rights in that portion of our Frontier. This occasioned a sudden burst of feeling which was displayed in increasing anathemas upon the Executive and the persons interested or connected in any way friendly to it. Therefore feeling solicitous for the peace and feelings of my friends and a desire to preserve civil order, and standing as I did determined never to see rights of my fellow citizens taken away or unjustly invaded, I advised a meeting in order to resolve what course should be pursued that if possible in a civil way any unjust intrusion might be avoided and thereby prevent the fatal results of rashness for a want of cool reflection and deliberations.

This was trouble indeed and smacked of a lynch mob. The colonel tried a little official reassurance, hoping to head off further ill feeling towards the perfectly innocent Mercer, who had absolutely no intention of violating citizens' rights.

Wheelock, May 12, 1845
Messrs Taylor and Others:
Gentlemen:
Through the politeness of Judge Reed I am informed that a report is in circulation that the Texas Association contemplates immediately to commence surveying over the locations and entries made in said colony from this county without any regard to vested rights. I as land agent of said colony have to state for the information of the community that, so far from being the instructions of said association, I have to respect all claims that are legitimate and not have any surveys made except on entirely public domains.
                                        Yours very respectfully, E.L.R.W.

On May 12 Wheelock received a letter from his friend and associate Thomas Johnson stating that he was to be appointed as one of the four Indian agents of the Republic. Three were in place, but the fourth slot had remained unfilled due to a lack of funds. If Wheelock was willing to work without stipend, he could have the post. Such an appointment would allow him to move freely through Indian country, using his expertise in the general pacification. Any trading he wished to do on the side would be perfectly all right with the government. The letter reads:

Dear Wheelock:
I have conversed with Major Western and the President, in relation to the subject matter of your letter.

Owing to the slight difficulty existing between the Comanches and the Delaware, it will be imprudent, just now, to engage in your intended exploration project. From the exertions now working by the government, with an eye to reconciliation, I doubt not that so desirable an object may be attained in a short time. In the meantime, it will be well to suspend operations. Major Western wrote about last Friday, which I presume you have received ere this. I will visit you immediately after court, some two weeks hence.

In token to the agency, from what Houston said to me, I presume a commission will accompany this. The government has already three agents, the public service requires four, but the appropriation of the last Congress is insufficient to allow any additional expense, so that if you accept it, it will be necessary for you to risk some future appropriation. This matter you can think of.

In relation to the first project, Western says it will be necessary to have new passports, from the present executive, and passports for all your associates. I shall have time to arrange all these matters as soon as the Indian difficulty is removed.

Write to Mr. Stroud. I would have written, but have not had time. I am so pressed with the examination of the black catalogue of human inequity that I have scarce time to breath. This will be an apology for not dispatching James sooner. I've not slept for three hours at any one time since last Monday night til last night, Saturday. It was impossible for me to have consulted sooner than yesterday, as it was necessary to confer with the President and Major Western. before I could write understandably.
Your friend, (Judge) Thomas Johnson.

PS—The President's proclamation you now have on this. Please use all your influence to give it efficacy.

On May 15 Wheelock began an attempt to survey for the Mercer Colony, taking with him his two eldest sons, George Ripley and William. He wrote to Dr. Chalmers, the Mercer surveyor, from Torrey's Trading House on the frontier, about eight miles south of present day Waco:

> I send this by William. I find a great deal of hostility to our operations in the Mercer Colony. You had better be careful. I could barely make a demonstration of surveying. I wish you to copy the enclosed and mail it yourself and forward it to the appropriate attorney. And also to answer and perform all the duties of my situation while absent that it is possible for me to substitute you for. Which trouble I will compensate you for satisfactorily. Give my kind regards to Capt. Killough and my daughter.
>   Yours truly. E.L.R. Wheelock.
> PS File the enclosed claim and sign my name to the copy which I send. I have to write on my knees. My health is improving. Ripley sends friendship. If you write to Mercer inform him I am in the woods. If any letters should come to me from him, please write to him to that effect and give him all the information you can for me.

The protest detailed the county surveyor's illegal conduct in withholding documents and filed a confirmation of the Mercer Colony and Wheelock's position in it.

Chambers was in no better case. His attempt to survey and section sixteen townships for immediate settlement under Wheelock's sub-agency encountered opposition led by Thomas I. Smith, captain of the Texas Rangers, and W. R. Hower, who lived on Chambers Creek. When Chambers was instructed to survey the "vacant land not claimed by any person, excepting the claims of the Association" in the neighborhood of Chambers Creek, he was prevented by threats and notices from settlers in the region.

Wheelock consulted Ebenezer Allen, the attorney for the Texas Association, who advised conciliation. When Chambers attempted to establish an office near Melton, he was hounded out and stranded some thirty miles above Franklin. C. C. Taylor, surveyor of Robertson County, declared that no surveyor of General Mercer would ever run a line in his county. Allen advised either an indemnity from the government or a redress by process of a mandamus against the municipal officers.

On May 28, Wheelock wrote to Mercer:

> I start with my son as secretary to my mission with an escort of Indians tomorrow to the heads of the Brazos to accomplish the government's object. In my route I shall examine generally that part of the Association's territory and upon my return anticipate I shall be able to make a report for the benefit of the company of the natural advantages discovered, etc. And also my formal quarterly report of my acts and doings. I am happy to say I have incurred no extra expenses but that of postage for the Association. I wish you to write me fully and in case of anything of importance should occur that requires immediate attention you will have the goodness to address as to the care of J. W. Kellogg Esq., Postmaster of Wheelock, whom I authorized to open and answer during my absence so far as practicable. Accept the assurances of fidelity and that devotion to your interest while I have the pleasure of being your faithful, humble servant.
> E. L. Ripley Wheelock.
> Camp Torrey's Trading House, May 20, 1845

To the Hon. E. Allen:
Sir: Agreeable to my instructions from General Charles F. Mercer, as chief agent for the Texas Association, to inform you and enquire for advice:

I have to report to you that on my way to the colony through Franklin I was informed on the 15th instant by Col. Tyten, commanding the militia, that any attempt by agents of said company to have any surveys performed even on vacant land in this territory set apart for them would be repelled by armed force. I have not been able to obtain plots from the county surveyor. There appears to be a general conspiracy to defeat the operations of every individual that is employed by said company. I have advised B. I. Chambers, the surveyor, to make a demonstration and in case of difficulty to refer it to you during my absence which I presume will be about two months in the woods for the purpose of examining said territory and other objects. Please to direct your letters to me at Wheelock, Robertson County.

Yours respectfully, E. L. Ripley Wheelock, Sub Agent

Worried though he must have been about continued threats to the Mercer enterprise, Wheelock now turned to the other objects which concerned him during his two months in the woods.

CHAPTER 19

SILVER AND STATEHOOD: 1845

Silver Fever

In addition to his new position as sub-agent for General Mercer, his small law practice, his trading with the Indians, and his plantation (in the hands of a tenant), E.L.R. Wheelock had another iron in the fire, more glamorous and more ephemeral. He thought he had found one of the lost silver mines of Texas legend.

Accounts of silver in Texas had always hovered just on the brink of reality, from the seventeenth century tales of a silver hill to hidden mines hinted at by LaSalle's men and eighteenth century rumors of a treasure on the Llano River. When the Spanish established a mission to the Apache on the San Saba, rumor labeled it a cover-up for a fabulous silver mine. Was this the mine Jim Bowie claimed to have found? If so, he died at the Alamo with his lips sealed.

"Shades of dead dreamers," cried the incomparable J. Frank Dobie, "is there somewhere on the Llanos a Hill of Silver, somewhere three suns west of the San Gabriel a ledge of Comanche ore, somewhere about the shattered and silent ruins

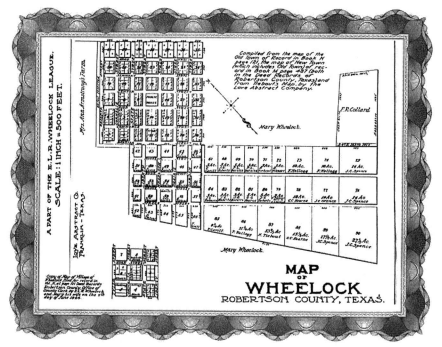

—Courtesy Love Abstract Company, Franklin, Texas

of the Mission San Saba a shaft down to thousands of bars of . . . bullion . . . is there somewhere a Lost Bowie Mine?" [1]

E.L.R. Wheelock thought there was. He had become one of Coronado's Children. Exactly when this silver fever first manifested itself is uncertain, perhaps as early as 1824 during his first exploratory journey of Mexican Texas. Belief that he had found a silver mine could have motivated his later determination to seek his fortune in Texas.

Wheelock's special relationship with the Indians is spotlighted in a letter he wrote on May 28, 1845, to an unknown recipient, reflecting in secret his confidence that he had located such a mine.

I wrote you last night after dark but the Delaware not starting I now write you again. If the Caddos are going near the point you wish to go, you will be perfectly safe with them. You had better go on. Mark your spot with R.T.W. with the date with pick near a rock, say north or south, east or west or to the point where the

sun rises or sets on the day you make it. Let measurements be
taken to some known stream with a lariat or rope which you bring
and let Ripley make them. You and Jack (Harry) act as Measure-
men. Make some figures such as you fancy, the North Star or the
sun will answer, for the corners from the beginning which should
be for 2 S or 10,000 N one way and 5,000 the other, as the case
is. Be careful to keep hidden as are the Indian people.

If you cannot get with Winkler now or wait for Capt.
[Benjamin] Stout [Indian Agent] without too much trouble, never
mind. You must accomplish your object. But under no circumstances move without having the protection of the Jose Maria band
[Chief of the Anadarko Tribe]. . . . me they will lead . . . in perfect
safety. I . . . will make the Cherokee Village my headquarters.
Tomorrow I make start down home to be gone 16 days and bring
up some more supplies, hoping that Red Bear [Caddo tribe] will
return by that time so that I can obtain a peep at the other point
and load back with something that will make a show. I know where
to find it.

Keep the Cherokees in good spirits for they are faithful. We
can be their friend. Tell Jack Ivy to not give up ship. All will be
made good to him. I have never told you all, but intend to as
soon as we are in the woods so you have no idea of the extent. If
you get with Winkler, he will aid muscular Ripley in marking the
spot, and he has verbal instructions from me.

That is the letter of a successful prospector, or one right on
the brink of success. Red Bear knew where the silver was, and so
did Wheelock.

Evidently, he had already brought small amounts of silver
home. Annette Killough's grandson, Roy De Lafayette Killough,
remembered that she had often spoken of sterling silver tea-
spoons, marked with an *M* for Mary, which her father had caused
to be crafted in Philadelphia from ore taken from his own mines.

But a large-scale mining effort had to await Indian pacification. In 1845 Wheelock finally applied to the Texas government for a license to mine. Dr. Anson Jones, secretary of state,
replied to Wheelock's application:

Sir:
I have the pleasure of acknowledging the receipt of your communication addressed to this department under the date of 21st.

inst. with view to perpetuate the testimony of rights and privileges which you may have acquired by reason of certain discoveries made by you in 1834 and 1835.

Your communication will be laid before His Excellency, the President, for his consideration immediately upon his return to the Seat of Government. In the meantime this department is prepared to grant you, whenever it may be desired, a license under the provisions of the Act of Congress entitled An Act to Incorporate the Colorado Mining Company and other companies for similar purposes, approved 17 January 1843, provided the mines discovered by you be situated south of the Indian line established by the Seventh Congress. If they be situated, however, north of this line, the license should come from the Executive Department.

Wheelock answered, laying forth his ideas for the betterment of tribes within whose territory his mineral claim might lie:

Sir:

In reply to the communication of the Department of State dated the 8th inst. the undersigned has the honor to observe that from the best information he has been able to acquire of the locality of the Indian Territory, he is induced to believe that his discovery of mineral copper is within its bounds and the supposed silver mines at or near the south easterly line, but he had to remark that he knew of no such territory until lately.

For the purpose of obviating all difficulties which might possibly arise with government in reference to the pending negotiations with the Indians, he takes the liberty of asking permission to suggest to the Hon. Secretary the propriety of making it in the interest of the Indians in the immediate neighborhood, say Delaware, Shawnee and Caddos, to have it worked by the following inducements:

First they shall receive a percent out of the net proceeds to be applied to the purposes of teaching them the useful arts under the direction of the government. Secondly, they shall agree for a reservation of not less than four leagues for mining purposes in addition to my head right labor which I conceive I have a right to have surveyed upon opening of the mines.

Thirdly, that a commissioner shall be appointed by the government to locate and mark the reservation, the same being paid for his services by the undersigned. Fourthly, the undersigned shall be allowed to erect sufficient buildings for defense introduced by paying [here a line is obliterated] merchandise as may be necessary for his workmen and to supply the wants of those Indians immediately in the vicinity under the contract of the government.

The undersigned is confidently informed that the foregoing arrangement or something of a similar nature would not only be beneficial to the Indians by identity of interest but would result in a happy extension of the government's views to the object of Christian Philanthropy.

With sentiments of respect, I have the honor to be etc.
E.L.R. Wheelock

The impoverished government, although concerned with sealing yet another Indian treaty, was immediately interested in Wheelock's prospects. He received the following letter:

August 20, 1844
Washington (on-the-Brazos)
Dear Wheelock:
Your favor of the 17th inst is before me. I have seen and conversed with the Sec. of State, pretty much at length, in relation to our matter, also with the Sec. of War. They are willing, nay, anxious, to further our views and will have the matter specially attended to in the treaty. Dr. Hill thinks that the section of county you refer to will not fall into the Indian boundary, but if there should be any probability of its doing so will make the reservation. He will be present at the treaty. The Pres. will probably attend . . . If you are not mistaken in the character of the mineral, I mean its quantity and richness, it presents the first prospect for Fortune in the world. I would not exchange it for the richest mine in Mexico. If our Indian difficulties are settled this fall, we must commence operating forthwith. By establishing a trading post with a good supply of merchandize, our goods will put up all the necessary buildings, build block houses, furnaces, and all, pay our hands, meet all the expenses out of the profits, leaving the Capital Stock wholly untouched. Nothing need be apprehended from Mexico now at all events. I write advisedly. . .

I urged your claims to the Superintendency of Indian

Affairs when the Sec. of State approved, which proves the entire incompetency of Austin. I spoke in flattering terms of your qualifications, and, I must say, of the Indian character. etc. IF we realize these matters . . . we shall be in town with our pocket full of rocks. I start on Thursday for the circuit, will be with you early in October. If this matter of ours should succeed, I will resign so as to devote my whole time to it.

Your friend, Thomas Johnson. (Judge)

The Indian Line was drawn roughly east-west along the row of trading posts established by the government to supply the tribes, about level with or a little above the present city of Waco.

On October 9, 1944, the Republic signed a treaty with Texas's Indian tribes at Tawakoni Creek, near present-day Mexia. Article Seven confirmed the establishment of trading houses along the line to supply the Amerinds, who promised in return to trade only with Texas government representatives, and, in Article Sixteen, to treat prospectors for minerals well. The president of Texas promised to send missionaries to the Indians to teach them not only the advantages of the Christian religion but also of western civilization, including useful trades. Texas promised to appoint good and honest men as Indian agents and traders.

Red Bear signed for the Caddos, Jose Maria for the Anadarkos, and St. Louis for the Delawares. All three were special friends of Colonel Wheelock. John F. Torrey, whose trading post was nearby, signed as a witness.

Wheelock's company, the North West Mining Company, was officially launched on February 3, 1845, with himself as its first president. Edwin Morehouse, now authorized to sell shares in the company, was one of the three commissioners who signed the treaty at Torrey's Trading House and a New Yorker who arrived in Texas by way of Missouri in 1826. A Republic of Texas senator, he had also served as adjutant general of the Texas Army and brigadier general of militia. His association with Wheelock's mining company gave it considerable credibility.

Where was Wheelock's mine? Geologically speaking, silver and copper mines could best be found in the Llano Uplift, a boundary where the stratified rocks of the eastern United States come into contact with the crystalline masses of the Rocky

Mountains. Here the batholith known familiarly as Enchanted Rock raises the tip of its granite vastness. C. E. Eckhardt explained: "Granite uplifts like the one called the Llano Uplift . . . are the primary source of mineral wealth—gold, silver . . . copper, precious jewels, in the world."[2] Wheelock must have known his way around this storied area as well as any white man.

Wheelock's guide was Red Bear, a Delaware. Transportation was slow and the Comanche still dangerous west of the Colorado River, where the Central Mineral District is located. Yet if the mines were on or inside the Indian line, they must have been north of Waco. The Mercer Grant, which Wheelock was at this time exploring, also began north of Waco. Some place in or near present-day Brown County, about seventy-five miles west of the Mercer Grant, is perhaps a reasonable guess as to the location of Wheelock's find. "Good paying ore has been taken out (of this area) by geologists in the twentieth century," according to Eckhardt.[3]

Later in the same month Wheelock wrote to General Morehouse, as an officer of the North West Mining Company:

> My Dear General:
> I now write in relation to our copper and silver mines. I shall start up for the purpose of making surveys about the 15th of next month. To tranquilize the natives I have procured four hundred dollars worth of goods which I hope will enable me to effect my object. I expect to return with one or two mule loads of specimens, one of which I desire you to operate with and the other for our friend Judge Johnson.
>
> Mrs. W. sends her kind respects and has always a plate for Gen. Morehouse. My health is rather poor yet, but improving. No news. W.

Very likely Wheelock was already suffering from the malady which would take his life two years later.

The Stroud brothers, who were also involved in the mining venture, wrote from the frontier:

> Rosa Mas Village, 29 May 1845
> Dear Col:
> The Delaware have waited til I have held a meeting with Rosa. He

has shown me the Comanche trails. Perhaps we will go to the Fork of the Brazos where he will unite with [obliterated] and explain to me. He has as yet said nothing of his doing, neither have I used him yet. He is displeased with the President. I am somewhat discouraged about his going. He will go or send some men with us to the Town, ten miles above here . . . feel assured if he will not go, I will then have my Comanches and influence them to being more kindly.

It is necessary for you to be somewhere up country for I am determined to stay for at least two mining operations. We shall have to be here for at least two months. You can stay at the - or on Trinity or where you please until we see you. We will succeed in part if not all. We shall buy some mules to pack and proper things will be given for presents. Stroud M.[4]

Annexation Games

Politically, the pot was still boiling. Most Texans again wished to join the United States. Gazing into a clouded crystal ball, the Texas Senate promised America that "Texas would form an iron band which would hold the Union together."[5]

Finally, after almost ten years of wrangling, the U.S. House of Representatives passed a bill admitting Texas to the Union as a full state, allowing her to keep all her public lands, giving her the power to split into four more states, and giving the U. S. president the power to negotiate if these terms were not pleasing to Texas. Texas had until January 1, 1846, to accept or decline the honor. After the U.S. Senate approval, cannons boomed in Washington, D.C., to welcome the twenty-eighth state, but Texas had yet to answer.

The last Texas Congress settled down to write a state constitution, with its peculiarly Texan items of separate property rights for married women, the homestead law, an anticorporation law, and a provision that no minister of the Gospel could serve in the Texas legislature. On October 13, in a very light turnout, the citizens of Texas voted 4,000 to 200 in favor of annexation to the United States of America. They also approved their new State Constitution. The Texas Congress had still to speak.

Colonel Wheelock continued to grapple with the fruits of his unpopular association with the Mercer Colony. The first petty manifestation of resentment came in the form of intercepted mail. In March a business letter from Illinois complained that many previous letters had remained unanswered. Wheelock had never received them. From now on, instead of trusting his letters to the post, he chose a private path through an intermediary in New Orleans, adding, "All curse Mercer's Colony."

Wheelock's desire to proceed to the frontier was further delayed by Indian and bureaucratic troubles. Western, as Superintendent of Indian Affairs in Washington-on-the-Brazos, now wrote:

> Dear Sir:
> In the line of my duty I have to apprise you that a slight misunderstanding exists between the Comanche and the Delaware, and that the Comanche Chief Pah-hah-yuco (Chief of the Penateka or Honey Eaters Comanche) has notified this Govt that no white man or Delaware would be safe in that country until this difficulty should satisfactorily be arranged. They express themselves in the most friendly terms and decidedly inclined to peace, but say they cannot control their men, as foolish young men in their rage are determined to avenge the death of their companions, who were murdered by some bad Delaware from the United States. I regret that it is out of my power to grant your request as regards an interpreter.
>
> Respectfully yr. obt. servt,
T. G. Western, Sup. Ind. Afrs.
>
> They will not seek to molest our people, but should a small party of our men throw themselves in the path of these deranged despoilers, they the chiefs will not they say be answerable for consequences. I would not create alarm in your breast. I would merely discharge my duty as a fellow citizen and as a public officer by affording you the best information in my possession, and at your own sound judgement dictate your cause touching your own welfare and that of your companions.[6]

Two days later Western wrote to L. H. Williams, agent at Indian Post No. 2, stating that Wheelock was coming, enjoining on him the strictest compliance with regulations and to be present at all times to receive the Comanches if they came. The government was of course very anxious to see peace made, but Williams had his own agenda and would later play a key role in bringing about Wheelock's downfall as Indian commissioner.

Domesticity

While great affairs unfolded in the two Washingtons, small affairs continued to occupy folks at home. By 1845 Wheelock was the best known town in Central Texas. "It was on the main stage and mail routes; ox-wagons passed over its streets and great herds of cattle were driven from the town to distant markets. Cotton was loaded in the fields and consigned to ports on the Texas coast and in Europe. Teamsters returning from Galveston and Houston brought building materials and store stock to the merchants. State Street was lined with good homes. The people had visions of greatness for their prairie."[7]

But visions are in the eye of the beholder. The private journals of John C. Roberts give a mixed facetious and admiring description of the town. "Wheelock is a ragged, dirty little up-country town to a stranger fresh from the states, but it is a pretty fair place to a trained Texan."[8] . . . "The residences there appear to be connecting links between a rail fence and a corn crib . . . Wheelock is a business place and Texas is a great country and bids fair to become THE state of the Union."[9]

Colonel Wheelock had been ill most of the winter, probably with the mercury poisoning which weakened him during the last years of his life and ultimately killed him.[10] But, misguided though it was, he had medical care which was state of the art for his time and place. Dr. John Cameron had just arrived in Wheelock from Scotland and was said to have been educated at Edinburgh University itself.

There were now Methodist, Baptist, and Presbyterian congregations in the neighborhood. The latter was the faith of the Prickett family. What Mary Wheelock may have thought about religion was not recorded. Unchurched by the wilderness, perhaps she did not greatly regret the loss of formal worship, although she may have missed the social nexus.

But in the Wheelock family a strain of religious piety ran strong, skipping a generation here and there but breaking through again as the family tree branched outward. The founder of Dartmouth College had it and Colonel Wheelock's sister had it, as her letters clearly show. Although his family may not have known it, Colonel Wheelock had it too, hidden for a very long time and about to emerge, to the consternation of his protestant family.

Bedridden, he composed essays for the newspaper of his good friend Mr. Miller:

> I take the liberty of forwarding the effusions of a leisure moment of convalescence only after a protracted illness this winter. If you think they are worthy of preserving you can correct them and insert them in your paper. But don't criticize like an Edinburgh reviewer. I am truly happy to hear of your success in business. My health has prevented my attending to the obtaining of subscriptions, . . . but as it returns I shall exert myself in your behalf. I shall trouble myself no more with posey but will send you some time hence other matters and things. Be good enough to write when you have leisure as I assure you it would afford great pleasure to a sick friend to hear of your doings.
>
> I am truly yours, E. L. Ripley Wheelock.

On December 29 a decade of hopes and fears culminated in Washington City as James Knox Polk signed the bill which merged Texas into the United States of America, fulfilling a wish expressed by the Republic in its first election in 1836, and repudiated and revived so many times since.

But the Lone Star flag was not to come down just yet.

CHAPTER 20

MERCER COLONY PART II: MAY-DECEMBER 1845

Indian Commissioner

By the middle of 1845 E.L.R. Wheelock and Robertson County had come to the parting of the ways, the former thoroughly embroiled in combating the latter's insurrection against the Mercer Colony. "Unfortunately for Mercer, his colony lay across the path of sunburned, weather-beaten squatters, whose political and economic philosophy was shaped by a frontier environment."[1] These squatters cared little for law and were determined to block Wheelock's attempt to colonize Mercer's grant.

The convention called by President Jones for July 4, 1845, in Austin to consider annexation by the United States of America and write a new state constitution temporarily saved the Mercer Colony. The Texas legislature was under heavy local pressure to cancel Mercer's grant. However, J. Pinckney Henderson, afterwards Texas's first American governor, pointed out that state nullification of the contract would ignore the U.S. Constitution fiat that no state should pass any law impairing the obligation of a contract. This was no time to defy the U.S. Constitution. Mercer troubles were temporarily set aside.

Wheelock, hearing the good news, was just starting out on a foray north and had written to his employer:

General C. F. Mercer, My Dear Sir:
I start in one hour. I shall examine closely the natural advantages of the colony. In the meantime I authorized S. W. Kellogg Esq to represent me in so far as practicable and to watch the moves of our enemy.

A month later, he was home again with good tidings. He wrote:

July 8, 1845 Washington-on-the-Brazos
To General Charles F. Mercer
My Dear Sir: . . . I returned from my excursion through the northwest part of the Mercer Grant, having ascended the Brazos to the neighborhood of the Comanche Peak, having found a desirable section of the country upon Nolan's River combining many important advantages such as good soil, water, timber, hydraulic power to a great extent, and appearance of mineral wealth, all of which will in due season be made the subject of another letter.

Wheelock was in the capital to confer with Ebenezer Allen, attorney to the Mercer Colony and Texas secretary of state, asking for official sanction as a Indian trader and confiding his personal ideas on Indian policy:

July 13, 1845, Washington-on-the-Brazos
To the Hon. Sec. of State, Sir:
The ideas which you had the goodness to advance in our casual conversation of yesterday in relation to the true policy of government with the Red men, that of paralyzing their natural propensities for war by adopting a system of benevolence and philanthropy in the extension of the useful arts and the distribution of moral and religious instruction to the different bands, have struck me forcibly. For the last twenty years I have been induced to believe it to be the only true course of an enlightened government when the savages are not the aggressors.

If the government should conceive that the object within intimated should be worthy of consideration, it will afford me great pleasure to facilitate their wishes without any remuneration other than such as can be afforded in the Indian Trade, with proper checks and securities.

With highest sentiment of respect,
I have the honor to be your humble
Servant, E.L.R. Wheelock[2]

The permissions to trade and to act as agent without pay were taken for granted, but it was not until mid-July that Wheelock's anticipated appointment as Indian commissioner arrived:

July 14, 1845,
In the name and by the authority of the Republic of Texas,
To all to whom these presents shall come, Greeting.
Know ye, that I, Anson Jones, President of said Republic of Texas, reposing special trust and full confidence in the honor and patriotism, fidelity and capacity of Col. E.L.R. Wheelock, have constituted and appointed, and do by these presents constitute and appoint him the said Col. E.L.R. Wheelock to the office of Indian Commissioner for the purpose of cultivating friendly intercourse with all the various tribes of Indians residing within the limits of said republic, and to induce them to encourage the extension of the useful arts as well as the cultivation of moral and religious principles and to make a treaty with them for that purpose. The said Wheelock is also empowered to make the proper locations that are contemplated by the 15th and 26th articles of the Indian treaty signed at Tawakoni Creek Oct. 9th 1844 for the furtherance of his objects and for his own benefit, which is considered the only compensation the said Wheelock has a right to require for his services in the premises.
In testimony whereof, I have cause the Great Seal of the Republic to be hereunto affixed.
Done at Washington this 14th day of July, in the year of our Lord one thousand eight hundred and forty-five, and of the Independence of Texas the tenth.

Anson Jones.[3]

Also on July 14, President Jones wrote to A-cah-quash:

My Brother,
I have heard your talk with Col. Wheelock in Council at Tawakoni
Hills last month. . . Col. Wheelock will take this talk to you and
he will tell you all I wish you to do. He is a good man and my
friend, and the friend of the Indians. I want you and all the
Indians to listen to his words. He will go with his son to see Pah-
hah-yuco. If convenient I wish you to go with him. I hear there
will be a great Council to the Choctaw Nation next month. I wish
you to attend it and to tell the Chiefs.[4]

He wrote similarly to Pah-hah-yuco, of the Honey Eater
Comanche.
Wheelock now hoped to combine another trip north of the
Indian line for the government with Mercer Colony business. By
the end of July Wheelock was again at the Tawakoni Hills. He
wrote:

July 27, 1845
Camp near Tawakoni Hills
To Major T. G. Western
My dear friend:
I am now on my way to camp with the object and in effect the
wishes of government in relation to the 15th and 26th articles of
Indian Treaty (with my son) and hope I shall be able to write you
fully in a short time that I have accomplished the wishes of the
president in treaty making. . . .
                                                    E.L.R. Wheelock[5]

Five days later he was able to write to Western:

Trinity River, August 1, 1845
To Thomas G. Western, Supt Indian Affairs
Sir:
I herewith transmit to the proper department the Invoice contemplated by the 10 section of the Indian Law of 1842. I have to
report that everything is progressing harmoniously and rapidly
at this point and great praise and credit is due to Judge S. for his

great exertions. I start on my mission to Keechi Village today. In the meantime I have appointed C. M. Winkler Esq. agent pro tem by virtue of my authority as Indian Commissioner, feeling that the public peace and serenity required it. He will remain at this point until I return from Peasika, whose delegates accompany me. . . I am sir yours very respectfully, E.L.R. Wheelock.[6]

The full events of this dramatic and fateful trip are best expressed in Wheelock's letter of September 20, 1845, to the Honorable William G. Cooke, Secretary of State:

Sir:

In obedience to instructions received from His Excellency, the President, I beg leave to report to you that during your and the Superintendent of Indian Affairs' absence from the seat of Government in the month of July last, that, in addition to the commission of Indian Agent without pay, I received the appointment as Indian Commissioner from the Government and was specially directed to repair to the Keeches, Wacos, Tawakani, and Wichita bands and to the Comanche Chief Pianca in order to communicate the President's talk of peace, etc., and other objects for the interest of the Government.

On my route I went by the way of Capt. Thomas I. Smith's dwelling, and reported my entrance into the Indian Country, he commanding the Rangers in Viesca. On my arrival at the Trading Post No. 1, I ascertained satisfactorily that there was a regular traffic carried on by a few individuals who lived in the Cross Timbers (by means of Arkansas Indians) in ardent spirits with Indians within our territory. I immediately took measures to prevent it by temporarily appointing an agent to remain immediately at Post No. 1 until properly advised from the Government.

On the 8th of August I arrived at Keechis, Tawakoni, and Waco Villages on the Brazos with my son, George Ripley Wheelock, and a muleteer and in company with William Richie and Jack Ivy, who were taking goods to the Comanches from Post No. 1, and had agreed to interpret the talk from the President, etc. Immediately on my arrival my son, the muleteer, Richie, and Ivy were directed to camp on the opposite side of the river and I was conducted to the strangers' wigwam of the Principal Keechis

Chief. Upon his ascertaining that I was a Texian, he became enraged and attempted to take my saddle bags, etc.

Instantly the whole village strung their bows and mounted their feathers as harbingers of war, then placed a guard around me, keeping me in close custody about twenty hours without any nourishment except water. A short distance away they were dancing a war dance of savage fury. Circumstances led me to believe that their object was to intimidate for the purpose of obtaining a large quantity of presents. In this they were disappointed. I at last succeeded in getting them to send for Jack Ivy to interpret for us. This permission was obtained through the friendly offices of a Caddo Indian who resided in the United States.

Upon Jack Ivy's appearance, I ascertained that since the Indians had sent their talk to the president of which I was the bearer from near Tawakani Hills, that they had become dissatisfied with the Texas government, in consequence, as they alleged, of the Texian Officer having endeavored to induce a band of Comanche Indians to commence hostilities against their village as a retaliation for the murders committed on the Colorado by the Comanches themselves. The Texian Officer said that he had authority to do so, and they called in their braves, who were on their way to Mexico, to protect their wives and children and were to scout in a few days for a frontier settlement for plunder.

By observing that I was half Indian and half Whiteman representing Texas, which was a part of the United States, I succeeded in getting them to go to council, which was represented by nearly all of the Keechis, Tawakanis, Wacos, and Wichita chiefs. They listened to the president's talk, said it was good if true, but they were dissatisfied because Sam Houston promised them that he would fix the time and point at which they were to receive their presents, not Anson Jones.

I succeeded in allaying their unkind feeling by promising to write to the president on the subject and they agreed to steal no more horses for ninety days, the time allowed to get an answer from the government. This object was accomplished without making any pledges. I smoked the pipe of peace with the principal Wichita chief upon his pledging himself to return all property in their hands when demanded by a proper officer.

I have no doubt that my timely arrival has prevented cruelty and blood being shed on our Border.

From the village Jack Ivy and William Richie were dispatched to Pravia with the President's talk and were successful in the object of the government. He, Pravia, expressing an anxious desire to cultivate a friendly intercourse, particularly with the whites when he ascertained we were shortly to be part of the United States. He was willing that the Brazos River should be made the dividing line.

On my return to Post No. 1, I was accompanied by seven chiefs of the Keechi, Wacos, Tawakoni, and Wichita bands.

I was fully aware that their sole object was for the purpose of begging and was properly impressed that upon my success in procuring such articles as they wanted depended their faith, and the temporary security of the frontier families. . . I deemed it advisable for the interest of the government to purchase a few necessary articles from Isaac C. Spencer Esq., trader at Post Number 1, which I did on the account of the Government.

Wheelock's assertion that he was half Indian and half white man referred of course not to ancestry but to sympathies. Unfortunately for Wheelock, one month before he wrote thus, L. H. Williams (agent at Post #2) had written to Thomas G. Western at the Indian Agency, accusing the colonel and Mr. Spencer (agent at Post #1) of improper conduct, specifically, of informing the Indians that the coming council was to be held not at Post No. 2 but at Post No. 1 on the Trinity River. This, Williams complained, would confuse the Indians. For some reason, the imputed offense was considered heinous, probably because it offered a chance to impeach a Mercer man.

Williams also stated that Wheelock had "gone up among the Indians and intends to use all his influence to bring the Indians in to the Trinity Post No. 1 to Council. For the truth however of these reports I am not able to vouch, but conclude from the smoke that there must be some fire."[7] The fire had been lit by Mercer Colony opponents, seizing their chance to get rid of Mercer's sub-agent.

On September 5 Western replied to Williams stating:

I hope the rumors you have heard concerning the conduct of Col. Wheelock may not be true. I cannot get my own consent to believe that white folks much less one such as he would wilfully mislead the Indians or attempt to deceive them, as to the point

where the council will be held or attempt to obstruct the views of
the government or counteract the orders of its officers. I think
there has been some mistake.[8]

There had been mistakes. Wheelock's deportment, as
usual, was correct but tactless. His connection with the Mercer
Colony, his sympathy for the Indians, his interruption of the illegal trade in whiskey through Post No. 1—all combined to turn
the frontiersmen against him. It is more difficult to understand
why Anson Jones was so ready to believe their libels. Perhaps his
foot was in the anti-Mercer camp. At any rate, on Jones's orders,
Western was obliged to dismiss his friend from his brief office as
Indian Commissioner.

Wheelock's report to Western concerning these events, in
which he pointed out that the Indians were not nearly so pacified as Texas thought, that they were being abused by Anglos
selling them forbidden whiskey, and that his coming had averted
a serious incident, was either suppressed or discounted.

The Waiting Game

Still, the Mercer party was not yet ready to lie down and
play dead. In July and August the noble and naive General
Mercer visited Texas himself, and went home persuaded that all
difficulties had been ironed out.[9]

Dr. Rowlett, who had been having no trouble east of the
Trinity River but was beginning to hear disquieting tales, then
approached Colonel Wheelock:

Dear Sir:
Today I received a communication from New Orleans via
Galveston addressed to me by General C. Hillman in which he
says he has received two very discouraging letters from you on the
subject of his colonial grant, and he prays me to open a correspondence with you on the subject . . . Yesterday I was in company
with Mr. James E. Patton, a surveyor employed last winter to do
some work in Mercer's Colony between the Navasota and the
Trinity Rivers. I had heard nothing for some time from Mr. Fuller
and hearing while in the colony last month that there was a vio-

lent opposition to the grant and that Capt. Smith and others had prevented the progress of this work to be done . . . I fear all is not right.

Wheelock continued to work for the colony and promote immigration, advertising in American newspapers. In September, he wrote to Mercer:

Wheelock, Sept 29, 1845
To Gen. Charles F. Mercer
My dear sir:
My last communication was made to you some time in July from Washington. Since that time I have been taking a general tour through the Association's grant on the west side of the Trinity River. I arrived home on the 15 Instant from my tour having traveled and as far as the Keechis, toward the Waco and Wichita villages 160 miles N 60 West from Dallas [near present day Mineral Wells] traversing the country in various directions, examining closely the upper and lower crops and timbers of the southwest fork of the Trinity N bound river and the Brazos River 150 miles above the Comanche Peak, a topographic map of which will be shortly made out and transmitted. I will remark that I found several sections of the country admirably situated for farming purposes and a geological and mineralogical assessment will accompany it.
    I could not from the situation of Public Hostility towards the colonial contractors, fanned into a flame by a few disgruntled public demagogues, without the hazard of my life and property issue a certificate publicly. Although my being your agent has positively prostrated my influence with the ignorant, vulgar, and designing, you may rest assured that I shall do all my feeble ability will allow me for the interest of the Association as an honest man. I have opened a Land and General Agency office at my town, "Wheelock," and have made a branch of it in the colony under the superintendence of the Rev. Mr. Byess, who is secretly watching the movements of the enemy and taking notes for the use of the Texas Association. I was thrown from my mule about 15 days ago and am yet unable to write, My health has improved much this summer.

P. S.
I am now enabled to give a topographical sketch from the natural advantages and I believe a pretty correct estimate of the mineral wealth, which is considerable. I shall prepare a formal report of my tour for the association and will have forwarded to you in a few weeks. The country is more valuable than I anticipated.

Whatever Wheelock's hopes may have been, the prospect of American citizenship did nothing to right the wrongs suffered by the Mercer Colony under the Republic of Texas. After the adoption of the new state constitution, Taylor, the county surveyor for Robertson County, recorded every maverick application for land handed in, regardless of Mercer's prior claim. Wheelock observed that various members of the Constitutional Convention from Robertson and other counties were taking out large illegal grants within the Mercer Colony, naming Irion, Rusk, and Edward Tarrant. In Wheelock's opinion, nothing could be done on the Mercer grant "until the judicial arm of the United States" should be properly extended.[10] Dr. Rowlett agreed. He wrote:

It is certain that officers of the government are to be found among the foremost in the mob resisting the laws of the land. Such men are too corrupted to merit further remark, but I hope that when Uncle Sam sees the laws faithfully executed that such persons may come to a sense of their duty to the government and to themselves. . . . That they should be able to get up an excitement against one of the best projects for settling the country ever devised by the government is to me matter of astonishment. But so it is, and if this selfish class of our country are to locate and sell the whole of the public domain they will to an injurious extent retard the settlement of the country for many years.

Of his dangerous contact with the Indians Wheelock wrote to Mercer:

I learned from their chiefs that they had made a treaty (with Texas) but that no line had definitely been settled, and the Indian Agents had instructed them to seize all persons above the

Thomas I. Smith Road or the road leading from Dallas to the Falls of the Brazos, and that they were determined to do so.

After my explaining my official capacity, and that we were Americans as well as Texans, they were willing with Pianca, the principal Comanche Chief, to enter into a treaty with me, and I was fully authorized. I mention this to prove that, so far from being at peace with this government, that they were hostile and were in the act of coming together upon the settlements in the Association's colony but were prevented by my timely arrival and the Wichita's conciliator, who had never made overtures toward peace with Texas. They swore I was the first Texian who had ever entered their villages. These facts, which can be proved by my son, Mr. Wm. Rupe, and myself, conclusively show that the change of government only has preserved the frontier and only since August 8 last.

During the months of July, August, and September I traveled 2700 miles within the limits of the association's grant and west of the Trinity river, exploring and noting the natural and local advantages of every sector.

. . . Even in the face of opposition the number in my Book of Contracts is equal to 21 families and applications by letter equal today thirty more.

I am assured that nothing can be done until the United States government takes over and enforces the law. . . and that in such a manner as not to come in contact with the selfish interest of demagogues who lead the Ignus Vulgus, that powers will give the Association their legitimate rights which any disinterested Texian of honor admits they deserve . . . .

Signed E. L. Ripley Wheelock

In fear of any enemy interest, I send this privately. Dr. Rowlett sent me a letter which was stopped at the Post Office for nearly two months.

He had yet to learn that nothing now could save the Mercer Colony or himself.

CHAPTER 21

THE HOUND OF HEAVEN: 1846

Change of Command

During the winter of 1845-46, Col. E.L.R. Wheelock had been chronically ill again at his home in Wheelock. It was a bad time for him to be out of circulation. Early in the new year he wrote to Major Western, the loyal friend who had supported his appointment as Indian commissioner and dismissed him from that position reluctantly on the orders of President Jones. Wheelock was worried that Western might believe some allegations, which had been floated by enemies of the Mercer Colony. He wrote:

Wheelock, Robertson County, Jan. 23, 1846
To Major Western:
My Dear Sir:
I am hardly able to write from my protracted illness, which is the only apology I have to offer for not writing an old friend. I am truly sorry that when you passed up the country you did not call upon me, although I was partially insensible of objects around me. Since my recovery I have learned with regret that design or perhaps interest of a few designing land speculators were deter-

mined to make me as many foes as possible. I was and am yet the agent of the Mercer Colony. This alone was sufficient to (cause them) to endeavor by every means in their power, even by the subversion of Truth, to destroy my influence in the country. They have failed, for Truth is powerful and will prevail. I am conscious that I never had any other but kind feelings toward you. . . . I believe that my communications to you (which were in due form) were suppressed at the Post House for objects unknown to me. I have delayed from my extreme illness to wait upon you personally. I forward my report so far as it relates to your concerns.

I leave it in your hands to do justice and am satisfied. If my health improves as it has for a few days, I hope to have the pleasure of seeing you during this session of the Legislature.

Mrs. Wheelock requests that you will accept the salutations of friendship, while I ask you to believe that I remain yours in the bonds of Masonic love, E.L.R. Wheelock.[1]

On February 19, at a ceremony on the capitol steps, President Anson Jones declared that "the Republic of Texas is no more," and with his own hands lowered the Lone Star flag. As the Texas banner came down, its staff shattered, as if loath to bear other colors. The star spangled banner was raised on a temporary pole.

Texas was now officially the twenty-eighth state of the United States of America, as in some secret way she had always been.

Annexation made little difference on the domestic scene. Mary Prickett Wheelock's father had been dead for some time and now she learned of her mother's passing. For being matriarch of the Texas branch of her family, which included not only her own children, son-in-law, and grandchild, but also her brother George, his wife and child, and her husband's widowed sister-in-law and niece now living in Wheelock, she received her share of money and real property from her parents' estate, but no memento, no dish, or second-best bed. She had been away too long.

Wheelock grandchildren had been hard to come by. George Ripley's first marriage had been childless. William and David were still bachelors. Annette, losing one husband to yel-

low fever and another to border warfare, had endured the death
of her first baby at the age of three weeks and her second and
third (Killough twins born in 1842) before their second birth-
days. She must have felt singled out for grief. When Nancy Jane
Killough was born on August 14, 1845, she became a much cher-
ished child. By 1846 she was the apple of her grandparents' eye.

His health seeming to improve and the Mercer Colony
crumbling, Colonel Wheelock was now determined to visit the
Eastern seaboard in search of capital for the development of his
North West Mining Company. He also wished to settle once and
for all his financial affairs in Illinois, where he still owned substantial property. Accordingly, he sold 250 acres of land to his
neighbor Cavitt Armstrong, paid up his bills, and settled his affairs in anticipation of a year's absence. As was the custom of the
day, he began to collect letters of introduction from friends who
had connections in the East. They were addressed to prominent
men in Washington City, Baltimore, Philadelphia, New York,
and Boston, and came from Brenham, Houston, and Galveston.

As he prepared for travel, one last war came his way, one in
which he was too old and too ill to participate, a Mexican War
perhaps inevitable as the United States fumbled for its new
southern and western borders.

Sometime in April 1846, a new company of Rangers was
formed at "a little place called Wheelock." Buck Barry, the or-
ganizer, recalled that they "killed two large beeves, barbecued
them, and set out for the scene of the action."[2] William
Wheelock had been too young to participate in the Texas
Revolution. Now his turn had come and Mary Wheelock waved
her second son good-bye as he went off to war.

Company K, composed of personnel recruited primarily at
Wheelock, was mustered into federal service on July 18, 1846, as
part of the First Texas, most famous of the Ranger units of the
Mexican War. On August 30 they joined the main army in China,
Mexico, and later took part in the Battle of Monterrey. William
H. Wheelock, age twenty-one, was third sergeant in this com-
pany under Capt. Eli Chandler and Col. John C. Hays and part
of the First Regiment of Texas Mounted Riflemen.

In June of the following year David P. Wheelock would be
mustered in as a private in Company I, recruited in Rusk County

by Capt. Isaac Ferguson. Three other members of Mary's family fought in the Mexican War: her nephews George W. Prickett, Thomas Jefferson Prickett, and John Adams Prickett, the latter serving as a first lieutenant in Company E, Second Regiment of Illinois Volunteers, under Colonel Bissell. After John's left shoulder was shattered by a bullet in the Battle of Buena Vista, he was sent home to Illinois and would be convalescing there when Colonel Wheelock made his last visit to his wife's family.

As the Mexican War wore on, Wheelock continued to gather together the necessaries for his trip east. General Morehouse wrote:

> May 16, 1846, Trading House
>
> Dear Col.
>
> I will be with you in a few days as I intend to leave this place for Wheelock Prairie tomorrow. The Treaty has been concluded. I refer you to Captain Killough for the news in general. No doubt you are all ready for our contemplated trip. There is no doubt but that we shall succeed. My regards to your family. Capt. K. is about leaving.
>
> I am anxious to arrive in Washington before the Congress may adjourn.
>
> > Yours with high consideration
> > Morehouse.

The fact that Wheelock now felt free to turn his full attention toward the North West Mining Company was based on disappointing legal developments in regard to the Mercer Colony. Instead of improving under United States of America rule, General Mercer's position had been deteriorating. On May 11 the Texas State Legislature enacted a law requiring the attorney general to institute legal proceedings against all colony contractors who had entered into contracts with a president of Texas. Mercer himself had given up, and would soon pass on the affairs of the Texas Association to his nephew, Theodore S. Garnett.

On May 1, 1846, Colonel Wheelock received a legal paper stating he was entitled to a 100th part of all lands or money made by the Association during the previous calendar year plus

$500 for expenses. This may have been his last contact with Mercer interests.

In 1848 a Texas District Court would declare the Mercer contract void, a ruling overturned ten years later by the Texas Supreme Court. Litigation dragged on until 1883, when the United States Supreme Court finally refused compensation to Mercer's Texas Association. Conflicting claims in the Mercer Colony were to fill courtrooms until 1936.

Change of Soul

When Colonel Wheelock announced to his wife that he planned to travel to New York and points east to be gone for at least twelve months, he had something of even greater importance to tell her. The treatment he had received from the citizens of Robertson County (people he had long considered friends) while sub-agent for the Mercer Colony and Indian commissioner had cut him to the quick. Their rejection of his bid for the Senate still rankled. As he was determined to make himself and his family rich from silver, so he was determined to shake the dust of Robertson County off his feet forever. He could not live among the perfidious again.

But merely moving house was not enough. No one in his family was aware that he had finally taken a step which he perhaps had been considering as long ago as his visit to Tampico in 1824. Somehow, gradually, secretly, and finally, he had cast away his natal Protestantism, which he perceived as having betrayed him, not only in New Hampshire as a boy but also as a man in Texas, by throwing in his lot with the established church of Mexico, the country he had hoped to make his final home. Nothing is known of the exact circumstances of his conversion. Its revelation produced results all too predictable.

Mary Pope Prickett Wheelock had forgiven him the months and years of absence, the wrenching upheaval of moving her family to foreign parts, the worry of a soldier's wife, and the pain of poverty. This new treachery she could not forgive. To her staunchly Presbyterian spirit such a religious commitment was the final betrayal, the ultimate infidelity. In her world, religious tolerance was not a virtue. He had gone over to the scarlet woman. The horrified children sided with their mother. The family was torn apart, not by theology, which they barely understood, but by cultural treason. Their final good-byes were cold.

By the middle of July, Colonel Wheelock was in Galveston awaiting transportation to New Orleans and wrote Mary the following letter, the first which she kept of the many he must have written to his only love during his long and frequent absences from home. In it he gives her final counsel on financial affairs and shares his hopes for his sons, including his plans for David, whom he had placed in an attorney's home for instruction.

July 24, 1846, Galveston

My dear wife:

I have delayed writing to you . . . from the circumstance of not knowing what to write. In the first place my health is gradually improving but I am still weak and nervous. I am here waiting for a passage to New Orleans which I expect I shall take on board the ship Bangor which sails tomorrow if the steamship New York should not arrive today. I have completed arranging our business about the Quincy papers and have gotten the opinion of Judge Webb, Col. Mayfield, and Mr. Allen. They say there is no difficulty about our holding the property.

I left David at Judge Johnson at Brenham and have paid in my horse, $150 for board and $12 towards tuition. I think that in the little time I was absent I could discover an improvement in his manners. This I think is from being placed in a situation where the society of girls will have its influence. Mrs. Johnson will be a mother to him. She is an excellent woman. I made an arrangement for his future clothing and purchased what was necessary for the present.

I heard from William at Bastrop. He appeared to be doing well.

I pray to God that they may take a worthy course; they both have capacity if they will properly extend it. I have left all of our papers about lands in the hands of Judge McFarlin of Washington, who is directed to hand them over to Captain Killough. There is no difficulty about our lands upon the Trinity River that I could learn.

Give my kind love to the Captain, Annette, and kiss our little grandchild for me. Tell Capt. K. I will write when I get to New

Orleans. Give my love to Ripley, your brother, wife, and little Georgia, and accept the assurance of the affection of your husband,

E.L.R. Wheelock.

PS. I have our deed recorded for the lots in LaGrange. It is in the hands of Judge McFarlin.

Although where and how the colonel received knowledge and instruction in his new faith is unknown, his conversion was painfully sincere. Four days later he wrote again, including the unwelcome news that he had visited the Bishop. This must have been John Mary Odin, a French priest who first came to Texas in 1840 as Vice-Prefect Apostolic and was consecrated bishop in 1842. Bishop Odin had been in Europe to recruit missionaries and had just returned to Galveston on July 2, 1846. No record exists of Wheelock's baptism in Galveston, but of course this rite might have been administered elsewhere. He apparently asked Bishop Odin how he ought to handle his family's horrified reaction to his change of creed. Wheelock wrote to his wife:

Galveston, July 28, 1846

My dear wife:

I have been detained here in consequence of the non-arrival of the steamship New York and the sickness of the Captain of the ship Bangor. I am determined not to sail unless I am satisfied of a good vessel and a pleasant captain. Thus far I have succeeded well in my business. I think this fall to be able to place myself where I can have the company of her I most love in this life.

I have been to church. I have seen the Bishop and now feel as if I should be glad to see you and my dear children. Pray for me; at least think of him who has been your partner for years.

I hope David will do well. William I understand will come back with his Company as I understand General Taylor is about discharging all of the volunteers unless they will enlist for 12 months.

This is a pleasant place. The people appear more like civilized beings compared with the Pudlyfunks of the Border. My health is rather improving. I now weigh 182 lbs. and still going down. I am weak. I eat nothing, drink a little tea, and eat a piece of toast three times a day. Gov. Runnells, Mr. Merrand, and other

friends here have treated me kindly. Such is the contrast of ignorance and prejudice on the one side and intelligence on the
other. It is impossible to compare the community of the border
with this place.

I shall drop you a line frequently believing that you will read
it, at least with the same pleasure you would one from an old
friend. On the management of your affairs, I would never presume to offer an opinion to you as the best course of your interest. Of that of your children, however, I am determined to provide a home for us elsewhere and without any aid from your
estate.

Yours forever, Affectionately, E.L.R. Wheelock.

Change of Direction

Colonel Wheelock took his leave of Texas for the last time
on July 30, 1846. He left his family life in shambles, his children
refusing to speak to him, and his wife estranged. He was to write
home frequently, eloquent letters begging for reconciliation,
which was never granted. Shocked though he was by the tidal
wave of revulsion his dip into Romish holy water had occasioned, he never wavered. But he mourned.

By the middle of August he had reached Edwardsville,
Illinois, where he was to visit his wife's family and untangle the
Wheelocks' snarled business affairs in that state. During his stay
in Illinois he had a serious relapse and was forced to seek medical attention. He wrote later of this experience:

. . . I had a severe attack of my old complaint on the 11th of
November which confined me to my room for six weeks and two
days, about three of which I had to lie upon my face from a car-
buncle on my back. I had to have a servant night and day for 32
days to attend me. . . I had the skill of Dr. Nichols, formerly of
the Boston Hospital and Dr. Birdsall, eight years a surgeon in the
United States Army. They say they do not know how I got here
alive. They say that the sympathetic nerve glandular system and
the gall duct were perfectly clogged with glutinous bile and that
my physicians had given me so much calomel that it would not

act upon my system, besides the rheumatism in my bowels. But they have with the aid of Divine Goodness in mercy restored me to my wonted feelings of health. I am weak yet, and weigh about 180 lbs. Everybody has been kind to me and I have not suffered for anything. The sickness has cost me nearly $300 but I have paid it.

It is indicative of the state of his relationship with his own children that he wrote first to his son-in-law, Samuel Killough:

August 17, 1846
Edwardsville
Capt. S. B. Killough
My dear son:
I have barely time to say I arrived here a week ago today. My health is much improved. . . Brother Elisha came up and made a surrender of the Trust estate and was surprised at David and George's conduct. I think I will be able to settle.
        I start for Springfield in the stage and shall arrive there on the 20th and at Quincy about the 23rd. Tell Mary to be cautious of her sister-in-law. From what I can learn she is not the clean thing in any respect. Beware of your talk.
                                        Your father truly, E.L.R. Wheelock.

From Alton he wrote to Mary, imploring her to answer his letters:

October 3, 1846
My Dear Wife:
Although I have written several letters, I cannot boast of one from you. I hope you have not forgotten. At least you think of me and you will remember the love and enjoyment of our youth. I have always adored you and my life has been devoted to the happiness of yourself and children. They are mine and I love them with all the fondness of a father. They have neglected me. I forgive them. I hope you will write me and I can say you are well and happy. Tell me about Annette, Ripley, William, David, and our pretty little grandchild. My health is unimproved.
        Our relatives are all well. I shall succeed in all of our busi-

ness and be able I hope to give you a home where I can be satisfied if you choose it. This I leave entirely to your discretion. I am determined to do all in my power to render you happy and comfortable. You are my only love and the only woman I would wish to live for, but I must always be master of my own affairs. . . .
I send prayers of affection. Be pleased to consider me yours truly and a husband until death, E.L.R. Wheelock.

This letter was intercepted by E.L.R.'s son William in Galveston as he returned from fighting in the Battle of Monterrey. He added a post script:

Dear Mother:
I arrived here last evening from Galveston and found this letter from father to you and took the liberty of breaking it open. I never have heard from you since I left home. I have been very sick since I left Camargo. I have had measles which came near to taking my life. I start this evening for home with Barnard's wagon but whether I will be able to get home or not I am not able to say for I am very weak . . . Yours in haste. William Wheelock.

A later note from E.L.R. to William reflects a father's satisfaction at having received an official letter commending his son's courage at the Battle of Monterrey.
Ill as he was, Colonel Wheelock had been obliged to linger in Illinois and file suit against the brothers-in-law who had tried to defraud him and Mary of money and property. He wrote:

October 3, 1846, Alton
To Captain S. B. Killough
My dear son:
I have refrained from writing you in consequence of not knowing what to write about my Quincy matters. The property is valuable and from the best information I can get it is worth from 80 to 90 thousand dollars. I have had every difficulty that you could possibly imagine to contend with. I have traveled over one thousand miles in this state by stages to collect facts, etc., and have prepared myself for war or peace.
I am now on my way to Edwardsville to attend court as you

will discover by the papers I send you . . . Never was a man treated worse by a family than I have been by my wife's relatives. David is a scoundrel. George has acted as an honest man but is a great fool under the thumb of his wife!

Governor Ford has stood by me as an ancient friend, as also all my old acquaintances. My health is rather improving. I placed myself under the care of Dr. Nichols and Dr. Rodgers, who are the first Physicians who have prescribed for me, and who declare my disease is an affliction of the liver and the effects of calomel given during the Colony. They have put me upon a diet, a mixture of iron and hemlock of the antianto (contents?). It is working wonders and I have no doubt in a few months I shall be restored to health.

I have partially effected my object in regard to my Great Western Commercial project. I shall go to Washington City with Senator Sample of this state and thence to New York, Boston, and thence home in April. Governor Ford, Senator Sample, John Tillsen, Col. Bayley of Wall Street are interested etc. All is well.

Accept the kind assurances of a Father's love and believe me to be Yours Sincerely, E.L.R. Wheelock.

As a postscript, he added:

My dear Ripley:
Although you have not written to your old father, he has not forgotten you as a parent. It would at least be a pleasure to see a letter from you. Annette, my dear daughter, I kindly thank you for remembering me and telling me about your sweet, dear little daughter Nancy. Do plant a few dozens of kisses for her grandfather and remember me kindly to your affectionate husband to whom I will write from Washington City. I hope William is better and able to write to me at Washington. I shall be here all of the month of February next. If he wants to lead the life of a soldier I will get him appointed to the regular army. Send word to David to write me also.

Another long letter to Mary illustrates his anxiety about his sons, whose fate was much on his mind. It reads:

I wish you to write to me in Washington City, via Edwardsville, as all letters will be forwarded from that place to my whereabouts and say in the most positive terms what other point in Texas you would prefer for me to fix a home for you. I am determined to do my duty as a kind and affectionate husband, but in Robertson County I will not live if I perish elsewhere. Victoria, San Antonio, Goliad, LaGrange, Brenham are places that I prefer to that county. Houston, Galveston, Bastrop, anywhere else.

. . . if you only say that you are well it will afford me great pleasure. If you are unhappy, say so that I may at least feel part of it.

About the children . . . although old I still may be useful to them. But I cannot and will not submit to the indignities that they have shown me heretofore and live in their society. I will enjoy the liberty of conscience if I have to do it in the wilderness. My family have hurt my feelings in that particular, but I forgive them and love them better than myself. I pray for their prosperity and happiness daily. God has brought low my bodily strength but it has only more strongly fixed me in my faith in His only Son Jesus as a redeemer of fallen man as unfolded by the Holy Catholic Church.

My dear wife, upon you depends as great deal of the misery or woe that will befall to William and David, your maternal example and precepts may save their immortal souls. They are young. You can by your motherly care persuade them to be moral if not religious. Do try for your husband's sake. I wish to see them, but fear if I should I should feel unhappy and wish myself abroad again on their account. I love them as a parent should love his children but their disobedience to me is death to my feeling and all of my happiness at home. Don't fail to write me weekly.

Now my dear wife and children, I offer up to God my prayers for happiness in this world and Eternal Glory in that to come for each and every one of you, and I remain yours in the bonds of Love, until death, E.L.R. Wheelock.

PS—I go home to Edwardsville to deposit papers for the court and in the stage hence, to my sister Nancy where I shall remain two days only, thence by stage to Wheeling in Virginia, then to Washington City by stage and railroad. The weather is cold here. The river is frozen over. Not much snow but I shall wrap up in a Buffalo skin. It will cost me very little more to travel than to lie by. I can not come until June.

E.L.R. Wheelock.

Other letters home explained that Wheelock was paying Governor Ford, Browning, and Bushnell in property for pursuing his case in court to recover $25,000 misappropriated by relatives.

To his brother-in-law George Prickett, a partner in the mining scheme, he wrote:

> Dr. Brother: Thus far I have succeeded well in my enterprise in the company. I have added a good deal of influence and have gotten letters and all is going on well. Don't despair, for my health is spared. You will be rich enough in two years. I refer you to my letter to Mr. Kellogg for particulars.

His health seemed restored. The problems with the Illinois property were being settled. He headed east with his usual optimism and expectation of success.

CHAPTER 22

And Sudden Death: 1847

The altar must often be built in one place so that the fire from
Heaven may come down at another.
—Charles Williams

In Edwardsville, Illinois, Colonel Wheelock was able to gather additional letters of introduction to substantial citizens in New York, Boston, Hartford, Washington City, St. Louis, and as far away as London. Even after an absence of fourteen years, he still had many sincere friends in Illinois.

Mail from home having now caught up with him, Wheelock wrote to his wife, who had succumbed to his pleas for a letter:

Quincy, January 10, 1847
My Dear and Affectionate Wife:
Your kind favor of November 7 came to hand last night and I hasten to say that it has afforded me a great pleasure to hear you are well and the family is the same.
    The mail brought me ones from Capt. Killough and Mr. Kellogg, one of which is postmarked as late as Dec. 8, by which I learn you are well and that William our dear son has got home.

247

This is a great source of satisfaction to me. I hope he has profited morally by his experience with the world. David will also be benefitted by the change of position. As to myself, I am now in better health than I have been for twenty years, though I am yet weak from a sick bed. . . O my dear wife if you could have only known my suffering, how you would have felt for me, how you would have nursed me and with pleasure. . .

I do not expect to come to Texas before the 15th or 20th of June next, as I have to be at the May court next and I am doubtful whether I then get a final hearing, but that will not prevent my coming to see you and the children. I shall start this week for Washington City, New York, and Boston, and I believe with the aid of Ford, Bruses, Sample, Douglas, and the present Governor French, an old army friend, I shall carry the object of the North West Mining Company in full effect.

I may dispose of our property in part for merchandise. I have an offer by a Philadelphia house with a branch here, and, when there, shall determine.

By late January Wheelock was in St. Louis poised for his first trip to the eastern United States since 1818. His last letter from the Mississippi shows his concern for his sons. He wants them to become merchants, as security for any other vocations they wish later to follow, and has bought $12,000 worth of goods with which they can open their own establishment. He wrote:

January 29, 1847
St. Louis
My Dear Sons, Ripley, William, and David:
I have made arrangements to forward the amount of upwards of eleven thousand dollars worth of goods (Philadelphia price) in May next, all paid for. It is my wish for you to prepare yourselves for active commercial business.

William, I wish you to go to school if you prefer a profession. You can select it and go to work and shall be able I hope to pay the expense. If you choose to be a merchant, I will start you when I think you are able to judge correctly. Your conduct, I learn, was commendable on your Monterrey Campaign. I am well pleased at your course and you have a parent's thanks. Don't fail to go to school until I come back.

David, I wish you to study all of your time. Prepare yourself for business. I have learned you have been unkind to your mother. I hope and trust this is not true. Do endeavor to do right in all things. Upon your conduct depends your happiness in this life and hereafter. Let your good sense examine this matter and I am sure if the report is true you will correct the evil. Accept the kind feelings of your father for your prosperity.

Ripley, be good enough to write to me at Washington and give me your views as to what kind of goods will bear the best profit that are saleable in Texas and where is the best point to ship them to sale at retail.

Accept your father's love, E.L.R.; Wheelock.

A Gentleman of High Moral Character

Colonel Wheelock arrived in Washington City on February 14. Two days later he wrote to Mary exclaiming over the technical advances and other wonders revealed to him during his journey:

My dear Mary:
I arrived here on the 14th inst. by way of the Cumberland RR on which I have travelled 210 miles in 13 hours, and from Wheeling to that place in stage in 38 hours and from St. Louis to this place in 12 days.

My ship up the Ohio was a very pleasant one, but my fatigue in crossing the mountains was severe from cold, exposure, snow, ice, and all of the painful and beautiful scenery but my health is still improving although I have a bad cold and a slight cough.

Tonight I shall attend the President's Levee accompanied by Gen. Houston and Senator Johnston of Maryland. Tomorrow I shall present my letter of business to the Hon. Sec. Buchanan. My prospects are flattering of accomplishing my great object of putting into successful operation the North West Mining Company. I have more than 30 letters of the strongest kind to members of Congress which I hope will enable me to consummate my object; . . . I have made arrangements with Robert C. Gest Esq. to act as the company agent in London. I have procured the best of commercial letters for the company. This will supersede the necessity of my going to Europe as I was fearful I should be compelled to do, but now I feel as though I should see you in June next.

After having finished my object here, I shall proceed to Philadelphia and make my selection of goods from Mr. Smith, Murphy and Co. for the payment of $11,325, sale of a portion of the Quincy Estate, and then eastward to NY and Boston so as to give me time to be at the May court in Illinois. This will enable me to ship our goods about that time. I shall ship to Galveston. I wish you to get Killough and Ripley to write me what commercial house will be the safest to consign them to.

Remember me in your prayers and believe me your true and devoted husband until death.

Yours affectionately, E.L.R. Wheelock.

Did he have a premonition of death? He had been very ill and was torn by family turmoil. It would have been natural for him to want to get his affairs together as soon as possible, even by the awkward medium of nineteenth century mail. He wrote:

I am at a private boarding house, Mrs. Mounts, Pennsylvania Avenue, and boarding at $20 per week. This is about half what they charge elsewhere. I live very economically but I appear in the garb of a Gentleman as I am determined not to disgrace the family at home. I am careful to keep out of debt or responsibility. I wish to write you many particulars but have no confidence in the PO in Brownsville.

Wheelock still feared that his political enemies were monitoring his mail, and kept his business secrets out of his letters home. As things turned out, it was a great pity. On February 24 he wrote his wife again:

February 24, 1847
My dear Mary:
Tomorrow I leave this place for the City of Philadelphia and expect to arrive there about the 27th as I wish to stop at Baltimore for a few days for commercial purposes. I have made all arrangements about North West Mining Company that can be done at present. I shall therefore prepare for a return in some ten or fifteen days to St. Louis, Edwardsville, and Quincy, from which place I expect to depart for Texas some time in May or early part of June.

My health is improving but I am yet weak and have a severe cough which was contracted in crossing the Mountains, but I am still about. God only knows my fate. In Him I trust, for He is merciful and kind to me.

My dear Mary, please remember me to our children as an absent parent who has been devoted to them and their mother for life. Ascertain from them whether it is agreeable for me to live near them, or would they prefer my absence. I cannot live near them and be happy so long as they have no respect for my religious principles, nor regard for my moral principles, nor veneration for my age. No gratitude for their existence. No love for anything but money.

They are my children and for them alone have I toiled and to make you happy. No woman on earth can I love but you. Still, I fear you are unhappy with me through the influence of our children.

I want you at least to write me and say how you get along with them and whether they obey you. Write to me directed to Quincy, Illinois. State what necessities you would like to have brought out by me to Galveston for you, and also please state at what point you would like to have me settle for your comfort and pleasure.

And accept the devoted affections of your husband,

Unto death, E.L.R. Wheelock.

Back in Washington, Senator Houston, Senator Rusk, Congressman Kaufman, and Congressman Pillsbury addressed President Polk on Wheelock's behalf:

Washington City, March 1, 1847
To James K. Polk
President of the United States
Sir:
The undersigned delegation of Texas respectfully represent that Col. Wheelock of the said state is an applicant for a position under the general government, where his talents may be usefully employed.

Col. Wheelock is known, not only in Texas as one of the true patriots of that State, but throughout the whole union as a gentleman of high moral character, erudition, and experience. He has lived in Texas for the last thirteen years and the able and ef-

ficient manner in which he distinguished himself in the cause of
democracy have rendered him deservedly popular, both at home
and abroad. We earnestly press the great claims of Col. Wheelock
and with an abiding confidence in your favorable consideration
of his application, we subscribe ourselves,

> Your friends and obt. servants,
> D.S. Kaufman
> T. Pillsbury, (Congressman)
> Thos. J. Rusk (Senator)
> Sam Houston (Senator)[1]

　　Wheelock's application must have been for concessions or
rights necessary to carry out his mining project, not for employment in the usual sense, unless he was thinking of offering his
talents as Indian commissioner to the United States government. His subsequent death would of course have put an end to
any governmental considerations.

　　On March 8 Wheelock wrote to Mary from Philadelphia,
exhilarated by the tremendous speed made possible by contemporary railroading and the elegance of the Pennsylvania society,
but true to his love and hope for Texas. It was the last letter she
would ever receive from him.

My Dear Mary:
I have arrived here safe after passing from Washington City by
way of Baltimore at the rate of 20 miles an hour. This is a velocity that can hardly be conceived. I find everything changed since
I was here two years prior to our marriage. I am perfectly aston-
ished at the American people and character. Compare the natural advantages of this country with our dear adopted country of
Texas and we can not imagine what her growth will be in ten
years. I would not exchange our soil acre for acre with the best
here if I were to exist twenty years.

　　It is true that in social intercourse and refined feeling they
are years ahead of us. The ladies are gay, sprightly, and intelligent, but I have seen none even if I were free that I would exchange my Mary for. I have not visited any place of amusement.
Today I attended church, the sermon was the best I ever heard,
text St. John Third Chapter, 8th Verse. (The wind bloweth where
it listeth) The choir, organ, etc. were striking. I find wealth to

voluptuousness and poverty in all its shades of misery. We should be contented in Texas. I am, but not in Robertson County.

I believe I have made judicious arrangements for the company, but be assured I shall not involve myself and I shall not apply our means to accomplish any object where there is risk. I will write you in a few days defining my prospects. Give my kind respects to friends and love to our dear children, not forgetting little Nancy and Capt. Killough and believe me to be your affectionate husband. E.L.R. Wheelock.

My health is gradually improving. Don't forget to say to George that I have not forgotten my promise to him to whom I send a particular love and respect for self and family. Kiss little Georgia for her Uncle. Keep David and William in school until I return. Adieux. W.

Wheelock may have abandoned plans to go to New York and Boston because of success already achieved in obtaining backing for his mining venture and perhaps because his health was failing again. On March 11 he was able to write a fairly long letter to the firm which was exchanging merchandise for Quincy real estate. On March 20 he wrote from Washington to a former comrade in arms in regard to a contemplated publication, "Notes Upon Texas":

March 20, 1847
Washington City, D.C.
My Old Friend of the 21st Regiment
Dear Sir:
Yours of this past month is now before me, asking me to recommend the order of the material for the contemplated "Notes Upon Texas."
1. The causes which led to the Revolution in Texas with several dates and references—also express our reflections on this event including the history of the Republic.
2. The Military History, terrain, ranges of mountains. Geography.
3. Setting up the military heritage of the country and continuing as your own judgement and good sense may suggest.
4. A map of Texas, which I humbly opine is of vast importance.
5. Something about communication with California and the Pacific. Something about Indians. Etc.

But it was not to be.

All his life, Wheelock kept copies of the letters he wrote. This was the last.

The details of his journey west during the next three weeks are unknown, but he arrived back in Edwardsville on April 15.

Eleazar Louis Ripley Wheelock died in Edwardsville, Illinois, at the home of his brother-in-law on April 20, 1847, at the age of fifty-four, probably from chronic mercury poisoning.

On his body friends found the sum of seventeen dollars: $1.25 went to Dr. Hart, the physician who attended him; four dollars were charged for digging his grave; and eighty-seven and a half cents for washing his clothes. The remainder went to Daniel Anderson for nursing care. The family was informed that money was still owed to Dr. Weiss, Dr. Hart, S. L. McCorkle for the coffin, Q. Meeker for the shroud, and Anderson for the balance of his nursing fee.

Mary's brother Elisha wrote to her nine days later to describe the circumstances of her husband's death:

April 29, 1847
State of Illinois
Dear Sister:
I sit down to perform a painful duty, though it is probable that before this reaches you, you have received the sad intelligence of the death of Col. Wheelock, who departed this life at Edwardsville on the 20th of this month. He got to Edwardsville on Thursday the 15th and was taken with a chill the same day. He seemed to be a good deal fatigued and poorly for two or three days when he took off his trusz and was taken bad immediately and died on Tuesday night, about nine o'clock.

Let me prevail on you, my dear sister, not to grieve more than you can avoid on account of your husband's dying among strangers. He had a great many warm friends here that sympathize with you in your sore bereavement. I have a comfortable hope from the manner in which he expressed himself to many religious persons that he was prepared for death, and again let me prevail on you, not to grieve as those who have no hope. I would have been glad if it had been the will of the Lord to have spared him to get home, but it was not.

Sister, if you can come to Illinois, if I can arrange my business I will try to go home with you and see Texas. We are all well enough, your brother til death, Elisha Prickett.

Erstwhile Indian commissioner and regional land commissioner of the Republic of Texas, captain of the Texas Rangers, soldier, frontiersman, surveyor, a founder of towns who dreamed of founding a great university, lawyer, miner, trader, advocate of the Indians, Eleazar Louis Ripley Wheelock had ridden west to carve out a secure life for his wife and children in a foreign land. He had dared much and risked much and accomplished much and failed in much during his rich life, but to the very last he put each failure behind him and moved on. He never surrendered his own strict code of honor and never lost faith in Texas. In the latter case, at least, he was not mistaken. Texas has flourished more exuberantly than even he envisioned.

By the time his eldest son arrived in Edwardsville to wind up his father's affairs, the tightly strapped trunk containing all Colonel Wheelock's business papers had disappeared. It seems reasonable to suppose that the in-laws who had sought to cheat him out of his Illinois property took this opportunity to settle pending litigation. With Colonel Wheelock's death, the North West Mining Company died too, as the Texas University Company had died and the Mercer Colony and the fabric of his family life and even his affection for Robertson County itself.

Wheelock's altars remained desolate. Yet fire did descend. Silver was eventually recovered from the Texas hills, and Texas did open a university; North Texas was settled, and peace was made with the Amerinds; books about Texas were written, and the state prospered beyond promise until Sam Houston's name was the first human word spoken on the moon. "This is a velocity," Colonel Wheelock might well reaffirm, "which can hardly be conceived!"

Looking down from whatever heaven is reserved for loyal Texans, he can remember with satisfaction the words he wrote in Philadelphia the year of his death:

"Compare the natural advantages of this country with our dear adopted country of Texas and we cannot imagine what her growth will be! . . . I would not exchange our soil, acre for acre, with the best here . . . We should be contented in Texas."

So they should. Rest well, old heroes. Your Odyssey is finished.

EPILOGUE

Like an oak, Wheelock lives on and its branches spread wide over the Prairie. The branches of the tree are the families who lived and died here.

—J. W. Baker

Although the loss of her husband's business papers greatly reduced the financial security he had hoped to bestow upon her, Mary Wheelock continued to live comfortably in the town of Wheelock and watch it swell in importance, only to decline gently as the railroad passed it by. She died at the age of eighty-four, in the same house she was living in at the time of her husband's death, and is buried under the ancient oaks of gracious and peaceful Wheelock cemetery.

George Ripley Wheelock passed the rest of his life quietly as a rancher and farmer. He married for the second time in 1854 but was again left a childless widower. In 1858 he finally attained domestic happiness through his union with Mary Ann Jane, daughter of his father's old nemesis Francis Slaughter, whose casting of a double vote for a rival cost Colonel Wheelock a seat in the Texas Senate.

Annette Woodward Wheelock Kimble Powers Killough and her third husband Capt. Samuel Blackburn Killough continued to flourish. Captain Killough, an author of the Texas State Constitution, in time became chief justice of Robertson County and captain of the Home Guard of Wheelock during the Civil War.

William Hillman Wheelock was twice elected sheriff of Robertson County. He became an outstanding East Texas rancher.

David Prickett Wheelock followed the gold rush to California, but gained no profit by it and eventually returned to the family prairie. He was the only child of E.L.R. Wheelock to hand down the colonel's distinctive Christian names. David's great-grandson, the last E.L.R. Wheelock, now lives with his wife in the British Virgin Islands.

—Mary Foster Hutchinson
Austin and Dallas
AD 2002

Wheelock's original land grant, February 1834.

ENDNOTES

Unattributed primary material throughout the book is from the E.L.R. Wheelock Papers, Center for American History, The University of Texas at Austin.

Chapter 1

1. The exact origin of E.L.R.'s second name is unknown. No Lewises or Louises appear on either side of his family tree. The name, however, is common among the French and was given by them to many Amerinds in Canada. Several of these were connected to the Dartmouth family as students or relatives of students. There was also a doctor in Hanover named Lewis. No doubt Eleazar Wheelock, Jr. chose the name for his eldest son as a token of friendship for one of these. The custom of giving children second or third names of friends rather than family has persisted in the Wheelock line to the present day.

2. Foster, Bridgman, and Fay, *Town Records of the Town of Hanover,* p. 66.

3. Andreas Reichstein, *Rise of the Lone Star,* p. 23.

4. Thomas Jefferson Papers Series 1, General Correspondence, Image 1007 of 1330.

5. Roy C. Thompson, *The Schools of Claremont,* p. 10.

6. George T. Chapman, *Sketches of the Alumni of Dartmouth College,* p. 20.

Chapter 2

1. Alec R. Gilpin, *The War of 1812 in the Old Northwest,* p. 230.

2. Harry L. Coles, *The War of 1812,* p. 157.

3. John K. Mahon, *The War of 1812,* p. 274.

261

4. Ibid.

5. Ibid., p. 274-275.

6. Ibid., p. 275.

7. Coles, *The War of 1812*, p. 160.

8. Pension application, National Archives.

9. Coles, *The War of 1812*, p. 162.

10. Ibid., p. 163.

11. From this point forward, all unattributed material is from the E.L.R. Wheelock Papers, Center for American History, University of Texas at Austin.

12. Louis B. Wright, *Culture on the Moving Frontier*, p. 32.

13. Ibid., p. 31.

14. Theodore Calvin Pease, *The Story of Illinois*, p. 100.

15. In an attempt to keep this tangle of Ripleys straight, E.L.R. Wheelock will be henceforth called E.L.R. (which is how he signed himself for most of his life), his son George Ripley, and his cousin General Ripley.

16. Reichstein, *Rise of the Lone Star*, p. 16.

17. Malcolm McLean, *Papers Concerning Robertson's Colony*, Vol. I, p, 247.

Chapter 3

1. Edwin C. Bearss and Arrell M. Gibson, *Fort Smith*, p. 40.

2. Eugene Barker, *Stephen F. Austin*, p. 83.

3. McLean, II, p. 470.

4. G. W. Featherstonhaugh, *Excursion through the Slave States from Washington on the Potomac to the Frontier of Mexico, with Sketches of Popular Manners and Geological Notices*, p. 29.

5. Cecil Eby, *That Disgraceful Affair, the Black Hawk War*, p. 24.

Chapter 4

1. Hubert Howe Bancroft, *The Works of*, XVI, p. 5.

2. James Alexander Gardner, *Lead King, Moses Austin*, p. 132.

3. McLean, Intro, p. 43.

4. Powell A. Casey, *Encyclopedia of Forts, Posts, and Names Camps and Other Military Installations in Louisiana*, p. 93.

5. Turner, *The Life and Times of Jane Long*, p. 59.

Chapter 5

1. McLean, Intro p. 47.

2. Ibid., p. 46.

3. Ibid., I, p. lvi.

4. Reichstein, *Rise of the Lone Star*, p. 33.

5. McLean, Intro, pp. 303-304.

6. Ibid., p. 310-311.

7. Ibid., p. 267.

8. Reichstein, *Rise of the Lone Star*, p. 34.

9. McLean, Intro, p. 424.

10. Ibid., p. 474.

11. Ibid., p. 562.
12. Ibid., p. 566.

Chapter 6

1. The mystery of what happened to Robert Leftwich, last seen in East Texas in the spring of 1826, has never been solved.
2. McLean, III, p. 57.
3. S. H. Dixon quoted in J. W. Baker, *A History of Robertson County, Texas,* p. 32.
4. McLean, III, p. 61.
5. Ibid., p. 66.
6. Ibid., V, p. 45.
7. Ibid., p. 46.
8. Ibid., VIII, p. 23.
9. Ibid.
10. Reichstein, *Rise of the Lone Star,* p. 49.

Chapter 7

1. Roy DeLafayette Killough, Letter to his children, 12/6/1945.
2. Ibid.
3. McLean, VIII, p. 479.
4. William Bollaert, *Texas,* p. 116.
5. McLean, IX, p. 129.
6. Ibid., p. 140.
7. Ibid., p. 141.
8. Ibid., p 55.
9. Ibid., VIII, p. 86.
10. Ibid., p. 85.
11. Sue Watkins (ed.), *One League to Each Wind,* pp. 16-17.
12. McLean, X, p. 32.
13. Parker, p. 19.
14. George W. Bomar, *Texas Weather,* p. vii.
15. A. Y. Kirkpatrick, *The Early Settlers' Life in Texas and the Organization of Hill County,* pp. 16-17.

Chapter 8

1. Reichstein, *Rise of the Lone Star,* p. 23.
2. Wallace Hawkins, *The Case of John Charles Waltrous,* p. 23.
3. Reichstein, p. 69.
4. T. R. Fehrenbach, *Seven Keys to Texas,* p. 36.
5. Ibid.
6. Barker, *Stephen F. Austin,* p. 85.
7. Fehrenbach, *Seven Keys to Texas,* p. 38.
8. Ibid., p. 39.
9. Reichstein, p. 187.

10. Channing quoted in Muir, *Texas in 1837,* p. 137.
11. Fehrenbach, *Lone Star,* p. 185.
12. McLean, IX, p. 50.
13. Ibid.
14. Ibid., X, p. 69.
15. Ibid., pp. 69-70.
16. Ibid., XVIII, p. 31.
17. Ibid.
18. Ibid.
19. Ibid.
20. Ibid., XVIII, p. 32.
21. Ibid., p. 82.
22. Ibid., X, p. 28,
23. Ibid., XIV, p. 313.
24. Ibid., X, p. 71.
25. Reichstein, p. 190.
26. McLean, X, p. 71.
27. N. C. Duncan, *Reminiscences of the Early Days in Texas.*
28. Reichstein, p. 197.

Chapter 9
1. McLean, X, p. 309.
2. Ibid., p. 75.
3. Ibid.
4. Ibid., p. 77.
5. Ibid., XI, p. 66.
6. Reichstein, p. 133.
7. McLean, XI, p. 60.
8. Ibid.
9. Muir, *Texas in 1837,* p. 137.
10. McLean, XI, p. 61.
11. Ibid., p. 66.
12. Ibid., p. 48.
13. Ibid.
14. Ibid., pp. 57-58.

Chapter 10
1. John Holt Williams, *Sam Houston,* p. 111.
2. Stephen L. Hardin, *Texian Iliad,* p. 5.
3. McLean, XII, p. 31.
4. Paul D. Lack, *The Texas Revolutionary Experience,* p. xiii.
5. Hardin, *Texian Iliad,* p. 54.
6. McLean, XII, p. 33.
7. Hardin, p. 13.
8. McLean, XIII, p. 472.
9. Ibid., p. 492.

10. Ibid., XIV, p. 323.
11. Reichstein, p. 144.
12. Muir, p. 145.
13. Hardin, pp. 6-7.
14. McLean, XIII, p. 47.
15. Jo Ella Powell Exley, *Texas Tears and Texas Sunshine,* pp. 55-57.
16. I. T. Taylor, *The Cavalcade of Jackson County,* pp. 79-80.
17. Ibid., p. 80.
18. Muir, p. 122.
19. Taylor, p. 83.
20. Killough Letter.
21. Hardin, p. 184.
22. Ibid., p. 183.

Chapter 11
1. Muir, p. 140.
2. Fehrenbach, *Lone Star,* p. 472.
3. Ibid., p. 473.
4. Ibid.
5. W. W. Newcombe Jr., *The Indians of Texas,* p. 189.
6. Fehrenbach, *Lone Star,* p. 32.
7. Ibid., p. 33.
8. McLean, XV, p. 37.
9. Ibid.
10. Ibid., p. 118.
11. Fehrenbach, *Lone Star,* p. 451.
12. Ibid.
13. Ibid., p. 452.

Chapter 12
1. Michael C. Meyer and William Sherman, *Course of Mexican History,* p. 332-333.
2. Dorothy Louise Fields, "David Gouverneur Burnet," *Southwestern Quarterly,* Vol. XLIX, p. 228.
3. Stanley Siegel, *The Poet President of Texas,* p. 24.
4. Mary Whatley Clarke, *David G. Burnet,* p. 134.
5. Fields, "David Gouverneur Burnet," p. 228.
6. Ibid.
7. Yoakum, quoted in Dudley Wooten, *A Comprehensive History of Texas,* I, pp. 296-297.
8. Fields, "David Gouveneur Burnet," pp. 228-229.
9. Lack, p. 153.
10. William C. Binkley, *Official Correspondence of the Texas Revolution,* Vol. II, p. 879.
11. Muir, p. 135.
12. John H. Jenkins, *The Papers of the Texas Revolution,* VII, pp. 470-471.

13. Binkley, Official Correspondence of the Texas Revolution, p. 879.
14. Ibid., p. 882.
15. Ibid., pp. 892-893.
16. Jenkins, *The Papers of the Texas Revolution,* Vol.8, pp. 104-105.
17. Ibid., pp. 127-128.
18. Ibid., p. 374.

Chapter 13
1. Muir, p. 50.
2. Ibid., p. 51.
3. Ibid., p. 53.
4. E.L.R. Wheelock Papers, Center for American History, University of Texas at Austin.
5. Muir, p. 36.
6. James B. Wyngaarden and Lloyd H. Smith, Editors, *Cecil Textbook of Medicine,* pp. 1686-1689.
7. McLean, XIV, p. 553.
8. Private English-speaking schools in Texas date from 1823, but none was located in Indian-exposed Robertson's Colony until Republic days. Frederick Eby, *Education in Texas Source Materials,* pp. 99-129.
9. Muir, p. 12.
10. Baker, p. 346.
11. Ibid., p. 81.
12. Ibid.
13. Ibid., p. 345.
14. McLean, IX, p. 238.
15. Kathryn Carter, *Stagecoach Inns of Texas,* pp. 210-211.

Chapter 14
1. *Constitution of the Republic of Texas,* General Provisions, Section 5.
2. Muir, p. 135-136.
3. Ibid., p. 81.
4. Ibid., p. 34.
5. Ruth Wilson, *A Republic of Texas Township,* p. 5.
6. Siegel, *The Poet President of Texas,* p. 110.
7. Muir, p. 53.
8. Ibid., p. 162.
9. Ibid., p. 45.
10. Muir, p. 154.
11. Carter, p. 211.
12. Ruth Wilson, *Welcome to Old Cavitt House,* p. 4.
13. Baker, p. 361.

Chapter 15
1. Williams, *Sam Houston,* p. 186.
2. McLean, XVII, p. 61.

3. Baker, p. 229.
4. Muir, p. 158.
5. Baker, p. 82.
6. Ibid.
7. Ibid.
8. Williams, p. 188.
9. Ibid., p. 190.
10. Fehrenbach, *Lone Star*, p. 255.
11. Ibid.
12. Mildred Mayhall, *Indian Wars of Texas*, pp. 29-30.
13. Herbert Gambrell, *Anson Jones, Last President of Texas*, p. 172.
14. Ibid., p. 162.
15. Ibid., p. 163.
16. Siegel, p. 63.
17. McLean, XVII, p. 69.
18. Baker, pp. 340-341.
19. Killough Letter.
20. Siegel, p. 55.
21. McLean, XVIII, p. 34.

Chapter 16
1. Baker, p. 90.
2. Fehrenbach, *Lone Star*, p. 459.
3. Siegel, p. 88.
4. Gambrell, p. 198.
5. Diary of Adolphus Sterne, *Southwestern Historical Quarterly*, Vol. 31, p. 80.
6. Baker, p. 235.
7. Gambrell, p. 219.

Chapter 17
1. Gambrell, p. 231.
2. Ibid., p. 234.
3. Sam Houston Regional Library and Research Center, Liberty, Texas.
4. Gambrell, p. 264.
5. Sam Houston Regional Library and Research Center, Liberty, Texas.
6. Gambrell, p. 343.

Chapter 18
1. Nancy E. Eagleton, "The Mercer Colony in Texas 1844-1883," *Southwestern Historical Quarterly*, Vol. 39, p. 275.
2. Ibid., p. 288.
3. Ibid., Vol. 40, p. 144.

Chapter 19
1. J. Frank Dobie, *Coronado's Children*, p. 61.
2. C. E. Eckhardt, *The Lost San Saba Mine*, p. 140.

3. Ibid., p. 112.
4. After the Civil War a group of four men, including one called Wiley Stroud, tried to find one of the lost mines of the Llano. Could he have been a relative of the Stroud brothers who were Wheelock's partners in the Western Mining Company?
5. Gambrell, p. 378.
6. Dorman H. Winfrey and James M. Day, *The Indian Papers of Texas and the Southwest*, Vol. II, pp. 231-232.
7. Baker, p. 99.
8. Parker, p. 99.
9. Ibid.
10. I am indebted to Seymour E. Wheelock, M.D., of Denver, Colorado, for this historical diagnosis.

Chapter 20
1. Eagleton, "The Mercer Colony in Texas," p. 144.
2. Winfrey and Day, Vol. II, pp. 286-287.
3. Ibid., p. 287-288.
4. Ibid., p. 288-289.
5. Ibid., p. 303.
6. Ibid., p. 307.
7. Ibid., p. 327.
8. Ibid., p. 346.
9. Eagleton, "The Mercer Colony in Texas," Vol. 40, p. 47.
10. Colonization Papers, Texas State Library, 1843-45.

Chapter 21
1. I have been unable to find E.L.R. Wheelock's name in the incomplete lists of Masons during the 1840s, but he obviously believed himself to be a member. His father had been a Mason in Vermont. His son, George Ripley Wheelock, was a member of Gillespie Lodge No. 55 of Robertson County.
2. James K. Greer (ed.), *A Texas Ranger and Frontiersman, The Days of Buck Barry in Texas*, p. 33.

Chapter 22
1. Eugene Barker and Amelia W. Williams (editors), *The Writings of Sam Houston 1813-1863*, Vol. V, p. 9.

BIBLIOGRAPHY

Adjutant General's Office. *Roster of Ohio Soldiers in the War of 1812*. Columbus: Edward T. Miller Co., 1916.

Album Centennario de Tampico. 1823.

Andrew Jackson Houston Papers.

Armstrong, Perry A. *The Sauks and the Black Hawk War*. Springfield: Illinois, Rohler, Printer, 1887.

Asbury, Henry. *Quincy, Illinois*. Quincy: Published by Wilcox, 1882.

Atlas, Clermont County, Ohio. Philadelphia: Lake and Gordon, 1891.

Austin, Stephen Fuller. *Letters*.

Bakeless, John. *America as Seen by the First Explorers*. New York: Dover Publishing Company, 1961.

Baker, J. W. *A History of Robertson County, Texas*. Waco: Robertson County Historical Society, 1870.

Bancroft, Hubert Howe. The Works of, Vol. XVI. *North Mexican States and Texas 1801-1889*. San Francisco: The History Company, 1889.

Barker, Eugene C. *The Life of Stephen F. Austin*. Austin: University of Texas Press, 1926.

Barker, Eugene, and Amelia W. Williams. *The Writings of Sam Houston, 1813-1863*, Vol. V. Austin: Jenkins Publishing Company, 1970.

Bartlett, Rev. Samuel C. "Dr. Wheelock and Dartmouth College," *The Granite Monthly*. Vol. I, #8, 9, 10. August, September, and October, 1888.

Bateman, Newton, and Paul Selby. *Historical Encyclopedia of Illinois and History of Sangamon County*. Chicago: Munsell Publishing Company, 1912.

Bearss, Edwin C., and Arrell M. Gibson. *Fort Smith, Little Gibralter on the Arkansas*. Norman: University of Oklahoma Press, 1969.

269

Berry. *Early Ohio Settlers*. Baltimore: Genealogical Publishing Company, 1986.

Berton, Pierre. *Flames Across the Border*. Boston: Little Brown, 1981.

Binkley, Wm. C. *Official Correspondence of the Texas Revolution 1835-1836*. Volume II. New York: Appleton Century Company.

Bollaert, William. *Texas*. Norman: University of Oklahoma Press, 1956.

Bomar, George W. *Texas Weather*. Austin: University of Texas Press, 1983.

Bond County Historical Society of Greenville, Illinois. *Bond County*. Dallas: Taylor Publishing Co.

Brackenridge, Henry M. *History of the Late War between the United States and Great Britain*. Philadelphia: James Kay Jr. and Brother, 1844.

Bridge, F. Gardiner. "A Dedicated Man, A Good Idea," *Connecticut Traveler.* February 1966.

Brown, John Henry. *Indian Wars and Pioneers of Texas*. Austin: State House Press, 1988.

Brown, Lawrence. *The Episcopal Church in Texas, 1838-1874*. Austin: The Church Historical Society, 1963.

Cannon, LeGrand Jr. *Look to the Mountain*. New York: Holt, Rinehart and Winston, 1942.

Carter, Clarence Edwin. *Great Britain and the Illinois Country, 1763-1774*. Port Washington, NY: Kennikat Press, 1910.

Carter, Kathryn. *Stagecoach Inns of Texas*. Waco: Texian Press, 1972.

Casey, Powell A. *Encyclopedia of Forts, Posts and Named Camps and Other Military Installations in Louisiana 1700-1981*. Baton Rouge: Claifors Publishing Company.

Cavitt, Ellen B. *Some Tracings of CavettCavil Family History, 1725-1965*. Waco, Texas, 1965.

Chase, Francis. *Gathered Sketches from the Early History of New Hampshire and Vermont*. Garland Publishing Company, 1976.

Chase, Frederick. *A History of Dartmouth College and the Town of Hanover*. Brattleboro: The Vermont Printing Company, 1928.

Child, Hamilton. *Gazetteer of Grafton County, New Hampshire 1709-1886*. Syracuse, New York: Syracuse Journal Company, 1886.

————. *Gazetteer of Orange County, Vermont, 1762-1888*. Part First Syracuse, New York: The Syracuse Journal Company, June 1888.

Chapman, George T. *Sketches of the Alumni of Dartmouth College*. Cambridge: Riverside Press, 1867.

Clarke, Mary Whatley. *David G. Burnet*. Austin: The Pemberton Press, 1969.

Coles, Harry L. *The War of 1812*. Chicago: The University of Chicago Press, 1965.

Collins, Wm. H., and Cicero Perry. *Past and Present of the City of Quincy and Adams County*. Chicago: The S. J. Clarke Publishing Company, 1905.

Colonization Papers. Texas State Library.

Constitution of the Republic of Texas.

Cox, Roy Cameron. *The History of the Wheelock Family in America 1600-1984*. Ms.

Cronan, William. *Changes in the Land*. New York: Hill and Wang, 1983.

Cutrer, Thomas W. *The English Texans*. San Antonio: Institute of Texan Culture, 1985.

Dobie, J. Frank. *Coronado's Children*. Dallas: The South West Press, 1932.

Downes, Randolph Chandler. *Frontier Ohio: 1788-1803*. Columbus: The Ohio State Archeological and Historical Society, 1935.

Doyle, Don Harrison. *The Social Order of a Frontier Community, Jacksonville, Illinois, 1825-70*. Urbana: University of Illinois Press, 1946.

Dumble, E. T. First and Second Annual Reports of the Geological Survey of Texas, Austin, 1890-1891.

Duncan, N. C. *Reminiscences of the Early Days in Texas*. Franklin, Texas: Texas Power Plant, 1912.

Eagleton, Nancy E. "The Mercer Colony in Texas 1844-1883." Austin: *Southwestern Historical Quarterly*, Vols. 39, 40, 1936.

Earle, Alice Morse. *Customs and Fashions in Old New England*. Rutland, Vermont: Charles E. Tuttle Company, 1973.

———. *Home Life in Colonial Days*. Stockbridge, Mass.: The Berkshire Traveller Press, 1974.

Eby, Cecil. *That Disgraceful Affair, the Black Hawk War*. N.Y.: W. W. Norton and Company, 1973.

Eby, Frederick. *Education in Texas Source Materials*. University of Texas Bulletin #1824, April 25, 1918.

Eckhardt, C. E. *The Lost San Saba Mine*. Austin: Texas Monthly Press, 1982.

E.L.R. Wheelock Papers. The Center for American History, The University of Texas at Austin.

Evans. *The Story of Texas Schools*. Austin: Stock Publishing Company, 1955.

Exley, Jo Ella Powell. *Texas Tears and Texas Sunshine*. Voices of Frontier Women, College Station, TAMU Press.

Faulk, Odie S., and Billy Mac Jones. *Fort Smith: An Illustrated History*. Ft. Smith, Arkansas: Old Fort Smith Museum, 1983.

Fay, Mary Smith. *War of 1812 Veterans in Texas*. New Orleans: Polyanthos Press, 1979.

Featherstonhaugh, G. W. *Through the Slave States from Washington on the Potomac to the Frontier of Mexico, with Sketches of Popular Manners and Geological Notices*. NY: 1844.

Fehrenbach, T. R. *Lone Star*. NY: American Legacy Press, 1983.

———. *Seven Keys to Texas*. The University of Texas at El Paso, 1983.

Ferguson, John L., and J. N. Atkinson. *Historic Arkansas*. Little Rock: Arkansas History Commission, 1966.

Fields, Dorothy Louise. "David Gouverneur Burnet," *Southwestern Quarterly*, Vol. XLVIII, pp. 226-229.

Foote. *Texas and Texans*. II (103).

Ford, Thomas. *History of Illinois 1818-1847*. Vol. I, Chicago: The Lakeside Press, 1945.

Foster, Bridgman, and Fay. *Town Records of the Town of Hanover, 1761-1818*. Hanover, N.H., 1905.

Friend, Llerena. *Sam Houston the Great Designer*. Austin: The University of Texas Press, 1954.

Gambrell, Herbert. *Anson Jones, the Last President of Texas*. Austin: University of Texas Press, 1947.

Gardner, James Alexander. *Lead King: Moses Austin*. Sunrise Publishing Company, 1980.

Garvin, Donna and James. *On the Road North of Boston: New Hampshire Taverns and Turnpikes, 1700-1900*. Concord, New Hampshire: New Hampshire Historical Society, 1988.

Gilpin, Alec. *The War of 1812 in the Old Northwest*. Michigan State University Press, 1958.

Goebel, Dorothy Burne. *William Henry Harrison*. Philadelphia: Porcupine Press, 1974,

Gracy, David B. II. *Moses Austin, His Life*. Trinity University Press.

Graham, Ian Charles Cargill. *Colonists from Scotland: Emigration to North America 1707-1783*. Port Washington, NY: Kennikat Press, 1956.

Graham, Robert B. *The Dartmouth Story*. Hanover, New Hampshire: Dartmouth Bookstore, 1990.

Greer, James K. (ed.). *Buck Barry, Texas Ranger and Frontiersman*. Lincoln: University of Nebraska Press, 1978.

Greven, Philip. *The Protestant Temperament*. New York: New American Library, 1977.

Halbisch, Harry. "Clermont County, 1800-1950," Ohio, *The Clermont Courier*. December 1950.

Hale, Duane Kendall. *Prospecting and Mining on the Texas Frontier*. Norman: PhD Thesis, Oklahoma State University, 1977.

Hammond, Isaac W. *Revolutionary War Rolls and Documents Relating to Soldiers in the Revolutionary War*, Part II. Manchester: John B. Clarke, Public Printer, 1889.

Hardin, Stephen L. *Texian Iliad*. Austin: University of Texas Press, 1994.

Hawkins, Wallace. *The Case of John Charles Waltrous*. Dallas: University Press, 1950.

Heitman, Francis B. *Historical Register and Dictionary of the United States Army*, Vol I. Government Printing Office, Washington: 1903, Urbana, University of Illinois Press, 1965.

Hickey. *The War of 1812, A Forgotten Conflict*. Urbana and Chicago: University of Illinois Press.

History of St. Clair County, Illinois. Philadelphia, Brink, McDonough, and Co., 1881.

Hollon, W. Eugene (ed.). *William Bollaert's Texas*. Norman: University of Oklahoma Press, 1956.

Howard, Robert P. *Illinois: A History of the Prairie State*. Grand Rapids, Michigan: Wm. B. Eerdmans Publishing Co., 1972.

Howe, Henry. *Historical Collections of Ohio*. Cincinnati: Derby, Bradley, and Company, 1848.

Hunter, John W. *Rise and Fall of the Mission San Saba*. Bandera, 1905.

Huntington, Lee Pennock. *Brothers in Arms*. Woodstock, Vermont: Countryman Press Inc., 1976.

Illinois State Genealogical Society Quarterly. Vol. VII, No. 2, Summer 1975.

Illustrated Encyclopedia and Atlas Map of Madison County, Illinois. St. Louis: Brink McCormick Company, 1873.

Ingmire, Frances Terry. *Texas Frontiersmen 1839-1860*. Saint Louis: Ingmire Publishing Company, 1982.

James, Marquis. *The Raven*. Austin: University of Texas Press, 1929.

Jenkins, John H. *The Papers of the Texas Revolution 1835-1836*. Volumes 7 and 8. Austin: Presidial Press, Brig. Gen. Jay A. Matthews Publisher, 1973.

Johnston, Bob. *Court Records of Madison County, Illinois, 1818-1821*. Edwardsville, 1983.

Jones, Anson. *Memoranda and Official Correspondence Relating to the Republic of Texas and History of Annexation*. Chicago: The Rio Grande Press.

Kelly, Sarah Foster. *Children of Nashville*. Nashville: Blue and Gray Press.

———. *West Nashville, its People and Environs*. Nashville, TN.

Killough, Roy LaFayette, private letter.

Kirkpatrick, A. Y. *The Early Settlers Life in Texas and the Organization of Hill County*. Hillsboro, 1963.

Lack, Paul D. *The Texas Revolutionary Experience*. College Station: TAW Press, 1992.

Leach, Douglas Edward. *Flintlock and Tomahawk: New England in King Philip's War*. NY: W. W. Norton and Co. Inc., 1966.

Lord, John K. *A History of Dartmouth College 1815-1909*. Volumes I and II. Concord, New Hampshire: The Rumford Press, 1913.

Loso, Frank E. (ed.) *The Woodbine and Adjacent Strata of the Waco Area of Central Texas*. Dallas: SMU Press, 1961.

Lossing, Benson Jr. *The Pictorial Field Book of the War of 1812*. Comersworth: The New Hampshire Publishing Company, 1976 (Facsimile of 1869 edition).

Mahon, John K. *The War of 1812*. Gainesville: University of Florida Press, 1972.

Mayhill, Mildred. *Indian Wars of Texas*. Waco: Texian Press, 1966.

McClure, David, and Elijah Parish. *Memoirs of the Rev. Eleazar Wheelock D.D.* NY: Arno Press, 1972.

McCallum, James Dow. *Eleazar Wheelock, Founder of Dartmouth College*. Hanover, NH: Dartmouth College Publications, 1939.

McCarver. *Hearne on the Brazos*. Century Press of Texas, 1968.

McCusker, John J. *How Much Is That in Real Money? A Historical Price Index for Use as a Deflator of Money Values in the Economy of the United States*. Worchester: American Antiquarian Society, 1992.

McDonald, Archie. "Fredonia Rebellion." *New Handbook of Texas*. Austin: Texas State Historical Association, 1996.

———. *Texas, All Hail the Mighty State*. Austin: Eakin Press, 1983.

McLean, Malcolm Dallas. *Papers Concerning Robertson's Colony in Texas*. Compiled and Edited by Malcolm D. McLean. 19 Volumes, 1974-1993.

Vols. I-III were published by the Texas Christian University Press, Fort Worth, Texas, 1974-1976. Vols. IV-XVIII were published by The UTA Press, Box 19929, The University of Texas at Arlington, Arlington, Texas, 1977-1993. The Introductory Volume was published by the UTA Press in 1986. Volume I was reprinted by The UTA Press in 1980. All the volumes that are still in print can be purchased from the Special Collections, University of Texas at Arlington, Box 19497, Arlington, TX 76019-0497.

McNeill, John Timothy. *History and Character of Calvinism: A Compendium of Calvin's Institutes*. Westminster Press.

Meyer, Michael, and William Sherman. *Course of Mexican History*. NY: Oxford University Press, 1987.

Miller, Thomas Lloyd. *Bounty and Donation Land Grants of Texas 1835-1888*. Austin: University of Texas Press.

Moore, James Talmadge. *Through Fire and Flood: the Catholic Church in Frontier Texas 1836-1900*. Houston: St. Thomas University, 1992.

Morison, Samuel Eliot. *The Founding of Harvard*. Cambridge, Mass.: Harvard University Press, 1935.

Muir, Andrew Forest (ed.). *Texas in 1837, An Anonymous Contemporary Narrative*. Austin: University of Texas Press, 1958.

Nance, Joseph Milton. *The Early History of Bryan and the Surrounding Area*. Hunt's Brigade—Bryan Centennial Committee, 1962.

New Handbook of Texas. Austin: Texas State Historical Association, 1996.

Newcomb, W. W. Jr. *The Indians of Texas*. Austin: University of Texas Press, 1961.

Paddock, B. B. *A History of Central and Western Texas*. NY: Lewis Publishing Company, 1911

Parker, Richard Denny. *Historical Recollections of Robertson County, Texas*. Salado: Anson Jones Press, 1955.

Patten, Ruth. *Interesting Family Letters of the Late Mrs. Ruth Patten of Hartford, Conn*. Printed by D. B. Moseley, 1845.

Pease, Theodore Calvin. *The Story of Illinois*. Chicago: University of Chicago Press, 1965.

Pierce, Gerald S. *Texas Under Arms, 1836-1846*. Austin: Encino Press, 1969.

Power, John. *History of the Early Settlers of Sangamon County, Illinois*. Springfield, Illinois: Philips Brothers, 1970.

Pruett and Cole. *Goliad Massacre*. Austin: Eakin Press, 1985.

Reichstein, Andreas. *Rise of the Lone Star*. College Station: TAMU Press, 1989.

Richardson, T. C. *East Texas, its History and its Makers*. Vol. III. NY: Lewis Historical Publishing, 1940.

Richardson, Rupert N. *Texas the Lone Star State*. Englewood Cliffs, New Jersey: Prentice Hall, 1958.

Rockey, J. L., and R. J. Bancroft. *History of Clennont County, Ohio*. Philadelphia: Louis H. Everts, 1880.

Ryan Daniel. *Ohio in Four Wars*. Columbus: the Heer Press, 1917.

Sam Houston Regional Library and Research Center, Liberty, Texas.

Shaw, Joyce. *Three Wheelocks*. Privately Issued, 1977.

Siegel, Stanley. *The Poet President of Texas, the Life of Mirabeau B. Lamar*. Austin: Jenkins Publishing Company, The Pemberton Press, 1977.

Silliman, Silliman, and Dana. *American Journal of Science and Arts*. 2nd Series, Vol. II, 1846 and Vol. VI, 1848.

Slade, Robert K. "Early Days in Clermont County." *Manchester Signal*. Manchester, Ohio, 1964.

Smith, Maxine Hartmann. *Ohio Cemeteries*. Mansfield, Ohio: Ohio Genealogical Society, 1978.

Spurlin, Charles D. *Texas Veterans in the Mexican War*. Victoria College, 1984.

Sterne, Adolphus. "Diary," *Southwestern Historical Quarterly*. Vol. 31, p. 60.

Taylor, I. T. *The Cavalcade of Jackson County*. San Antonio: Naylor Company, 1938.

Thompson, Roy C. *The Schools of Clennont*. Cincinnati: Little Miami Lithopress, 1962.

Turner, Martha Anne. *The Life and Times of Jane Long*. Austin: Texian Press, 1969.

United States Biographical Dictionary. Chicago: American Biographical Publishing Company, 1876.

Wade, Richard C. *The Urban Frontier*. Chicago: The University of Chicago Press, 1959.

Wallace, Joseph. *Past and Present of the City of Springfield and Sangamon County, Illinois*. Chicago: the S.J. Clarke Publishing Company, 1904.

Webb, Irving H., A. B. Kelly, and Forrest Daniell. *One League to Each Wind*. Austin: Texas Surveyors Association, 1973.

Webb, Walter Prescott, Editor in Chief. *The Handbook of Texas*. Austin: Texas State Historical Association, 1952.

Wheelock, Eleazar, D.D. *Continuation of the Narrative of the Indian Charity School Begun in Lebanon in Connecticut, now incorporated with Dartmouth College in Hanover in the Province of New Hampshire*. Hartford, 1773.

Wheelock, Eleazar. *Memoirs of the Revolution*.

Whit, Aileen. *Clermont County, Ohio, Pioneers: 1789-1812: A Substitute Census for 1800-1810*. Privately Printed, New Richmond, Ohio, 1983.

White, Gifford. *Mercer Colonists*. St. Louis: Ingmire Publishing Company, 1984.

Wilbarger, J. W. *Indian Depredations in Texas*. Austin: Eakin Press, 1985.

Wilkins, Frederick. *The Highly Irregular Regulars, Texas Rangers in the Mexican War*. Austin: Eakin Press, 1990.

Williams, Byron. *History of Clermont and Brown Counties, Ohio*. Volume I. Baltimore: Gateway Press, 1987.

Williams, John Hoyt. *Sam Houston, A Biography of the Father of Texas*. NY: Simon and Schuster, 1993.

Williams, Rhea Houston. "History of Education in Robertson County." MA Thesis, SMU, 1937.

Winfrey, Dorman H., and James M. Day. *The Indian Papers of Texas and the Southwest, 1825-1916*. Austin: The Pemberton Press, 1966.

Wooster, Ralph A., and Robert A. Calvert (eds.). *Texas Vistas*. Austin: Texas State Historical Association, 1980.

Wooten, Dudley (ed.). *History of Texas*. Vol. I. Dallas: Wm. G. Scarff, 1898.

Wright, Louis B. *Culture on the Moving Frontier*. NY: Harper and Row, 1955.

Wyngaarden, James B., and Lloyd H. Smith, Editors. *Cecil Textbook of Medicine*. Philadelphia: W. B. Sanders Company, 1982.

Yoakum, H. *History of Texas*. Newfield, NY: 1856.

INDEX

277

U–
U.S. Constitution, 223
Ugartechea, Domingo de, 81, 90-91, 94
Ulster Scot Presbyterians, 72, 150
Upper Colony, 59, 63, 64, 72-73, 79, 81, 142
Urrea, Jose, 106, 128
Vaughn, Willis (Barker), 116, 132
Velasco, 121, 122, 132, 133
Velasco Rebellion, 125-127, 133-135, 147, 154
Velasco treaties, 124-125, 128
Vera Cruz, 50
Veramendi, Governor, 62, 63
Victoria, Texas, 177
Viesca, Agustin, 63, 82, 89, 194
Villa de Viesca, 69, 70, 88-89

W—
Waco Indians, 91, 114, 118, 185, 191, 193, 227, 228-229
Waco, Texas, 91, 157, 217
Walker, ———, 116
Walker, John, 92
Walker, Joseph, 132
War Party, 86-87, 89, 90, 94-95, 100, 103
Washington City, 115, 249
Washington, Kentucky, 17
Washington-on-the-Brazos, 104, 115, 190
Waterloo, 157, 177
Watrous, John C., 173, 179
Wavell, Arthur Goodall, 48-49, 51
Webb, A. J., 172
Webb, Mr., 105
Weiss, Dr., 254
Western, Thomas G., 205-206, 208, 220, 226, 229-230, 234
Wharton, William H., 56, 62, 79, 90, 101
Wheelock, Abigail, 5
Wheelock, Ann, 92
Wheelock, Annette Woodward, 24, 30, 67, 68, 93, 109, 123, 146-147, 172, 191
Wheelock, David Prickett (son), 31,

67, 68, 163, 168, 235, 236-237, 239, 240, 248, 258
Wheelock, Col. Eleazar Louis Ripley: ancestry of, 4, 5; birth of, 6; brand of, 160; business/speculation of, 20-21, 23-24, 29, 31, 34, 40, 141, 146, 149, 150-152, 158-159, 173, 191, 196, 217, 236, 249-253; childhood of, 6-8; children of, 18, 21, 23, 29, 30, 31, 34, 146-147, 151, 239, 242, 245, 257-258; and controversy with Robertson, 103-104; death of, 19, 254; described, 11, 65-67, 68-69, 70, 167, 186, 190, 251-252; education of, 4, 6; establishes town of Wheelock, 149-152, 153-161; home of, 163; illness of, 28, 204, 218, 221, 231, 234, 240, 241-242, 244, 250-251; and Indians, 71, 75, 114-115, 135, 151, 159, 178, 191, 196-197, 205, 208-209, 212, 213-219, 220-221, 224-230, 232-233; as Indian commissioner, 225-230, 234; joins Robertson's Colony, 63, 69; and land distribution, 72, 141-142, 173, 181-182, 183, 202; land owned by, 69-70, 84, 98, 166-167, 236, 239, 243-244, 246; law practice of, 17, 141-146, 148, 158, 202, 212; law studies of, 17, 141; marriage of, 19, 20; and Mercer Colony, 201-211, 223-233, 237-238; in Mexico, 29; military title of, 5, 13, 31; name of, 3-4; papers of, 255; in politics, 22-23, 178, 179, 180, 185-186, 190, 193, 257; portrait of, 191; as ranger, 101, 105-106, 107, 109, 115-118, 127-137, 141, 147, 159; religion of, 29, 80, 183, 222, 238-241, 245, 254; with Second Reg. Illinois, 32-34; with Second Reg. Ohio, 11-13; and silver mines, 212-219, 248, 249, 251-254; as surveyor, 73-75, 83-86, 92, 118, 166, 205-211, 212, 213-214, 219-222, 223-233; and Tennessee Colony, 30; in Third

MARY FOSTER HUTCHINSON is a graduate of Wellesley College, Wellesley, Massachusetts, and received an M.A. from Columbia University, NYC. She has earned her living as a writer, teacher, editor, and recreation director for the United States Air Force. She is a judge emeritus of the United States Figure Skating Association and served for a decade on its national public relations committee. The author of many magazine articles and several books on such diverse subjects as spies, real estate, figure skating, and history, Mrs. Hutchinson now spends her time on Texana (she is a contributor to the *New Handbook of Texas*), travel, genealogy, and volunteer work.